NOLS Wilderness Medicine
Fifth Edition

Tod Schimelpfenig
Illustrated by Joan Safford

A publication of the National Outdoor Leadership School and

STACKPOLE
BOOKS

Published by
STACKPOLE BOOKS
5067 Ritter Road
Mechanicsburg, PA 17055
www.stackpolebooks.com

Printed in the United States of America

10 9 8 7 6 5 4

ISBN 978-0-8117-1193-7

Cover photo by Brad Christensen

FSC
www.fsc.org
MIX
Paper from
responsible sources
FSC® C005010

NOLS books are printed by FSC® certified printers. The Forest Stewardship Council™
encourages responsible management of the world's forests.

Library of Congress Cataloging-in-Publication Data
Schimelpfenig, Tod, 1954–
    NOLS wilderness medicine / Tod Schimelpfenig ; illustrated by Joan Safford.
        p. cm.
    "A Publication of the National Outdoor Leadership School and Stackpole Books."
Previous editions had title: NOLS wilderness first aid.
    Includes bibliographical references and index.
    ISBN-13: 978-0-8117-3306-9
    ISBN-10: 0-8117-3306-8
    1. First aid in illness and injury. 2. Outdoor medical emergencies. I. Schimelpfenig,
Tod, 1954– . NOLS wilderness first aid. II. National Outdoor Leadership School (U.S.)
III. Title. IV. Title: Wilderness medicine.
RC88.9.O95S35 2006
616.02′52—dc22
                                    2006010138

To the students at NOLS.
I hope this text helps you to be better outdoor leaders.

To all NOLS instructors,
who on a daily basis teach and practice first aid
and safety in the wilderness and are the source of the
practical experience that is the foundation of this text.

To Betsy, Sam, Dave, Mark, and Emily
for their support and patience during
the time I devoted to this project.

To the St. Michael's College Rescue Squad,
where I first learned quality patient care.

QUICK-REFERENCE INDEX

CONTENTS

PREFACE

Traditional first aid programs are designed for the common medical problems, telephones, ambulances, and hospitals of urban areas. In wilderness medicine we take these practices and make them relevant to the medical problems we experience in the outdoors and the available equipment, transportation, and communication systems. Wilderness medicine training has become the standard for outdoor professionals, and the relevant training for the outdoor recreationist. When the first edition of *NOLS Wilderness First Aid* appeared on bookshelves in 1991, the concept of wilderness medicine seemed clear. Today, its very definition, at least in North America, has blurred.

In 1991, the traditional definition of medical care in remote locations, with improvised gear and challenging environmental conditions, applied to many wilderness areas. Today, technology and the growing popularity of outdoor pursuits has managed to effectively "shrink" many wilderness areas. Multiday evacuations with improvised litters are less common, largely replaced by helicopters. Communication technology now offers the chance of quick transport from remote areas to urban medical care, and many wilderness visitors have come to expect such service. In fact, much of what we call wilderness medicine is really a simple extension of modern emergency medical services into the wilderness by cell phone and helicopter instead of into a city by telephone and ambulance.

This doesn't mean wilderness medicine is obsolete. There are still areas where a radio or a cell phone will not work and where quick rescue service is not available. Weather and terrain can still hamper rescue. True wilderness medicine means we don't have the advantages of modern medicine. We don't have access to medications, diagnostic equipment and procedures, rapid transport, and specialty care. In reality, a medical emergency in the wilderness is a grave situation.

For over forty years, students and instructors on NOLS courses in remote locations around the world have received top-notch wilderness medical training in the outdoors. This book is an extension of those years of practical experience. It uses the insights and experience of NOLS instructors, who among their many talents must occasionally assess patients and make decisions about medical treatment and urgency of transport. Using the experience of our staff—who volunteer as members of the Fremont County (Wyoming) Search and Rescue—and our experience with NOLS instructors leading expeditions and evacuating people from all over the world, we can learn how skilled outdoors people, who are not medical professionals, make decisions. We can use our NOLS database of field risk management incidents—the most extensive in the industry—to look at what decisions wilderness leaders make. We gain insights into how and what we should teach and how to craft our decisions. The treatment and evacuation guidelines in this text are consistent with the same guidelines that guide the decisions of NOLS instructors in the field.

NOLS Wilderness Medicine reflects the changing field of wilderness medicine. In 1991, for example, there was no Wilderness Risk Managers Committee. In 1992, that group was started by this book's author, Tod Schimelpfenig. Today, it has combined wilderness leadership, risk management, and wilderness medicine into one of the most important conferences of its type.

Another very important move by NOLS in the past decade was the acquisition, in 1999, of the Wilderness Medicine Institute. One of the nation's leading wilderness medical trainers, NOLS WMI is the foremost wilderness medicine training center in the western United States. NOLS WMI provides wilderness first aid, first responder, and emergency medical technician training to more than 10,000 students each year.

Practical experience. Innovation. Vision. These are qualities that have made NOLS and this text a success. But no medicine is better than prevention. The prevention theme runs throughout this book. You'll read about it in chapters on hygiene, gender, and cold injuries. You'll also read about it in the chapter on leadership, teamwork, and communication for small groups. A foundation of wilderness medicine must be competence in basic outdoor skills and leadership. You can't learn this from a book. You need to go on your own wilderness trips or take a NOLS course.

John N. Gans
Executive Director

ACKNOWLEDGMENTS

I would like to thank the following people for their assistance in the preparation of this edition:

Shana Tarter of the Wilderness Medicine Institute at NOLS.

NOLS Field Program Supervisors Allen O'Bannon, Missy White, Pete Absolon, Kathy Brown, and Gary Cukjati for reviewing the chapters on cold injury, genitourinary, and hygiene and helping to assure the text reflects what really happens in the wilderness.

Karl Weller, longtime NOLS Rocky Mountain chef, for his advice on hygiene and foodborne illness.

Molly Doran for her review of the chapter on leadership, curriculum, and teamwork.

Herb Ogden, M.D., NOLS Medical Advisor and Chair of the NOLS Risk Management Committee, for review of the new sections of the text and his advice and support of NOLS instructors and students.

Louise Collins, M.D., for her assistance with the chapter on genitourinary concerns.

Wilderness Medicine Institute instructor Mike Ditola for his review of this edition.

Cynthia B. Stevens, M.D., for her comments and advice on the mental health chapter, and Sherwin Colter, Ph.D., for advocating for this topic in our wilderness medicine curriculum.

Linda Lindsey, Human Resources Director for NOLS, who coauthored the first three editions of this text. Linda's career in wilderness medicine includes extensive field work as a NOLS instructor. As the former coordinator of the Colorado Outward Bound first aid program, she has five years' experience as a staff nurse in obstetrics and neonatal intensive care. She served six years as a board member of the Wilderness Medical Society. Linda's work on the early editions of this text is deeply appreciated. You'll see her touch in much of the book, especially the gender-specific, respiratory and cardiac, heat, and altitude illness chapters.

INTRODUCTION

Wilderness has no handrails, no telephones, and no simple solutions for complex emergency situations. It does have dangers. Some are obvious: rock fall, moving water, stormy weather, avalanches, crevasses, and wild animals. Others are subtle: impure water, dehydration, cold and damp weather, altitude illness, and human judgment.

Although these risks can be minimized with skill, experience, and judgment, outdoor leaders know that despite their best efforts, accidents and illness will happen. Leaders prepare for the challenge of providing emergency medical care in remote and hostile environments with limited equipment and long and arduous transport to a hospital.

This book is designed as a text to accompany the wilderness first aid curriculum presented on NOLS field courses and the Wilderness First Responder (WFR) course taught by WMI.

Chapters one through eight cover fundamental topics in first aid—patient assessment, shock, soft tissue injuries, burns, fractures and dislocations, and chest, head, and abdominal injuries. Chapters nine though fifteen present environmental medical problems—heat, cold, water, altitude, and poisonous plants and animals.

Chapters sixteen through twenty-one cover medical topics—cardiac, respiratory, diabetes, allergies, anaphylaxis, genitourinary medical problems, and mental health concerns. The final section discusses a variety of topics pertinent to expedition medicine—water disinfection, hygiene, hydration, flulike illness, and dental problems, as well as leadership, stress, and legal topics. These concerns may not threaten life or limb, but they are the everyday medical experience of the wilderness leader.

The NOLS leadership skill curriculum has been woven together with current research in human factors in accidents to discuss the critical topic of leadership, teamwork, and communication among rescue groups. This chapter is unique within wilderness medical texts and curricula and sets this text apart from others in the field.

Many of the changes in this version are organizational and designed to fit the structure of the NOLS Wilderness Medicine Institute courses. Two new chapters have been added to discuss decision-making and mental health concerns. The evacuation guidelines have been highlighted to help the reader understand key points in deciding whether or not to evacuate a patient.

NOLS Wilderness Medicine may also be used as a text for any wilderness medicine course, as an information source for outdoor enthusiasts, or as a resource to tuck into your pack or kayak. This text covers the material commonly taught by reputable wilderness first responder (WFR) instructors or listed in the Wilderness Medical Society's recommended minimum WFR course topics and in the WFR Scope of Practice Document.[1] People using this as a WFR textbook should seek supplementary background information on cardiopulmonary resuscitation (CPR); obstetrical emergencies; oxygen use and mechanical aids to breathing.[2]

Simply reading the text or successfully completing a NOLS course does not qualify a person to perform any procedure. The text is not a substitute for thorough, practical training, experience in emergency medicine and the outdoors, critical analysis of the needs of specific situations, or the continued education and training necessary to keep skills sharp.

The majority of the first aid practices discussed in this text are common and accepted. Wilderness medicine expands the scope of practice beyond what may be routinely done when we are close to a hospital or physician. For example, in remote settings it is appropriate to attempt to reduce dislocations, clean wounds, and consider clearing a potential spinal injury. Wilderness leaders often make decisions on whether or not to seek the advice of a physician; decisions that are not made by ambulance personnel who routinely transport all patients; decisions that may end an expedition or place rescuers in jeopardy. The wilderness practices presented in this text are consistent with wilderness medicine protocols for NOLS Instructors and those taught by the NOLS Wilderness Medicine Institute (WMI). People leading trips or managing wilderness programs should be aware of the medical legal issues in wilderness medicine and consider utilizing written medical protocols, such as the *Practice Guidelines for Wilderness Emergency Care*[3] developed by the Wilderness Medical Society, and a physician medical advisor to guide the wilderness protocols specific for their program.

In addition to first aid, a NOLS course gives invaluable experience in critical areas of wilderness medicine: fundamental wilderness living and travel skills, expedition planning, prevention through risk management, and leadership and judgment. To care for your patient in the wilderness you first have to care for yourself.

The most effective first aid is prevention. Wilderness medicine training should prepare the student for serious illness and injury. It should also discuss prevention and treatment of common wilderness medical problems such as infected wounds, hygiene-associated illness, and treatment of athletic injuries. You will find prevention to be a recurring theme in this text.

Tod Schimelpfenig
Lander, Wyoming
October 2012

---

1. Johnson, D., et al. Wilderness First Responder Scope of Practice. (September 21, 2010, retrieved from http://www.outdoored.com/Community/blogs/wild med/archive/2010/05/21/wtr-scope-of-practice-draft.aspx).

2. Wilderness first responder recommended minimum course topics. (Wilderness Medical Society, 1999).

3. Wilderness Medical Society, *Practice Guidelines for Wilderness Emergency Care*, ed. Wm. W. Forgey, M.D. (Merriville, Indiana: ICS Books, 2005).

PATIENT ASSESSMENT

"Your ability to manage an emergency is rooted in your ability to assess the scene and the patient."

—Buck Tilton

Many outdoor leaders, skilled in wilderness living and travel yet inexperienced in first aid, have wondered if they will be able to care for an ill or injured companion. They can and do provide this care using the patient assessment system as their foundation—their tool for checking for life-threatening problems, surveying the patient for injury and illness, and gathering the information needed to prioritize the treatment and evacuation decisions. Generations of NOLS Field Instructors have proven this true. The foundation of their first aid and medical judgment has been common sense, good training, and the thoroughness and care by which they gather information in the patient assessment.

CHAPTER 1 | PATIENT ASSESSMENT SYSTEM

INTRODUCTION

Imagine yourself kneeling beside a fallen hiker, deep in the wilderness. As you examine the victim, thoughts of your remoteness, the safety of your companions, the incoming weather, evacuation, communication, and shelter possibilities swirl through your brain. The telephone, the ambulance, and those images and expectations we have of prompt advanced medical care don't apply to this situation. You are about to make decisions and initiate a series of events that will affect the safety and well-being of the patient, your group, and outside rescuers.

In the city, the patient could be quickly transported to a hospital. In the wilderness, patient care may be your responsibility for hours or days. You cope with improvised gear and inclement weather and take care of yourself, the other members of your group, and the patient. The rescue or evacuation may be strenuous and can jeopardize the safety of the group and the rescuers.

You need information to help you determine how to best care for and transport the patient. You will gather that information during the patient assessment, the foundation of your care.

SCENE SIZE-UP

Patient assessment begins immediately as you arrive on the scene. Your observations of weather, terrain, bystanders, and the position of the patient are your first clues as to how an injury occurred, the patient's condition, and possible scene hazards.

Scene Safety

Look for danger to yourself, bystanders, other rescuers, or the patient. Your top priority is the well-being of yourself and your fellow first responders. A patient can be served only by healthy rescuers, not by more patients.

Driving cold rain may make constructing on-the-spot shelter an immediate priority to avoid hypothermia. Falling rock or avalanche may dictate a move out of the path of danger. Protect your patient by protecting yourself.

Mechanism of Injury or Illness

Assess the mechanism of injury or illness (MOI). Look around. Your observations of the scene and questions of bystanders can give clues about what happened. Is the patient ill or injured? If ill, gather a short history of the illness. If injured, what is the mechanism? If the patient fell, find out how far and if he or she was wearing a helmet. Did the person land on soft ground, snow, or rocks? Did he or she fall free or tumble? Mechanism can give us critical information about the location and severity of injuries.

Find out if you have more than one patient. If so, a quick initial assessment may tell you who needs your immediate attention and how best to use your companions to organize the scene and care for the patients.

Body Substance Isolation

Health care workers practice body substance isolation (BSI) to protect themselves against infectious disease. It's impossible to know for sure if the patient is germ free. All body fluids and tissues are considered infectious, and appropriate precautions are taken as standard practice by health care workers. Protect yourself by washing your hands; using gloves, eyewear, and face masks; properly disposing of soiled bandages, dressing, and clothing; and avoiding needlestick injury.

Disposable latex, vinyl, or other synthetic or natural rubber gloves should be in your first aid kit (people allergic to latex will need nonlatex gloves). Wear them when there is a chance you may contact a patient's blood, other body fluids, mucous membranes, or broken skin, or if you handle bandages, clothing, or other items contaminated with blood or other body fluids. Hands should be thoroughly washed, ideally before and certainly after contact with a patient.

Long-sleeve shirts and pants and pocket masks for mouth-to-mask ventilation are recommended in situations in which splashes of blood and other body fluids are likely to occur. If there is splashing blood, vomit, or other fluids, wear a protective mask and glasses, or at least a bandanna over your nose and mouth. Wear your sunglasses or rain gear if nothing else is available. Items such as gloves and bandages that are contaminated should be placed in sealed plastic bags and labeled as a biohazard or incinerated in a hot fire.

Scene Size-up

- Identify hazards to self, other rescuers, bystanders, patient.
- Determine mechanism of injury.
- Form a general impression of seriousness.
- Determine the number of patients.
- Protect yourself with body substance isolation.

INITIAL ASSESSMENT

The initial assessment is a ritual performed on every patient to find and treat life-threatening medical problems. Besides attending immediately to vital functions, it provides order during the first frantic minutes of an emergency. You check, stop, and fix problems in the vital respiratory and circulatory systems. You assume disability and protect the spine. You assess and treat for environmental hazards.

Establishing Responsiveness

As you approach the patient, introduce yourself and ask if you may help. You're obtaining consent to treat, being polite, and finding out if the patient is responsive. If there is no response, attempt to arouse the patient by saying hello loudly—the person may just be asleep.

If this fails to arouse the patient, try a painful stimulus—pinch the shoulder or neck muscle or rub the breastbone.

At this point, if there is any mechanism of injury, control the cervical spine (neck). Place hands on the head to prevent unnecessary movement of the neck.

If the patient is awake and talking, the airway is not obstructed; the person is breathing and has a pulse. If the patient is quiet, you need to check the ABCs (airway, breathing, and circulation) immediately. In both responsive and unresponsive patients, you proceed through the entire initial assessment, and make a decision about possible disability, environmental threats, and hidden major injury.

ABCDE

The initial assessment checks the airway, breathing, and circulation, plus possible serious bleeding and shock. The airways are the mouth, nose and throat, and trachea. Oxygen is exchanged between the air and the blood in the lungs. Circulation is a function of the heart, the blood vessels, and the blood, which contains vital oxygen. We use ABCDE (airway, breathing, circulation, disability, environment, expose, examine) as a memory aid for the initial assessment sequence.

Airway. The airway is the path air travels from the atmosphere into the lungs. An obstructed airway is a medical emergency because oxygen cannot reach the lungs. If the patient is awake, ask the patient to open his or her mouth and check for anything, such as gum or broken teeth, that could become an airway obstruction. If the patient is unresponsive, assess the airway by opening it with the head-tilt–chin-lift method or the jaw thrust and look inside the mouth. If you see an obvious obstruction—a piece of food, perhaps—take it out.

The Initial Assessment

- Obtain consent to treat.
- Assess for responsiveness.
- Control the spine.

A—Assess the airway
- Open the airway.
- Look in the mouth and clear obvious obstructions.

B—Assess for breathing
- Look, listen, feel.

C—Assess for circulation
- Check pulse at the neck.
- Look for severe bleeding.

D—Assume disability
- Observe spine precautions.
- Avoid moving the patient.
- Consider the jaw thrust to open the airway.

E—Protect the patient from the environment
- Expose and examine major injuries.

The INITIAL ASSESSMENT

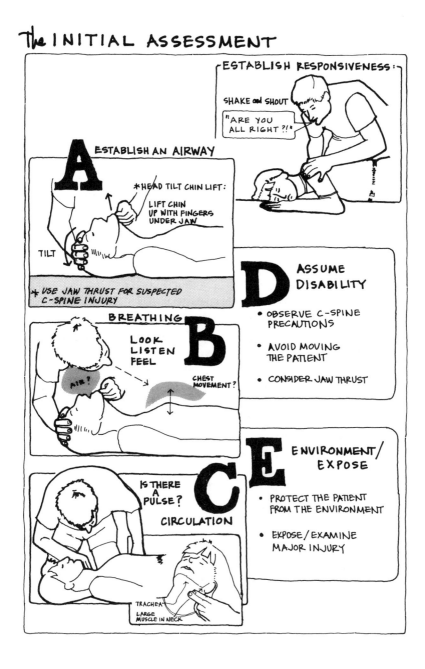

If you can see, hear, or feel air moving from the lungs to the outside, the airway is open. A patient making sounds is able to move air from the lungs and past the vocal cords. This indicates that the airway is at least partially open.

Signs of an obstructed airway are lack of air movement, labored breathing, use of neck and upper chest muscles to breathe, and pale gray or bluish skin. If you discover an airway obstruction, attempt to clear the airway before proceeding to assess breathing. The appropriate techniques are those taught in CPR for treating a foreign body–obstructed airway.

Breathing. If the patient is awake, ask him or her to take a deep breath. If the patient's breathing is labored or painful, expose the chest and look for life-threatening injuries. If the patient is unresponsive, any coughing, breathing, or movement is a sign of breathing effort. Look for the rise and fall of the chest as air enters and leaves the lungs. Listen for the sound of air passing through the upper airway. Feel the movement of air from the patient's mouth and nose on your cheek. If the patient is not breathing, give two slow, even breaths, then proceed with a check for a pulse.

Circulation. Check for the presence or absence of a pulse. Place the tips of your middle and index fingers over the carotid artery for at least 10 seconds. The carotid is a large central artery, accessible at the neck. Other possible sites are the femoral artery in the groin and the radial artery in the wrist (preferable for a responsive patient).

It may be difficult to feel a pulse if the patient has a weak pulse from shock, is cold, or is wearing bulky clothing. Finding a pulse is not always easy. If you are unsure about the presence of the carotid pulse, try the femoral or the radial pulse.

If the patient is moving or moaning, he or she must have a pulse. If there is no pulse, start CPR. If there is a pulse but no breathing, start rescue breathing.

Look for bleeding. Severe bleeding can be fatal within minutes. Look for obvious bleeding or wet places on the patient's clothing. Quickly run your hands over and under the patient's clothing, especially bulky sweaters or parkas, to find moist areas that may be caused by serious bleeding. Look for blood that may be seeping into snow or the ground. Most external bleeding can be controlled with direct pressure. Chapter 7 ("Soft Tissue Injuries") addresses bleeding control in detail.

Disability. Review the MOI and make a decision on the need to continue spine stabilization. If there is no spine injury MOI, there is no need to maintain spine stabilization. If there is a spine injury MOI, continue to maintain control of the head and spine. See chapter 4 ("Brain and Spinal Cord Injuries").

Environment/Expose. Without moving the patient, expose and examine for major injuries, which may be hidden in bulky outdoor clothing. Quickly unzip zippers, open cuffs, and look under parkas.

Assess and manage environmental hazards. You may need to move your patient off snow and onto an insulating pad, or out of a river onto dry ground.

THE FOCUSED EXAM AND HISTORY

Now pause a moment to look over the scene. The initial assessment is complete. Immediate threats to life have been addressed. Take a deep breath and consider the patient's and the rescuers' needs. If the location of the incident is unstable—such as on or near loose boulders or a potential avalanche slope—move to a safer position. Provide insulation, adjust clothing, rig a shelter. Assign tasks: boil water for hot drinks, build a litter, set up camp, write down vital signs. Establishing clear delegation of tasks helps the rescuers by giving everyone something to do and helps the

---

Focused Exam and History

PATIENT EXAM	VITAL SIGNS	MEDICAL HISTORY
• Look	• Responsiveness	• Chief Complaint (OPQRST)
• Listen	• Heart Rate	• SAMPLE
• Feel	• Skin	• AEIOUTIPS
• Smell	• Respiration	
• Ask	• Temperature	
	• Pupils	

FOCUSED ASSESSMENT and HISTORY

RESCUER CONDUCTING SURVEY:
INSPECT *THOROUGHLY*, INCLUDING UNDERNEATH CLOTHING.

HAVE ANOTHER RESCUER RECORD ALL OBSERVATIONS in WRITING.

MAINTAIN ABCs, MONITOR VITAL SIGNS.

LOOK
LISTEN
FEEL
SMELL

patient by creating an atmosphere of order and leadership. See appendix B ("Emergency Procedures for Outdoor Groups").

The focused exam and history is done after life-threatening conditions have been stabilized. It consists of doing a complete head-to-toe physical exam, checking vital signs, and taking a thorough medical history.

Head-to-Toe Examination

The head-to-toe exam is a comprehensive physical examination. Begin the head-to-toe examination by first making the patient comfortable. Except in cases of imminent danger, avoid moving an injured patient until after the exam. Your hands should be clean, warm, and gloved. Ideally, the examiner should be of the same gender as the patient; otherwise, an observer of the same gender should be present during all phases of the exam. Designate a notetaker to record the results of the focused exam and history.

As you examine the patient, explain what you are doing and why. Besides being a simple courtesy, this helps involve the patient in his or her care. This survey starts with the head and systematically checks the entire body down to the toes. One person should perform the survey in order to avoid confusion, provide consistent results, and minimize discomfort to the patient. Also, with a single examiner, the patient will be able to respond to one inquiry at a time.

The examination technique consists of looking, listening, feeling, smelling, and asking. If you are uncertain of what is abnormal, compare the injured extremity with the other side of the body or with a healthy person.

Head. Check the ears and nose for fluid and the mouth for injuries that may affect the airway. Check the face for symmetry; all features should be symmetrical down the midline from the forehead to the chin. The cheekbones are usually accurate references for facial symmetry. Feel the entire skull for depressions, tenderness, and irregularity. Run your fingers along the scalp to detect bleeding or cuts. Check the eyes for injuries, pupil abnormalities, and vision disturbances.

Neck. The trachea, or windpipe, should be in the middle of the neck. Feel the entire cervical spine from the base of the skull

HEAD-TO-TOE EXAMINATION:

HEAD
NECK
SHOULDERS
ARMS
CHEST
ABDOMEN
BACK
PELVIS
LEGS
FEET

VITAL SIGNS:

LEVEL OF RESPONSIVENESS
PUPILS
HEART RATE
SKIN SIGNS
BODY TEMPERATURE
RESPIRATIONS

The Focused Exam and History:
Head-to-Toe Patient Examination

- **Look** for wounds, bleeding, unusual movements or shapes, deformities, penetrations, excretions, vomit.
- **Listen** for abnormal sounds, such as crepitus and airway noises.
- **Feel** for wounds, rigidity, hardness, softness, tenderness, deformity.
- **Smell** for unusual odors.
- **Ask** if anything hurts or feels odd or numb.

---

to the top of the shoulders for pain, tenderness, muscle rigidity, and deformity.

Shoulders. Examine the shoulders and the collarbone for deformity, tenderness, and pain.

Arms. Feel the arms from the armpit to the wrist. Check the pulse in each wrist; it should be equal on both sides. Ask the patient to move his or her fingers, then check grip strength by having the patient squeeze your hands. Check for sensation by gently pinching the fingers or scratching the palm of the hand and fingers. If no injury is apparent, ask the patient to move each arm through its range of motion.

Chest. Feel the chest for deformity or tenderness. Push down from the top and in from the sides. Ask the patient to breathe deeply as you compress the chest. Look for open chest wounds. Observe the rise and fall of the chest for symmetry.

Abdomen. Feel the abdomen for tenderness or muscle rigidity with light pressure. If there is tenderness, localize it into a quadrant. Look for distension, discoloration, and bruising.

Back. Feel the spine. Feel each vertebra from the shoulders to the pelvis. It is important to slide your hand as far as possible under the patient. There may be a hidden injury. If you suspect a spine injury, logroll the patient to palpate the spine and see the back.

Pelvis. Press first in from the sides, and then, if there is no pain or tenderness, press down on the front of the pelvis. Is there deformity or instability?

Legs. Check the legs from the groin to the ankle. Check the pulse in each of the feet; they should be equal. Check for sensation and motor function in the feet by touching the patient's feet and by asking the patient to move his or her toes and to push his or her feet against your hands.

Vital Signs

Vital signs are objective indicators of respiration, circulation, heart and brain function, blood volume, and body temperature. Checking the vital signs helps further evaluate the ABCs. Airway and breathing are checked by noting skin color and respiratory rate and depth. Good color and easy and regular breathing are signs our airway and lungs are working well. Circulation is evaluated by pulse, skin color, skin temperature, and level of responsiveness. Effective circulation gives us warm, pink skin and enough oxygen to keep our brain alert.

As a general rule, measure and record vital signs every 15 to 20 minutes—more frequently if the patient is seriously ill or injured. The initial set of vitals—responsiveness, pulse, respiration, skin signs, pupils, temperature—provides baseline data on the patient's condition. The changes that occur thereafter provide information on the progress of the patient.

Level of Responsiveness. Brain function, also known as mental status and reflected in how responsive we are to our environment, may be affected by toxic chemicals such as drugs or alcohol, low blood sugar, abnormally high or low temperature, diseases of the brain such as stroke, circulatory or respiratory shock, or pressure from bleeding or swelling caused by a head injury.

I have chosen to use the term "responsiveness" rather than the more common "consciousness" to describe brain function. Consciousness is a vague term and difficult to measure. The more

---

Focused Exam and History: Vital Signs

- **Level of Responsiveness**—Assess with AVPU.
- **Heart rate**—Assess pulse rate, rhythm, strength.
- **Skin signs**—Assess skin color, temperature, and moisture.
- **Respiration**—Assess rate, rhythm, strength.
- **Temperature**—Assess temperature with a thermometer.
- **Pupils**—Assess reactivity to light.

specific responsiveness is a criterion we can evaluate on every patient and then describe with clarity and specificity.

When you assess responsiveness, first determine the initial state. Begin by approaching the patient, introducing yourself, saying "Hello," and asking if you can help. You're being polite as well as finding out if the patient is awake, asleep, or possibly unresponsive.

Then describe the stimulus you used to arouse the patient. If the patient opened his or her eyes and responded after a simple "Hello," the person may have been asleep or distracted. If you needed to shout loudly several times to arouse the patient, the person would be described as not awake but responsive to a verbal stimulus. If you needed to use pain to arouse the patient, the person would be described as not awake and responsive only to pain.

Awake. Normally, we are awake (or we wake quickly from sleep) and know who we are, where we are, the date or time, and recent events. This is described as A (awake) and O (oriented) times 0, 1, 2, 3, or 4, depending on whether the patient knows who he or she is, where he or she is, what date or time it is, and recent events:

- A+O×4 The person knows person, place, time, and event.
- A+O×3 The person knows person, place, and time, but not event.
- A+O×2 The person knows person and place, but not time and event.
- A+O×1 The person knows person, but not place, time, and event.

A patient who is awake but not oriented to person, place, time, or event is described as disoriented or A+O×0. The spoken response may be incoherent, confused, inappropriate, or incomprehensible.

Responsive to Verbal Stimulus. The patient is not awake but responds to a verbal stimulus, such as the rescuer saying, "Hello, how are

---

AVPU: Assessing Level of Responsiveness

- Awake
- Responsive to Verbal Stimulus
- Responsive to Pain
- Unresponsive

you?" If the patient does not respond, repeat louder: "Hey! Sir (or Ma'am)! Wake up!" The patient's response may be opening the eyes, grunting, or moving. Higher levels of brain function respond to verbal input, lower levels to pain. Test for responsiveness to verbal stimuli first, painful stimuli second.

Responsive to Pain. The patient is not awake, does not respond to verbal stimuli, but does respond to painful stimuli by moving, opening the eyes, or groaning. To stimulate for pain, pinch the muscle at the back of the shoulder or neck, or squeeze a fingernail.

Unresponsive. The patient is not awake and does not respond to voice or painful stimuli.

Report the patient's initial state, the stimulus you gave, and the response. For example: "This patient is awake and oriented times four." Or, "This patient is not awake, but is responsive to a verbal stimulus. When awake, the patient knows his name but is otherwise disoriented."

Heart Rate. Every time the heart beats, a pressure wave is transmitted through the arteries. We feel this pressure wave as the pulse. The pulse rate indicates the number of heartbeats over a period of time. For an adult, the normal range is 50 to 100 beats per minute. A well-conditioned athlete may have a normal pulse rate below 50. Shock, exercise, altitude, illness, emotional stress, or fever can increase the heart rate.

The heart rate can be measured at the radial artery on the thumb side of the wrist or at the carotid artery in the neck. Place the tips of the middle and index fingers over the artery. Count the number of beats for 15 seconds and multiply by four.

In addition to rate, note the rhythm and strength of the pulse. The normal rhythm is regular. Irregular rhythms can be associated with heart disease and are frequently rapid. The strength of the pulse is the amount of pressure you feel against your fingertips. It may be weak or strong.

A standard pulse reading includes the rate, rhythm, and strength of the pulse. For example: "The pulse is 110, irregular, and weak." Or, "The pulse is 60, regular, and strong."

Skin Signs. Skin signs indicate the condition of the respiratory and cardiovascular systems. These include skin color, temperature, and moisture, often abbreviated SCTM.

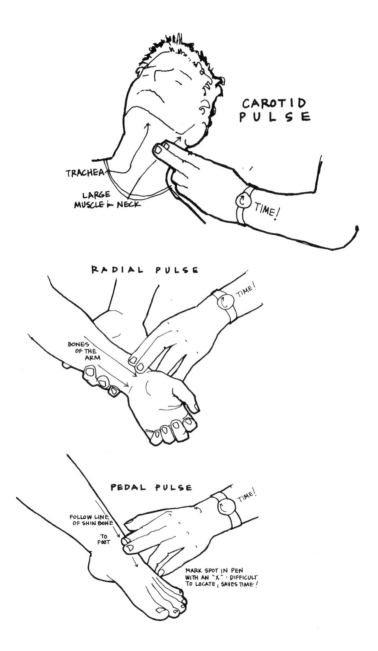

CAROTID PULSE

TRACHEA

LARGE MUSCLE in NECK

TIME!

RADIAL PULSE

TIME!

BONES OF THE ARM

PEDAL PULSE

TIME!

FOLLOW LINE OF SHIN BONE

TO FOOT

MARK SPOT IN PEN WITH AN "X" : DIFFICULT TO LOCATE ; SAVES TIME !

Pinkness. In a light-colored person, normal skin color is pink. In darker-skinned individuals, skin color can be assessed at the nail beds, inside the mouth, palms of the hands, soles of the feet, or lips.

Redness. Redness indicates that the skin is unusually flushed with blood. It is a possible sign of recent exercise, heatstroke, carbon monoxide poisoning, fever, or allergic reaction.

Paleness. Pale skin indicates that blood has withdrawn from the skin. Paleness may be due to fright, shock, fainting, or cooling of the skin.

Cyanosis. Blue skin, or cyanosis, appears when circulation to the skin is reduced or the level of oxygen in the blood falls. Well-oxygenated blood is brighter red than poorly oxygenated blood. Cyanosis indicates that oxygen levels have fallen significantly, or that the patient may be cold.

Jaundice. Yellow skin combined with yellow whites of the eyes—jaundice—is a sign of liver or gallbladder disease. The condition results from excess bile pigments in the blood.

Temperature and Moisture. Quickly assess the temperature and moisture of the skin at several sites, including the forehead, hands, and trunk. In a healthy person, the skin is warm and relatively dry. Skin temperature rises when the body attempts to rid itself of excess heat, as in fever or environmental heat problems. Hot, dry skin can be a sign of fever or heatstroke. Hot, sweaty skin occurs when the body attempts to eliminate excess heat and can also be a sign of fever or heat illness.

Skin temperature falls when the body attempts to conserve heat by constricting blood flow to the skin; for example, during exposure to cold. Cool, moist (clammy) skin is an indicator of extreme stress and a sign of shock.

A report on skin condition should include color, temperature, and moisture. For example: "The patient's skin is pale, cool, and clammy."

Respiration. Respiratory rate is counted in the same manner as the pulse: Each rise of the chest is counted over 15 seconds and multiplied by four, or 30 seconds and multiplied by two. Watch the chest rise and fall, or observe the belly move with each breath. Normal respiration range is 12 to 20 breaths per minute.

The patient's depth and effort of breathing enable you to gauge his or her need for air and the presence or absence of chest injury. In a healthy individual, breathing is relatively effortless.

A patient experiencing breathing difficulty may exhibit air hunger with deep, labored inhaling efforts. A patient with a chest injury may have shallow, rapid respirations accompanied by pain. Irregular respirations are a sign of a brain disorder. Noisy respirations indicate some type of airway obstruction. Assess and, if necessary, clear the airway.

Smell the breath. Fruity, acetone breath can be a sign of diabetic coma. Foul, fecal-smelling breath may indicate a bowel obstruction.

Report respirations by their rate, rhythm, effort, depth, noises, and odors. For example, a patient in diabetic ketoacidosis may have respirations described as "20 per minute, regular, labored, deep. There is a fruity breath odor."

Temperature. Temperature measurement is an important component of a thorough patient assessment, but it is the vital sign that is least often measured in the field. It can tell us of underlying infection or of abnormally high or low body temperatures. Although a normal temperature is 98.6°F (37°C), daily variation in body temperature is also normal, usually rising a degree during the day and decreasing through the night.

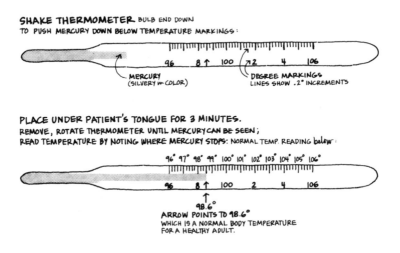

SHAKE THERMOMETER BULB END DOWN
TO PUSH MERCURY DOWN BELOW TEMPERATURE MARKINGS:

MERCURY (SILVERY IN COLOR)

DEGREE MARKINGS LINES SHOW .2° INCREMENTS

PLACE UNDER PATIENT'S TONGUE FOR 3 MINUTES.
REMOVE, ROTATE THERMOMETER UNTIL MERCURY CAN BE SEEN;
READ TEMPERATURE BY NOTING WHERE MERCURY STOPS: NORMAL TEMP. READING below:

98.6°
ARROW POINTS TO 98.6°
WHICH IS A NORMAL BODY TEMPERATURE
FOR A HEALTHY ADULT.

Temperature can be measured orally, in the ear (tympanic), on the forehead (infrared), or rectally. Axillary readings—taken under the armpit—are the least reliable. Rectal temperatures are the most accurate indication of the core temperature available to first responders. Rectal temperature is sometimes considered necessary for suspected hypothermia but is rarely measured due to patient embarrassment and cold exposure. Diagnosis of hypothermia in the outdoors, discussed in chapter 9 ("Cold Injuries"), is often based on other factors, such as behavior, history, appearance, and mental status.

Many thermometers are now digital. If you have an older mercury thermometer, shake down the thermometer to push the mercury below the degree markings. This is essential for an accurate reading. Place the thermometer under the patient's tongue for at least 3 minutes. The patient should refrain from talking or drinking during this time. A report on temperature should include the method, such as "100°F oral" or "37°C rectal."

Pupils. Pupils are clues to brain function. They can indicate head injury, stroke, drug abuse, or lack of oxygen to the brain. Both pupils should be round and equal in size. They should contract symmetrically when exposed to light and dilate when the light dims. Evaluate pupils by noting size, equality, and reaction to light.

In the absence of a portable light source, such as a flashlight or headlamp, shield the patient's eyes for 15 seconds, then expose them to ambient light. Both pupils should contract equally. When in doubt, compare the patient's reactions with those of a healthy individual in the same light conditions.

PUPIL   SIZE:

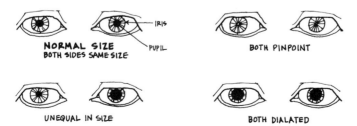

NORMAL SIZE
BOTH SIDES SAME SIZE — IRIS — PUPIL

BOTH PINPOINT

UNEQUAL IN SIZE

BOTH DIALATED

A patient whose brain cells are deficient of oxygen may have equal but slow-to-react pupils. A wide, nonreactive pupil on one side and a small, reactive pupil on the other side indicates brain damage or disease on the side with the larger pupil. Very small, equal pupils may indicate drug intoxication.

Blood Pressure. The concept of blood pressure is discussed in chapter 2 ("Shock"). Although blood pressure is routinely measured when professional medical care is being administered, accurate measurement requires a stethoscope and a sphygmomanometer—equipment rarely carried on wilderness trips. A strong radial or pedal pulse is a good sign and suggests the patient has a cardiovascular system healthy enough to pump blood to his hands and feet. The absence of a radial or pedal pulse, unless explainable by limb injury, suggests that blood pressure may be low. If this is the case, it's likely accompanied by other signs of shock.

Medical History

The patient's medical history provides background that is often relevant to the present problem. Gathering the history is an ongoing process that you typically carry out while measuring vital signs and performing the head-to-toe exam. Obtaining an accurate history depends greatly on the quality of communication between you and the patient. This rapport begins as soon as you approach the scene. Communicating clearly, acting orderly, and appearing to be in control make it easier to obtain an accurate history.

Chief Complaint. Obtain the patient's chief complaint—the problem that caused him or her to solicit help. Pain is a common complaint—for example, abdominal pain or pain in an arm or leg after a fall. In lieu of pain, a chief complaint may be nausea or dizziness. A memory aid for investigating the chief complaint is OPQRST.

Onset. Did the chief complaint appear suddenly or gradually?

Provokes/Palliates. What provoked the injury? If the problem is an illness, under what circumstances did it occur? What makes the problem worse, and what makes it better?

Quality. What qualities describe the pain? Adjectives may include

---

Focused Exam and History: Medical History

- Chief Complaint (OPQRST)
- SAMPLE

stabbing, cramping, burning, sharp, dull, or aching.

Radiate/Region/Referred. Where is the pain? Does it move, or radiate? What causes it to move? Chest pain from a heart attack can radiate from the chest into the neck and jaw. Pain from a spleen injury can be felt in the left shoulder.

Severity. On a scale of 1 to 10 (with 1 being no pain or discomfort and 10 being the worst pain or discomfort the patient has ever experienced), how does the patient rate this pain? This question can reveal the level of discomfort the patient is experiencing.

Time/Trend. When did the pain start? How frequently does it occur? How long does it last? Is it getting better or worse? Correlate the patient's complaints with the vital signs.

SAMPLE. This is a memory aid for a series of questions that completes the medical history.

Symptoms. What symptoms does the patient have? Nausea? Dizziness? Headache? Ask the patient how he or she is feeling, or if anything is causing discomfort. A symptom is something the patient perceives and must tell you about (e.g. pain). Tenderness, on the other hand, is a sign, something you can find when you touch an injury during a patient exam.

Allergies, Medications. Ask if the patient is currently taking any medications or has any allergies. If so, find out if he or she has been exposed to the allergen and what his or her usual response is. Ask about nonprescription, prescription, and herbal medications, as well as possible alcohol or drug use. Ask whether the patient is allergic to medications or has other environmental allergies to food, insects, or pollen.

Past History. The past history consists of a series of questions you ask the patient to discover any previous and relevant medical prob-

---

OPQRST:
Assessing the Chief Complaint

- Onset
- Provokes/palliates
- Quality
- Radiates/region/referred
- Severity
- Time/trend

SAMPLE:
Assessing the History

- Symptoms
- Allergies
- Medications
- Past history
- Last intake/output
- Events

lems. (If the patient has a broken leg, for example, it's unlikely we need to know about childhood illness.) First ask these general questions: Has the patient ever been in a hospital? Is the patient currently seeing a physician? Next, ask about specific body systems. Avoid medical jargon. For instance, asking the patient about any previous heart problems may be less confusing than asking, "Do you have a cardiac history?"

Additional sources of information may include a medical alert tag or a medical information questionnaire. A medical alert tag is a necklace, bracelet, or wallet card that identifies the patient's medical concerns. It reports a history of diabetes, hemophilia, epilepsy, or other disorders; allergies to medication; and other pertinent information. Medical forms are common to many outdoor schools, camps, and guide services. The NOLS student medical history form is filled out by the student prior to the trip and is available for review by field staff.

Last Intake and Output. Ask the patient when he or she last ate and drank. This information may tell you whether the patient is hydrated or give you important history if, for example, the patient is diabetic. Also find out when the patient last urinated and defecated. Clear, copious urine indicates good hydration; dark, smelly urine suggests dehydration. A patient with diarrhea or vomiting may be dehydrated.

Events. Recent events are unusual circumstances that have occurred within the past few days that may be relevant to the patient's present situation. Recent events might include symptoms of mountain sickness preceding pulmonary edema or changes in diet preceding stomach upset.

THE ASSESSMENT

The assessment is a review of the information gathered during the initial assessment and the focused exam and history. Examine the records of the head-to-toe examination, the vital signs, and the medical history. Review OPQRST and SAMPLE.

Rule out possibilities as you assess. Many diagnoses are made by physicians on the basis of what a condition isn't rather than what it could be. Is chest pain a muscle pull or a heart attack? Does the patient have the flu, mountain sickness, or early cerebral edema?

The Plan

Next, develop a Problem List to prioritize the patient's medical problems and develop a Treatment Plan for each.

The initial exam provides a baseline. Periodically repeat the exam to judge the patient's response to treatment and any changes for better or worse. If there is any change or deterioration in the patient, return to the beginning and repeat the initial assessment.

The Assessment

- Review available information.
- Rule out other possibilities.

The Plan

- Prioritize and treat.
- Review and repeat exam.

SOAP Notes

You may find it helpful to write down the results of your assessment. You may also need to communicate with an evacuation or rescue party or the emergency room physician. Health care professionals commonly organize their medical notes into the SOAP format: subjective or summary, objective or observations, the assessment, and the plan.

Subjective or summary information is told to you by the patient or bystanders. It is the "story" of this event. It includes age, sex, mechanism of injury, chief complaint, and OPQRST findings.

Objective information is measurable or observable: vital signs and results, what we call "findings," from the SAMPLE history and the patient exam.

The assessment section categorizes the patient's medical concerns in a problem list. For example, a problem list might be "sprained ankle, mild hypothermia," or "chest pain, possible heart attack." There should be a plan, or you should note interventions or treatment for each problem.

EXTENDED PATIENT CARE

Emergency medical care in the wilderness may be prolonged over hours or days in isolated locations. Splints, shelter, and litters may need to be improvised. In addition to first aid, basic nursing care is necessary to manage the physical and emotional needs of the patient.

Daily Needs

Keep the patient warm, clean, and comfortable. Remove soiled and wet clothing, and wash the patient. An individual immobilized on a litter may need extra insulation to keep warm and occasional position changes to avoid bedsores. Hot water bottles, heat packs, or fires may be needed as sources of warmth.

Drinking and eating are not appropriate in patients with an abnormal level of responsiveness.

If the patient can drink, give water or clear soups and juices. Avoid lots of coffee, tea, or other beverages with high concentrations of sugar or caffeine. Excess sugar can delay fluid absorption; excess caffeine increases fluid loss.

Over a period of a few days, fluid intake is more important than solid food, as dehydration can complicate any existing medical condition. Dehydration is discussed in chapter 23 ("Hydration").

Arrange for the patient to urinate and defecate as comfortably as possible. These basic body functions are essential to overall well-being, despite embarrassment or temporary discomfort. The first responder's sensitivity to and support for the patient are essential here.

For male patients, a water bottle usually works well as a urine receptacle. For female patients, a bedpan can be fashioned from a frying pan or a large-mouth water bottle, or an article of clothing can be used as a diaper. Bowel movements can be managed by assisting the patient with an improvised bedpan.

Emotional Support

An ill or injured patient experiences a variety of emotions, including fear about the quality of care and the outcome of the injury or illness, the length of evacuation, loss of control and independence, loss of self-esteem, and embarrassment. To help the patient cope with such roller-coaster feelings, maintain your calm, respond promptly and clearly to questions, and treat the patient with respect and sensitivity.

Respecting your patient means using manners as you would in an average social situation. Introduce yourself, call the patient by name, and ask permission to give treatment. In doing so, you also begin to involve the patient in his or her own care. As you examine and treat the patient, explain your actions. Warn the patient if you might cause pain. Involve the patient in evacuation decisions.

Reassurance, concern, and sympathy are appropriate, but avoid making promises you are unsure of, e.g., "You're going to be just fine." It's healthy to allow the patient to discuss the incident. Talking about an accident begins the process of emotional healing. Do not critique the incident or lay blame on any party involved. This will only increase the patient's anxiety and agitation.

Anticipate a lull in your enthusiasm and energy as the initial excitement wears off, fatigue sets in, and you realize the amount of work required to care for and evacuate the patient. These emotions are a reality of rescue. They should not be communicated to the patient as a lack of concern. See chapter 28 ("Stress and the Rescuer") for more on rescue stress.

FINAL THOUGHTS—THE EVACUATION DECISION

An incomplete patient assessment system—failure to measure vital signs or review history and physical findings—has been the source of unnecessary and needlessly rushed evacuations. Helicopters have flown into wilderness areas for simple knee sprains and for hyperventilation misdiagnosed as a head injury. Rescue teams have hiked through the night expecting to treat serious injuries, only to find a walking patient with minor injuries. The patient, rescuers, and expedition members are needlessly put at risk.

Likewise, the same mistake has delayed evacuations. Life-threatening fevers have been overlooked because a temperature was not measured. Diabetic complications have been missed because no one asked about the patient's medical history.

A significant difference between urban and wilderness medicine is seen in the decision-making process. In the urban emergency medical services system, ambulance personnel rarely make

NATIONAL OUTDOOR LEADERSHIP SCHOOL
FIELD EVACUATION REPORT

Name of Evacuee _____ Course/Section _____

Course Leader _____ Date & Time of Incident _____

SUBJECTIVE: Age___ Sex___ Location of Patient: Common name _____

Mechanism of Injury/Illness _____

_____

_____

_____

Chief Complaint (OPQRST*) _____

_____

_____

_____

OBJECTIVE: Vital Signs**

Date/Time	LOR	Pulse	RR	Skin	Pupils	T

Signs/Symptoms (patient exam) _____

_____

_____

_____

_____

Allergies _____ Medications _____

Past Medical History _____

Last Oral Intake _____

Events (recent, relevant) _____

ASSESSMENT: Problem list (prioritize) _____

_____

PLAN: Emergency Care Rendered/Changes in Patient's Condition _____

_____

_____

_____

_____

_____

Evacuation Plan (timetable, backup, pickup point) _____

_____

_____

_____

_____

Instructor Signature _____ Date _____ Time _____

*OPQRST = onset, provocation, quality, region/radiation, severity, time sequence.
**LOR = alert x 4 (person, place, time, event), verbal, pain, unresponsive; pulse = rate, strength, and rhythm; RR = respiratory rate, depth, and rhythm; skin = color, temperature, moisture; pupils = equality, roundness, reactivity to light; T = temperature.

a decision whether or not to transport a patient. If they are called to help, an ambulance crew either transports the patient or the patient signs a refusal of treatment form. In the wilderness, the leader must decide if a patient needs to see a physician, and if so, with what urgency. The patient assessment system is an invaluable tool for these decisions.

Throughout this text I will suggest evacuation decision points. I'll note the thresholds for when patients should be evacuated, and when they need to be evacuated rapidly. These are guidelines that you can use, in conjunction with your physician advisor, to develop a protocol for your expedition or program.

There are many stories of outdoor leaders who, though they lacked medical experience, performed a simple and methodical assessment, checked the ABCs for life-threatening problems, then followed the focused history and exam protocols. They used a checklist, took their time, and made a written record of their findings. The information gathered was the foundation for quality first aid. Good medical decisions and judgment made for a sound evacuation plan.

TRAUMATIC INJURIES

The incident data collected over three decades by the National Outdoor Leadership School shows that sprains, strains, and small wounds are the common injuries experienced on wilderness expeditions. Serious injury is uncommon. Regardless, in the wilderness we need to be prepared to manage fractures and dislocations as well as head, spine, or chest injuries until we can deliver the patient to the physician. This section covers field first aid treatment principles for this spectrum of injuries, from bleeding control and wound care to splinting, moving, and immobilizing a possible spine injury, stabilizing a chest injury, taping an ankle, and aiding a person in shock.

SHOCK

INTRODUCTION

Shock is a simple name for a complex disorder of the circulatory system. Mid-nineteenth-century descriptions of shock as "a deadly downward spiral" and "a rude unhinging of the machinery of life" accurately portray a condition in which the circulatory system collapses in apparent disproportion to the initial injury. Shock is often the lethal component of burns, serious illness, fractures, injuries to the chest and abdomen, severe bleeding, and catastrophic injury. A first responder must anticipate, recognize, and treat shock.

THE CIRCULATORY SYSTEM

The circulatory system is composed of the heart, the blood vessels, and the blood. Its primary function is to deliver a constant supply of oxygen to the tissues. An interruption causes cells and tissues to malfunction and eventually die. The circulatory system also transports carbon dioxide from the cells to the lungs, keeps the electrolyte environment stable, delivers hormones from their source to their place of action, and mobilizes body defenses.

The heart is a two-sided pump that propels blood through a system of pipes (arteries, veins, and capillaries). The right side receives blood from the veins and pumps it through the lungs for

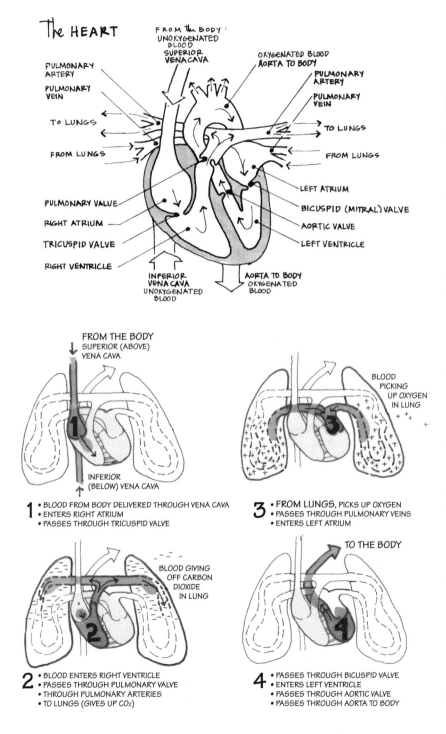

The HEART

FROM the BODY:
UNOXYGENATED BLOOD
SUPERIOR VENA CAVA

OXYGENATED BLOOD
AORTA TO BODY

PULMONARY ARTERY

PULMONARY VEIN

PULMONARY ARTERY

PULMONARY VEIN

TO LUNGS

TO LUNGS

FROM LUNGS

FROM LUNGS

LEFT ATRIUM

PULMONARY VALVE

BICUSPID (MITRAL) VALVE

RIGHT ATRIUM

AORTIC VALVE

TRICUSPID VALVE

LEFT VENTRICLE

RIGHT VENTRICLE

INFERIOR VENA CAVA
UNOXYGENATED BLOOD

AORTA TO BODY
OXYGENATED BLOOD

FROM THE BODY
SUPERIOR (ABOVE) VENA CAVA

INFERIOR (BELOW) VENA CAVA

1 • BLOOD FROM BODY DELIVERED THROUGH VENA CAVA
• ENTERS RIGHT ATRIUM
• PASSES THROUGH TRICUSPID VALVE

BLOOD GIVING OFF CARBON DIOXIDE IN LUNG

2 • BLOOD ENTERS RIGHT VENTRICLE
• PASSES THROUGH PULMONARY VALVE
• THROUGH PULMONARY ARTERIES
• TO LUNGS (GIVES UP CO_2)

BLOOD PICKING UP OXYGEN IN LUNG

3 • FROM LUNGS, PICKS UP OXYGEN
• PASSES THROUGH PULMONARY VEINS
• ENTERS LEFT ATRIUM

TO THE BODY

4 • PASSES THROUGH BICUSPID VALVE
• ENTERS LEFT VENTRICLE
• PASSES THROUGH AORTIC VALVE
• PASSES THROUGH AORTA TO BODY

oxygen replenishment. The left side pumps the oxygen-rich blood from the lungs to the rest of the body. Blood leaves the heart through arteries, which narrow into smaller vessels called arterioles and eventually become a vast network of microscopic vessels called capillaries.

Capillaries are woven throughout the tissues. The exchange of nutrients and waste products from the blood to the cells takes place across capillary walls only one cell thick. Blood vessels leaving the capillary beds widen into veins, conduits for blood returning to the heart. The venous blood returns to the right side of the heart and then to the lungs to be replenished with oxygen. The circuit is complete.

The circulatory system adjusts automatically to our energy demands, activity level, position, and temperature. The rate and force of pumping, the diameter of the vessels, and the amount of fluid in the system vary to meet the requirements of exercise, stress, sleep, and relaxation.

SHOCK

Cardiologist and wilderness medicine specialist Dr. Bruce Paton suggests the following analogy for shock: Imagine the body as a healthy wetland with a river running through lush vegetation. The vegetation depends on the river's flow of pure, unpolluted water and the nutrients it carries. If the river dries up or the water becomes poisoned, the plants shrivel and die. The maintenance of a healthy, well-oxygenated flow of blood through the tissues is called good perfusion.

Shock is the inadequate perfusion of tissue with oxygenated blood. It is a failure of any or all of three basic components of the circulatory system—heart, blood vessels, and blood—to deliver oxygenated blood to the tissues. Insufficient blood flow to the tissues causes inadequate oxygen and nutrient delivery and waste product removal. Shock is a state in which poor perfusion leads first to reversible then irreversible tissue damage. Bodily processes slow, and tissues begin to die.

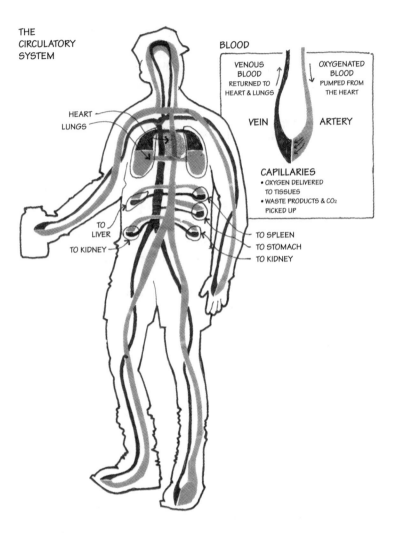

THE CIRCULATORY SYSTEM

BLOOD

VENOUS BLOOD RETURNED TO HEART & LUNGS

OXYGENATED BLOOD PUMPED FROM THE HEART

VEIN   ARTERY

CAPILLARIES
• OXYGEN DELIVERED TO TISSUES
• WASTE PRODUCTS & CO_2 PICKED UP

HEART
LUNGS

TO LIVER
TO KIDNEY

TO SPLEEN
TO STOMACH
TO KIDNEY

Causes of Shock

Adequate blood pressure, like a healthy river flowing at a proper level into the wetland, is essential to maintaining perfusion of vital organs. Three factors influence blood pressure, and changes in any of them can have serious consequences. The three critical factors are blood volume, cardiac output (the volume of blood pumped per minute by the heart), and the state of constriction or dilation of the blood vessels (peripheral resistance).

Fluid Loss. Fluid loss is a major cause of shock. The primary causes of fluid loss are bleeding, infections, extensive burns, and metabolic disorders. Massive bleeding results in a reduced blood volume; blood vessels are inadequately filled, and blood pressure falls. Shock can also develop from fluid loss during watery diarrhea, from dehydration, from illness such as diabetes, or from hidden bleeding into fractures of the femur and pelvis.

The average adult has 6 liters of blood. A 10 percent loss (.5 liter) is enough to affect blood pressure. A 25 percent blood volume loss (1.5 liters) can cause moderate shock. A 30 percent loss (2 liters) is considered serious shock.

Decreased Cardiac Output. The heart muscle may become so damaged by a heart attack that it cannot maintain adequate output (pump failure). Shock secondary to a heart attack is referred to as cardiogenic shock.

Blood Vessel Dilation. Dilated blood vessels cause blood pressure and perfusion to decrease despite the extra pumping of the heart in response to the shock. Fainting, a mild form of shock, results when momentary dilation of blood vessels occurs in a person's body as a response to a strong emotional stimulus. As the volume of blood returning to the heart diminishes, blood pressure falls and the person may faint. If a spinal cord injury damages nerves controlling vessel diameter, they may widen and cause shock. Changes in blood vessel diameter, however, are generally not an important cause of shock, except in overwhelming infection in which there is widespread dilation of small vessels.

Assessment of Shock

A patient in shock has a rapid pulse rate that may feel weak and irregular. The skin is pale, cool, and clammy. These signs and symptoms are due to our "fight or flight" response—our body's response to danger—wherein release of adrenaline increases heart rate, causes the skin to pale and sweat, and causes nausea and restlessness. Blood is routed away from the digestive tract and concentrates around the muscles and essential organs. These changes pump the blood faster, reduce the size of the blood vessels, and route the blood to essential organs, possibly enabling the body to compensate for the shock.

Signs and Symptoms of Shock

EARLY CHANGES

- Rapid and/or weak pulse
- Rapid and/or shallow respirations
- Pale, cool, clammy skin
- Anxiety or restlessness
- Nausea, thirst

LATER CHANGES

- Decreasing level of responsiveness
- Slow-to-respond pupils
- Falling blood pressure

Most people, when frightened, injured, or ill, have a "fight or flight" or acute stress response. Your heart beats strong and fast; you sweat, become pale, and feel nervous. If you're not seriously ill or injured and your circulatory system is healthy, this response should abate in a short time. The heart rate slows, you relax, and the skin returns to its normal color. When you measure a series of vital signs over time, you may see this initial acute stress diminish as you recover from the initial fright. If the circulatory system is unable to adjust, a downward spiral of deterioration may begin in which first tissues, then organs, and finally entire systems fail from lack of oxygen.

A progressively increasing pulse rate is a bad sign, indicating continuing blood loss or increasing shock. The skin becomes sweaty and pale, and the patient looks very ill. The patient may exhibit shallow, rapid breathing and be restless, anxious, irritable, and thirsty. Level of responsiveness is variable. If shock prevents the brain from being perfused with oxygen-rich blood, the level of responsiveness will deteriorate.

Treatment of Shock

Although shock is more likely with multiple injuries, serious illness, severe bleeding, dehydration, or a major fracture, initially you should treat every patient for shock. If the mechanism of injury is not serious and signs and symptoms stabilize or do not deteriorate, the patient is probably experiencing only a stress reaction.

Always assume that shock may occur, and begin treatment before signs and symptoms are manifested. Treatment begins with the triad of basic life support—airway, breathing, and circulation (ABC)—as well as control of bleeding and stabilization of fractures and other injuries. Thereafter, shock treatment moves to a second triad: temperature maintenance, position, and fluids.

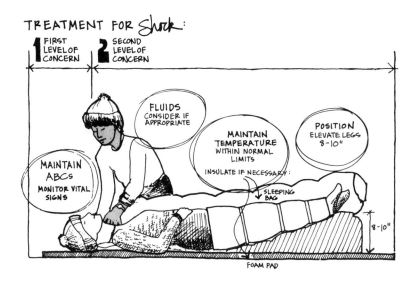

TREATMENT FOR Shock:

1 FIRST LEVEL OF CONCERN **2** SECOND LEVEL OF CONCERN

FLUIDS CONSIDER IF APPROPRIATE

MAINTAIN TEMPERATURE WITHIN NORMAL LIMITS

POSITION ELEVATE LEGS 8-10"

MAINTAIN ABCs MONITOR VITAL SIGNS

INSULATE IF NECESSARY:

SLEEPING BAG

8-10"

FOAM PAD

Maintain Temperature. Protect the patient from excess heat and cold. Your goal is to maintain body temperature within normal limits. Insulate the patient from the cold ground, provide protection from wind and weather, and remove wet clothes and replace them with dry.

Elevate Legs. Unless the patient has a head injury, or injury to the legs or pelvis prevents it, position the patient with the legs elevated 8 to 10 inches. Whether this helps return blood to the heart is debatable, but it doesn't harm the patient. Whether we are treating for shock or simply providing long-term patient comfort, it is good to support the patient's low back by adjusting leg position. Even with apparently minor injuries, this position can be used until you have assessed the problem and ruled out shock.

Consider Fluids. In the urban setting we rarely give the patient oral fluids. In the wilderness, fluids may be given if surgery does not seem likely, the patient does not have an altered mental status, and he or she can tolerate the fluids.

When giving fluids by mouth, plain water is adequate. Using one teaspoon of salt per liter is accept-

---

Treatment for Shock

- ABCs: open and maintain airway.
- Control bleeding, stabilize fractures.
- Maintain temperature.
- Elevate legs.
- Consider fluids.

able, as are diluted bouillon drinks. Beware of strong salty or sweet drinks.

FINAL THOUGHTS

Shock, an insidious and complicated disturbance in the circulatory system, is difficult to treat in the backcountry. Paramedics, nurses, and physicians in urban medical systems are trained to quickly assess, transport, and use technical medical procedures to fight shock. None of this is available in the wilderness.

The basic treatments of bandages, splints, and physical and emotional support, reinforced by temperature maintenance, position, and fluids, are all assets in the wilderness management of shock. The definitive treatment of shock in the backcountry, however, is evacuation.

Evacuation Guidelines
- Evacuate any patient whose vital signs do not stabilize or improve over time.
- Evacuate rapidly any patient with decreased mental status or deteriorating vital signs.

CHAPTER 3 | CHEST INJURIES

INTRODUCTION

Chest injuries range from simple but painful rib fractures to life-threatening lung injuries. NOLS' incident data shows that rib fractures are most common. *Accidents in North American Mountaineering* has documented more than a few instances of mountaineers who've suffered serious chest and lung injuries from falls. Paddlers can experience chest injuries from impact with rocks or from blows by the bows of kayaks. Horsepacking and backcountry skiing are other wilderness activities in which there are mechanisms—falls and collisions—for chest trauma. In the backcountry, our role is to recognize the injury, support the patient, and make a sound evacuation decision.

CHEST AND LUNG ANATOMY

Chest injuries concern us because they can compromise the respiratory or cardiovascular system. The respiratory system provides oxygen to and removes carbon dioxide from the body. The cardiovascular system transports these gases as well as nutrients and waste products to and from the cells. Contained within the chest cavity are some of the structures responsible for these processes: the airway passages, lungs, heart, and major vessels—the vena cava and aorta.

The clavicles, rib cage, and diaphragm form the boundaries of the chest cavity. The rib cage consists of twelve pairs of ribs. All

PARTS OF THE RESPIRATORY SYSTEM :

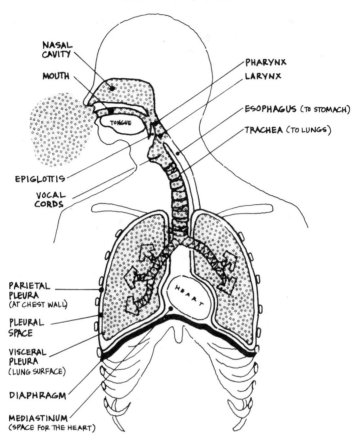

NASAL CAVITY

MOUTH

PHARYNX

LARYNX

ESOPHAGUS (TO STOMACH)

TRACHEA (TO LUNGS)

TONGUE

EPIGLOTTIS

VOCAL CORDS

PARIETAL PLEURA (AT CHEST WALL)

PLEURAL SPACE

VISCERAL PLEURA (LUNG SURFACE)

DIAPHRAGM

MEDIASTINUM (SPACE FOR THE HEART)

HEART

the ribs are attached to the spine in the back. The upper seven pairs are attached to the sternum by cartilage; the next three pairs are attached to cartilage only; and the lowest two pairs ("floating ribs") are attached only to the spine.

The components of the respiratory system are the nose, mouth, pharynx, larynx, epiglottis, trachea, bronchi, bronchioles, and alveoli. The diaphragm and muscles of the chest wall move air in and out of the lungs.

The average healthy adult breathes 12 to 20 times per minute, moving half a liter of air with each breath. Respiratory rate increases with exercise, altitude, illness, or injury.

Nose, Mouth, Pharynx, Larynx. As air enters the nose or mouth, it is warmed and humidified by mucous membranes that line the respiratory tract. The mucus produced by the membranes and the cilia (hairlike structures) helps keep foreign material out of the lungs. Air passes from the nose or mouth into the pharynx, past the larynx, and into the trachea. The larynx consists of tiny bones, muscles, cartilage, and two vocal cords. Air forced past the vocal cords causes them to vibrate, producing sound.

Epiglottis. The epiglottis sits above the larynx and prevents food from entering the trachea by closing over the larynx during swallowing. If solids or liquids inadvertently enter the larynx, the vocal cords spasm, causing us to cough.

Trachea. The trachea is approximately 5 inches long and is composed of cartilage, which prevents the trachea from collapsing. At the bottom of the trachea, the tube divides into the right and left bronchi. After air enters the lungs via the bronchi, it follows smaller passageways called bronchioles until it enters the alveoli.

Alveoli. The alveoli are small air sacs surrounded by capillaries where red blood cells release carbon dioxide and pick up oxygen. Blood then flows into the pulmonary veins, which carry it to the heart and the rest of the body.

Lungs. The lungs occupy most of the chest cavity. Each lung is enclosed by a double-layered membrane called the pleura. The layer that attaches to the lung is called the visceral pleura, and the layer attached to the chest wall is called the parietal pleura.

Between the two layers is a thin film of fluid that lubricates the membranes and allows them to move freely. This area is called the pleural space, and under normal conditions, it is a potential space under negative pressure. If air enters the pleural space, as in a pneumothorax, the potential space becomes an actual space, and the lung collapses.

Inspiration is the active motion of breathing. The diaphragm moves downward, and the intercostal muscles (muscles between the ribs) move the chest wall outward. As the ribs move outward, the negative pressure in the lungs increases, and air is sucked into the lungs. When the pressure within the lungs and the atmospheric pressure are equal, air stops entering the lungs. At this point, the diaphragm and chest muscles relax, elastic recoil reduces lung size, and air is exhaled (expiration).

Diaphragm. The diaphragm is a specialized muscle that works both voluntarily and involuntarily. The level of carbon dioxide in the blood determines how fast and deeply we breathe. If the level of carbon dioxide in the blood increases, the respiratory center in the brain tells the diaphragm to increase the respiratory rate. If the level of carbon dioxide is too low, the brain tells the diaphragm to slow down. We can directly control the diaphragm by taking deep breaths or by holding our breath, but only for short periods of time, after which the involuntary control centers of the brain take over again.

RIB FRACTURES

The most commonly fractured ribs are ribs five through ten. Ribs one through four are protected by the shoulder girdle and are rarely fractured. The floating ribs—ribs eleven and twelve—are more flexible and will give before breaking.

Signs and Symptoms. Rib fractures cause deformity and/or discoloration over the injured area. The patient complains of tenderness over the fracture (point tenderness) when touched. Breathing or coughing causes sharp, stabbing pain at the site of the fracture. Respiratory rate increases as the patient breathes shallowly in an attempt to decrease the pain. The patient may clutch the chest on the fractured side in an attempt to splint it. Carefully observe rib fracture victims for other injuries.

Treatment. A single fractured rib that is not displaced (simple rib fracture) does not require splinting. Pain medication such as acetaminophen or ibuprofen may be all the treatment necessary.

Tape the Fracture Site on One Side of Chest. If the pain is severe, tape the fractured side from sternum to spine with four or five pieces of 1-

---

Signs and Symptoms of Rib Fractures

- Point tenderness over the fracture
- Pain on inspiration, shallow breathing, coughing
- Shortness of breath during exertion

Treatment of Rib Fractures

- Tape the fracture site.
- Sling and swathe.

to 2-inch adhesive tape. This decreases movement at the fracture site and diminishes pain. Tape should never be wrapped completely around the chest, as this can restrict breathing. You may also find that a simple sling and swathe on the arm on the injured side limits movement and provides comfort. If the patient is not in respiratory distress, he or she may be able to walk out.

FLAIL CHEST

A flail chest occurs when 3 or more adjacent ribs are broken in two or more places, loosening a segment of the chest wall. When the patient breathes in, the increased negative pressure pulls the flail segment inward, and the lung does not fill with air as it should. When the patient breathes out, the opposite occurs, and the flail segment may be pushed outward. The flail segment moves in a direction opposite of normal breathing, thus the term "paradoxical respirations."

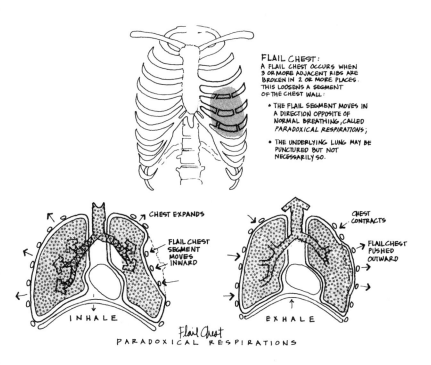

FLAIL CHEST:
A FLAIL CHEST OCCURS WHEN 3 OR MORE ADJACENT RIBS ARE BROKEN IN 2 OR MORE PLACES. THIS LOOSENS A SEGMENT OF THE CHEST WALL:

• THE FLAIL SEGMENT MOVES IN A DIRECTION OPPOSITE OF NORMAL BREATHING, CALLED PARADOXICAL RESPIRATIONS;

• THE UNDERLYING LUNG MAY BE PUNCTURED BUT NOT NECESSARILY SO.

CHEST EXPANDS

FLAIL CHEST SEGMENT MOVES INWARD

INHALE

CHEST CONTRACTS

FLAIL CHEST PUSHED OUTWARD

EXHALE

Flail Chest
PARADOXICAL RESPIRATIONS

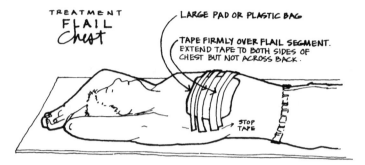

TREATMENT
FLAIL
Chest

LARGE PAD OR PLASTIC BAG

TAPE FIRMLY OVER FLAIL SEGMENT.
EXTEND TAPE TO BOTH SIDES OF
CHEST BUT NOT ACROSS BACK.

STOP
TAPE

Signs and Symptoms of Flail Chest

- Paradoxical chest movement
- Respiratory distress

Signs and Symptoms. A flail chest develops only with a significant chest injury, such as a heavy fall against a rock. The patient may be in respiratory distress. Put your hands under the patient's shirt, and you may feel a part of the chest moving in while the opposite part of the chest is moving out. This may also be visible upon inspection.

Treatment. Stabilize the flail chest:

- Position the patient whichever way makes breathing most comfortable. This may be on the injured side with a rolled-up piece of clothing underneath the flailed segment.
- Apply pressure with your hand to the flailed area. This works only as a temporary measure, as it is difficult to hold pressure while transporting the patient.
- Tape a large pad firmly over the flail segment (without circling the chest).

Treat the patient for shock and evacuate.

INJURIES TO LUNGS

In addition to injuries to the ribs, the underlying lungs may be damaged. Blood vessels can be ruptured and torn, causing bleeding into the chest, and lungs can be punctured, causing air to leak into the chest.

Pneumothorax. This occurs when air leaks into the pleural space, creating negative pressure that collapses the lung. Pneumothorax can be caused by a fractured rib that lacerates the lung (traumatic pneumothorax), a weak spot on the lung wall that gives way (spontaneous pneumothorax), or an open chest wound.

Hemothorax. This occurs when lacerated blood vessels cause blood to collect in the pleural space. The source can be a fractured rib or lacerated lung. If more than 1 liter of blood leaks into the pleural space, a hemothorax may compress the lung and compromise breathing. The loss of blood may also cause shock.

Spontaneous Pneumothorax. A congenital weak area of the lung may rupture, creating a spontaneous pneumothorax. The highest incidence occurs in tall, thin, healthy men between the ages of 20 and 30. Eighty percent of spontaneous pneumothoraxes occur while the person is at rest. The patient complains of a sudden, sharp pain in the chest and increasing shortness of breath.

Tension Pneumothorax. If a hole opening into the pleural space serves as a one-way valve—allowing air to enter but not to escape—a tension pneumothorax develops. With each breath, air enters the pleural space, but it cannot escape with expiration. As pressure in the pleural space increases, the lung collapses. Pressure in the pleural space eventually causes the mediastinum to shift to the unaffected side, putting pressure on the heart and good lung. If the pressure in the pleural space exceeds that in the veins, blood cannot return to the heart, and death occurs.

As pressure builds, you may see the trachea deviate toward the unaffected side, tissue between the ribs bulge, and the neck

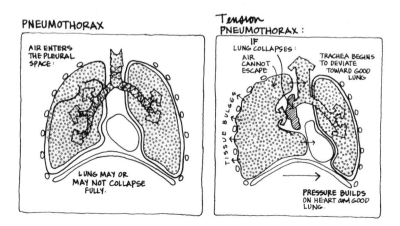

PNEUMOTHORAX

AIR ENTERS THE PLEURAL SPACE:

LUNG MAY OR MAY NOT COLLAPSE FULLY.

Tension PNEUMOTHORAX:

IF LUNG COLLAPSES:

AIR CANNOT ESCAPE

TRACHEA BEGINS TO DEVIATE TOWARD GOOD LUNG

TISSUE BULGES

PRESSURE BUILDS ON HEART and GOOD LUNG.

Injury to Lungs

SIGNS AND SYMPTOMS
- Obvious chest trauma
- Shortness of breath
- Rapid, shallow respirations
- Cyanosis
- Shock
- Coughing up blood

Pneumothorax
- Sudden, sharp chest pain

Tension pneumothorax
- Tracheal deviation

Open chest wound
- Sucking noise

TREATMENT
- Seal open chest wounds.
- Immobilize rib fractures.
- Stabilize impaled objects.
- Position patient for comfort.
- Monitor for shortness of breath.
- Evacuate.

veins distend. Respirations become increasingly rapid. The pulse is weak and rapid; cyanosis occurs.

Open Chest Wounds

If a wound through the chest wall breaks into the pleural space, air enters, creating a pneumothorax. If the wound remains open, air moves in and out of the pleura, causing a sucking noise.

The goal of treatment is to limit the size of the pneumothorax. Quickly seal the hole with any nonporous material—a plastic bag or petroleum jelly–impregnated gauze, for example. Tape the dressing down on all four sides to seal the hole. If signs of a tension pneumothorax develop, you can release and then reseal the hole. This might allow trapped air to escape and relieve the tension in the chest.

RESPIRATORY DISTRESS

Respiratory distress is an overall term that covers any situation in which a patient is having difficulty breathing. Respiratory distress can occur after an injury, during an illness such as pneumonia, during a heart attack or an asthma attack, or after inhalation of a poisonous gas.

Signs and symptoms of respiratory distress are anxiety and restlessness; shortness of breath; rapid respirations and pulse; signs of shock, including pale, cool, and clammy skin and cyanosis of the skin, lips, and fingernail beds; and labored breathing using accessory muscles of the neck, shoulder, and abdomen to achieve maximum effort. The patient is usually more comfortable sitting than lying.

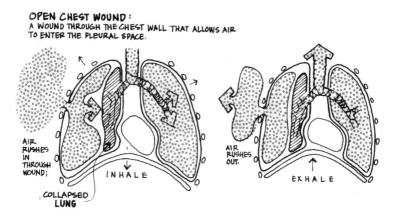

OPEN CHEST WOUND:
A WOUND THROUGH THE CHEST WALL THAT ALLOWS AIR
TO ENTER THE PLEURAL SPACE.

AIR RUSHES IN THROUGH WOUND;   INHALE

COLLAPSED LUNG

AIR RUSHES OUT.   EXHALE

Respiratory distress is a frightening experience for both the patient and the rescuer. If the underlying cause is emotional, as in hyperventilation syndrome (see chapter 17), reassurance may be all that's needed to alleviate the problem. If a chest injury with underlying lung damage or an illness such as pneumonia or a pulmonary embolus occurs, treatment in the field is difficult. Evacuation is the course of action. The airway can be maintained, the patient placed in the most comfortable position for breathing, the injury splinted or taped, wounds dressed, and the patient treated for shock.

FINAL THOUGHTS

Chest injuries range from painful but not life-threatening simple rib fractures to serious injuries of the chest wall, lungs, and heart. Chest injuries are often complicated by other injuries as well.

Evacuation Guidelines
- The simple rib fracture does not necessarily need to be evacuated unless the patient is uncomfortable with pain, unable to travel, or has shortness of breath.
- Patients with shortness of breath following a blow to the chest, open chest wounds, or other obvious signs of serious chest injury will need to be rapidly evacuated.

CHAPTER 4 | BRAIN AND SPINAL CORD INJURIES

INTRODUCTION

Head injuries range from simple scalp lacerations to life-threatening swelling of the brain. Spine injuries range from fractured vertebrae to actual spinal cord injuries that can result in paralysis. According to the data kept by NOLS, serious brain and spine injuries are rare in the wilderness, yet the urgency and care with which we must assess and handle these patients make them some of the more challenging problems to manage in remote areas.

CENTRAL NERVOUS SYSTEM

Together, the brain, spinal cord, and peripheral nerves monitor and control all body functions.

The brain governs thoughts, emotions, senses, memory, and movement, as well as basic physiological functions. The brain processes information from our senses, initiates motor responses, remembers, solves problems, and makes judgments.

The three main divisions of the brain are the cerebrum, the cerebellum, and the brain stem. The cerebrum is the largest part of the brain, the center for our "higher" cognitive functions: problem solving, memory, speech, hearing, sight, and so forth. The cerebellum, in the lower rear of the skull, regulates posture, co-

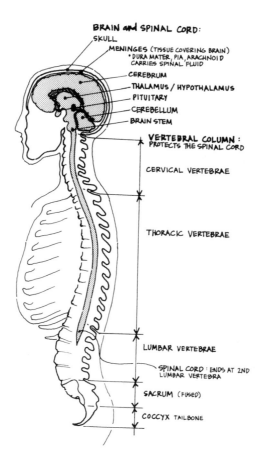

BRAIN and SPINAL CORD:
SKULL
MENINGES (TISSUE COVERING BRAIN)
• DURA MATER, PIA, ARACHNOID
CARRIES SPINAL FLUID
CEREBRUM
THALAMUS / HYPOTHALAMUS
PITUITARY
CEREBELLUM
BRAIN STEM

VERTEBRAL COLUMN :
PROTECTS THE SPINAL CORD

CERVICAL VERTEBRAE

THORACIC VERTEBRAE

LUMBAR VERTEBRAE

SPINAL CORD : ENDS AT 2ND
LUMBAR VERTEBRA

SACRUM (FUSED)

COCCYX TAILBONE

ordination, and motor responses. The brain stem, at the base of the brain, maintains consciousness, heart rate, blood pressure, and breathing.

The skull houses and protects the brain. The brain is covered by three layers of tissue, known collectively as the meninges: the dura mater, the pia, and the arachnoid. Cerebrospinal fluid (CSF), nourishing and cushioning the brain, flows within these layers. Blood vessels are located within the brain and the meninges.

Central nervous system tissue is extremely sensitive to oxygen deficiency. Depriving the brain of oxygen for only a few minutes can result in permanent damage.

BRAIN INJURIES

Head injuries include scalp, skull, and brain injuries. Scalp and skull injuries can be serious by themselves, but we're more concerned with possible injury to the brain.

A large blood supply feeds the scalp, causing it to bleed profusely when cut. A bruised or lacerated scalp can mask underlying injury to the skull or brain. Examine scalp injuries carefully to see if bone or brain is exposed or if an indentation, which might be a depressed fracture, is present. Bleeding from the scalp can be controlled by applying gentle pressure on the edges of the wounds, being careful to avoid direct pressure on possibly unstable central areas.

The skull consists of 22 fused bones. The strongest are the bones forming the top and sides of the protective box encasing the brain. Fractures of the skull are not in themselves life-threatening except when associated with underlying brain injury or spinal cord injury, or when the fracture causes bleeding by tearing the blood vessels between the brain and the skull. Many serious brain injuries occur without skull fractures.

Skull fractures can be open or closed. Open skull fractures expose the brain to infection.

Brain injury can be fatal when it disrupts heartbeat and breathing. In the long term, a severe brain injury may leave the patient physically immobile or mentally incompetent, with severely impaired judgment and problem-solving ability or an inability to process or communicate information properly.

The brain can be injured by a direct blow to the head or by twisting forces, which cause deformation and shearing against the inside of the skull. Some movement between brain and skull is possible. A blow to the head can make the brain "rattle" within the skull, tearing blood vessels in the meninges or within the brain itself, stretching and shearing brain cells and the connections between cells.

A mild brain injury (also known as a concussion) is temporary brain dysfunction or loss of responsiveness following a blow to the head. There may be no or only mild brain injury in this case. Contusions (bruising of brain tissue) and hemorrhages or hematomas (bleeding within the brain) are more serious injuries that can lead to increased pressure in the skull. Encased in this rigid box, a swelling or bleeding brain presses against the skull; the body has no mechanism to release such an increase in pressure. As pressure rises, blood supply is shut off by compression of swollen vessels, and brain tissue is deprived of oxygen. The brain stem can be squashed by the pressure, affecting heart and lung function.

Signs and Symptoms of Brain Injury

Signs and symptoms of brain injury depend on the degree and progression of injury. Some indications of brain injury appear immediately from the accident; others develop slowly.

Changes in Level of Responsiveness. Loss of responsiveness may be short or may persist for hours or days. The patient may alternate between periods of responsiveness and unresponsiveness or be responsive but disoriented, confused, and incoherent—exhibiting changes in behavior and personality or verbal or physical combativeness.

Headache, Vision Disturbances, Loss of Balance, Nausea and Vomiting, Paralysis, Seizures. Headache, vision problems, loss of balance, nausea and vomiting, and paralysis may accompany brain

---

Signs and Symptoms of Brain Injury

MILD BRAIN INJURY
- Brief change in mental status or brief loss of responsiveness
- Short-term amnesia
- Temporarily blurred vision or "seeing stars"
- Nausea and/or isolated vomiting
- Headache, dizziness, and/or lethargy

SERIOUS BRAIN INJURY
- Disoriented, irritable, combative, unconscious
- Heart rate decreases and bounds
- Hyperventilation, erratic respiration
- Skin warm and flushed
- Pupils become unequal (late-changing sign)
- Worsening headache, vision disturbances, protracted vomiting, lethargy, excessive sleepiness, ataxia, and seizures

---

injury. In serious cases, the patient may assume abnormal positions, with the legs and arms stiff and extended or the arms clutched across the chest. A brain-injured patient may have seizures.

Combativeness. A brain-injured patient may become combative, striking out randomly and with surprising strength at the nearest person. If the brain is oxygen-deprived, supplemental oxygen and airway maintenance may help alleviate such behavior. Restraint may be necessary to protect the patient and the rescuers.

Blood or CSF Leakage, Soft Tissue Injury to Skull, Obvious Skull Fracture, Raccoon Sign, Battle's Sign. Blood or clear cerebrospinal fluid (CSF) leaking from the ears, mouth, or nose is a sign of a skull fracture, as are pain, tenderness, and swelling at the injury site or obvious penetrating wounds or depressed fractures. Two other signs of skull fracture—bruising around the eyes (called the raccoon sign) and bruising behind the ear (Battle's sign)—usually appear hours after the injury.

Slow Pulse, Rising Blood Pressure, Irregular Respirations. Changes in vital signs that indicate a serious and late-stage brain injury are a slow pulse, rising blood pressure, and irregular respiratory rate. These contrast with the rising pulse, falling blood pressure, and rapid, regular respirations seen with shock.

Assessment for Brain Injury

Initial assessment of brain injury can be difficult. The symptoms of a mild brain injury are similar to those seen in more serious injuries.

JAW THRUST AIRWAY OPENING FOR SUSPECTED C-SPINE PATIENTS :
- *DO NOT MOVE NECK OR SPINE.*
- *DO NOT TILT HEAD BACK*

PLACE FINGERS IN FRONT OF EARLOBE.

PUSH JAW FORWARD AND UP.

ONE HAND ON EACH SIDE OF HEAD :

JAW

EAR

The assessment may also be complicated when the patient's mental status is affected by drugs, alcohol, or other traumatic injuries.

Assessment of a brain injury begins by checking the airway, breathing, and circulation (ABC); bleeding; and cervical spine. A patient with a brain injury is at high risk for cervical spine injury. Avoid movement of the neck. If you suspect brain or neck injury, use the jaw thrust to open the airway.

After a thorough physical assessment, including vital signs, evaluate the nervous system. Note the level of responsiveness and the patient's ability to feel and move extremities. Use the AVPU (awake and alert, not awake but responsive to a verbal stimulus, not awake but responsive to pain, or not awake and unresponsive) system to assess mental status. Question the patient or bystanders as to a loss of responsiveness. Was it immediate, or was there a delay before the patient became unresponsive? Has the patient been awake but drowsy, sleepy, confused, or disoriented? Has the patient been going in and out of responsiveness?

Watch any brain-injured patient carefully, even if the injury does not at first appear serious. Let the patient rest, but wake him or her up every couple of hours and assess responsiveness.

Treatment of Brain Injury

Brain injuries can be difficult to assess, and some that appear initially benign may over time become serious. Thus, we have a low threshold for evacuation. Evacuation is recommended for any patient who has become unresponsive, even for a minute or two, or

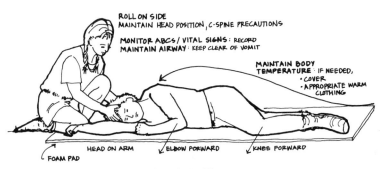

ROLL ON SIDE
MAINTAIN HEAD POSITION, C-SPINE PRECAUTIONS

MONITOR ABCS / VITAL SIGNS : RECORD
MAINTAIN AIRWAY : KEEP CLEAR OF VOMIT

MAINTAIN BODY
TEMPERATURE : IF NEEDED,
• COVER
• APPROPRIATE WARM
CLOTHING

HEAD ON ARM   ELBOW FORWARD   KNEE FORWARD

FOAM PAD

CARING FOR A BRAIN-INJURED PATIENT

Treatment of Brain Injury

- ABCs.
- Assume cervical spine injury.
- If patient is vomiting, position on side.
- Control scalp bleeding.
- Do not control internal bleeding or drainage.
- Elevate head.
- Record neurological assessment.

---

who exhibits vision or balance disturbances, irritability, lethargy, or nausea and vomiting after a blow to the head regardless of whether they were knocked out. A patient who experiences loss of responsiveness but who awakens without any other symptoms may be walked out of the wilderness with a support party capable of quickly evacuating the patient if his or her condition worsens.

ABCs. An injured brain needs oxygen. Ensuring an open airway is the first step in treatment.

If Vomiting, Position Patient on Side. Brain-injured patients have a tendency to vomit. Logrolling the patient onto his or her side while maintaining cervical spine stabilization helps drain vomit while maintaining the airway. Use the jaw thrust to open the airway.

Control Scalp Bleeding. Cover open wounds with bulky sterile dressings as a barrier against infection. Although it is acceptable to clean scalp wounds, cleaning open skull injuries may introduce infection into the brain, so leave them as you find them. Stabilize impaled objects in place.

Do Not Control Internal Bleeding or Drainage. Do not attempt to prevent drainage of blood or clear CSF from the ears or nose. Blocking the flow could increase pressure within the skull.

Elevate head. Keep the patient in a horizontal or slightly head-elevated position. Do not elevate the legs, as this might increase pressure within the skull.

Record Neurological Assessment. Watch the patient closely for any changes in mental status. These observations will be valuable to the receiving physician. Record changes in your patient report.

SPINAL CORD INJURIES

As with head injuries, spinal cord injuries primarily involve young people, with most cases occurring in men between the ages of 15 and 35. An estimated 10,000 new spinal cord injuries occur each year in the United States, and because central nervous tissue does not regenerate, victims are left permanently disabled—half as paraplegics and half as quadriplegics. Motor vehicle accidents account for the majority of spinal injury cases, followed by falls and sporting injuries.

The spinal cord is the extension of the brain outside the skull. A component of the central nervous system, the spinal cord is the nervous connection between the brain and the rest of the body.

The spinal cord is protected within the vertebrae, 33 of which form the backbone, or spine. A force driving the spine out of its normal alignment can fracture or dislocate the vertebrae, thereby injuring the spinal cord. There can be vertebral fractures or ligament and muscle damage to the backbone, however, without damage to the spinal cord. Fractured or dislocated vertebrae can pinch, bruise, or cut the spinal cord, damaging the nervous connections.

The smallest vertebrae with the greatest range of motion are in the neck—the most vulnerable part of the spine. From there, the vertebrae become progressively larger as they support more weight. The location of damage to the spinal cord determines whether the patient may die or be left paralyzed from the neck down (quadriplegia) or the chest down (paraplegia).

Signs and Symptoms of Spinal Cord Injury

Signs and symptoms of spinal cord injury include weakness, loss of sensation or ability to move, numbness and tingling in the hands and feet, incontinence, soft tissue injury over or near the spine, and tenderness in the spine.

Assessment for Spinal Cord Injury

Check for strength, sensation, ability to move, and weakness or numbness in the hands and feet. Ask the patient to wiggle fingers or toes, push his or her feet against your hands, or squeeze your hands with his or hers. Ask the patient to identify which toe or finger you are

Signs and Symptoms of Spinal Cord Injury

- Pain or tenderness on the spine
- Weakness in extremities
- Loss of strength or ability to move extremities
- Loss of sensation in extremities
- Tenderness on spine
- Numbness and tingling in hands and feet
- Incontinence
- Signs and symptoms of shock
- Shortness of breath

IMPROVISED CERVICAL COLLAR

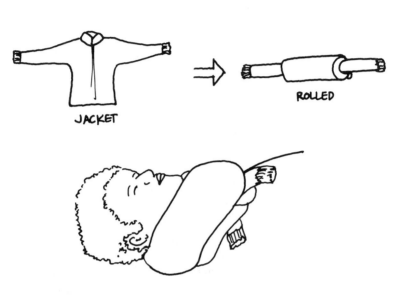

JACKET

ROLLED

touching. Ask if there are any unusual sensations of hot or cold, pins and needles.

Treatment of Spinal Cord Injury

Treatment for a spinal cord injury is to stabilize the spine to prevent further damage. Although it may be necessary to move a spine-injured patient, your first choice should be on-scene stabilization.

Stabilize the Spine. If spinal immobilization devices are not available, one person should always be at the head of the patient, controlling the head and maintaining stabilization of the neck. A clothing or blanket roll may be used as an improvised cervical or neck collar to aid in stabilization, freeing rescuers for other tasks. A strap of cloth or bandage across the forehead secured with wrapped clothing stabilizes the head and neck.

Move with Logroll or Lift. Assume that the patient may have to

---

Treatment of Spinal Cord Injury

- Stabilize spine.
- Hands on patient's head.
- Clothing or blanket roll.
- Move with logroll or lift.
- Immobilize spine.
- Cervical collar.
- Backboard.
- Check CSMs before and after movement.

STABILIZING THE HEAD:

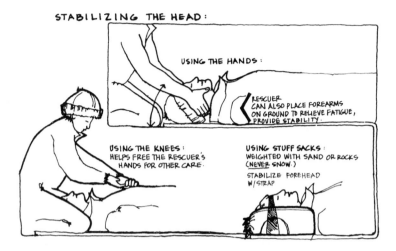

USING THE HANDS:

RESCUER CAN ALSO PLACE FOREARMS ON GROUND TO RELIEVE FATIGUE, PROVIDE STABILITY.

USING THE KNEES:
HELPS FREE THE RESCUER'S HANDS FOR OTHER CARE.

USING STUFF SACKS:
WEIGHTED WITH SAND OR ROCKS (NEVER SNOW.)

STABILIZE FOREHEAD W/STRAP

be moved at least twice during the rescue—once to place insulation underneath the body to prevent hypothermia, and a second time to place the patient on a litter or backboard. Two common techniques for moving the patient are the logroll and the lift. Practice these under the guidance of an emergency care instructor.

A patient can be assessed and immobilized while lying facedown or on his or her back or side. Unless airway, breathing, or bleeding problems are present, you should take the time required to carry out the logroll or lift and explain your actions to the patient.

The Concept:

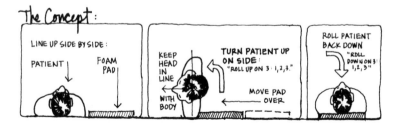

LINE UP SIDE BY SIDE:

PATIENT | FOAM PAD

KEEP HEAD IN LINE WITH BODY

TURN PATIENT UP ON SIDE:
"ROLL UP ON 3 · 1,2,3."

MOVE PAD OVER

ROLL PATIENT BACK DOWN
"ROLL DOWN ON 3: 1,2,3"

How to Perform a Four-Person Logroll

1. The rescuers take positions:
   - Rescuer One maintains stabilization of the head throughout the procedure and gives the commands.

- Rescuer Two kneels beside the patient's chest and reaches across to the patient's shoulder and upper arm.
- Rescuer Three kneels beside the patient's waist and reaches across to the lower back and pelvis.
- Rescuer Four kneels beside the patient's thighs and reaches across to support the legs with one hand on the patient's upper thigh, the other behind the knee.

2. The rescuers roll the patient onto his or her side:
   - Rescuer One, at the head, gives the command, "Roll on 3; 1, 2, 3," and the rescuers slowly roll the patient toward them, keeping the patient's body in alignment. Rescuer One supports the head and maintains alignment with the spine. Once the patient is on his or her side, a backboard or foamlite pad can be placed where the patient will be lying when the logroll is complete.
3. The rescuers roll the patient onto his or her back:
   - When Rescuer One gives the command, "Lower on 3; 1, 2, 3," the procedure is reversed, and the patient is slowly lowered onto the backboard or foamlite pad while the rescuers keep the spine in alignment.

Lifting Technique. The patient can be lifted by four people, enabling a fifth person to slide a backboard, foamlite pad, or litter underneath. The rescuer at the head again maintains stabilization during the entire procedure and gives commands. The other three

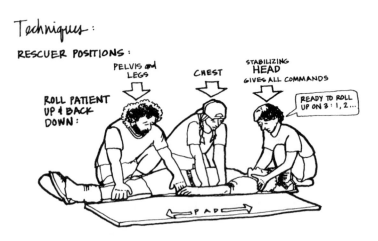

Techniques:

RESCUER POSITIONS:

PELVIS and LEGS   CHEST   STABILIZING HEAD GIVES ALL COMMANDS

ROLL PATIENT UP & BACK DOWN:

READY TO ROLL UP ON 3: 1, 2...

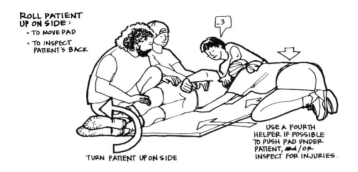

ROLL PATIENT UP ON SIDE:
- TO MOVE PAD
- TO INSPECT PATIENT'S BACK

..3

USE A FOURTH HELPER IF POSSIBLE TO PUSH PAD UNDER PATIENT, and/or INSPECT FOR INJURIES.

TURN PATIENT UP ON SIDE

rescuers position themselves at the patient's sides, one kneeling at chest level and another at pelvis level on the same side, while the third rescuer kneels at waist level on the opposite side. Before lifting, the rescuers place their hands over the patient to visualize their hands in position under the chest, lower back, pelvis, and thighs. They then slide their hands under the patient as far as they can without jostling the patient. On the command, "Lift on 3; 1, 2, 3," rescuers lift the patient to a standing position, then lower him or her onto the pad or litter.

THE LIFT
The Concept:

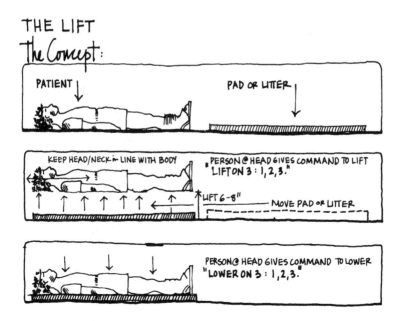

PATIENT

PAD OR LITTER

KEEP HEAD/NECK in LINE WITH BODY

PERSON @ HEAD GIVES COMMAND TO LIFT "LIFT ON 3 : 1, 2, 3."

LIFT 6-8" — MOVE PAD OR LITTER

PERSON @ HEAD GIVES COMMAND TO LOWER "LOWER ON 3 : 1, 2, 3."

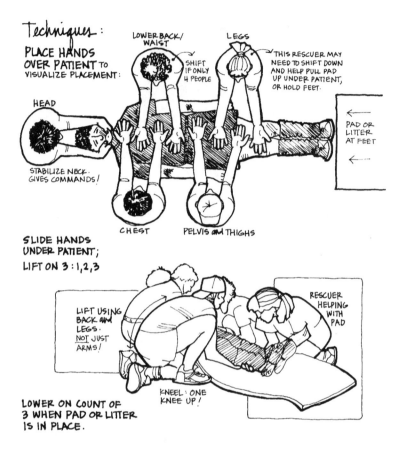

Techniques :

PLACE HANDS
OVER PATIENT TO
VISUALIZE PLACEMENT:

LOWER BACK/
WAIST

LEGS

SHIFT
IF ONLY
4 PEOPLE

THIS RESCUER MAY
NEED TO SHIFT DOWN
AND HELP PULL PAD
UP UNDER PATIENT,
OR HOLD FEET.

HEAD

PAD OR
LITTER
AT FEET

STABILIZE NECK.
GIVES COMMANDS!

CHEST   PELVIS and THIGHS

SLIDE HANDS
UNDER PATIENT;
LIFT ON 3 : 1,2,3

LIFT USING
BACK and
LEGS.
NOT JUST
ARMS!

RESCUER
HELPING
WITH
PAD

LOWER ON COUNT OF
3 WHEN PAD OR LITTER
IS IN PLACE.

KNEEL : ONE
KNEE UP!

Immobilize the Spine. Ideally, the patient should be moved as few times as possible, and preferably after immobilization on a backboard, Kendrick Extrication Device, SKED litter, vacuum litter, or other spine-splinting device, and with a cervical collar and head immobilization. Until such equipment arrives, insulate and shelter the patient.

Wilderness treatment may require caring for a patient during prolonged immobilization. It's uncomfortable to lie still on a hard surface for hours. Current advanced trauma life support (ATLS) curriculum recommends that patients on backboards be logrolled off the backboard approximately every 2 hours to prevent pressure sores on the back. Padding is important. A little bit under the lower back and behind the knees goes a long way to make the patient comfortable. Strapping over bony areas helps tie the patient down, but the straps should be padded and can be loosened when the patient is not being carried.

The Focused Spine Assessment. If a mechanism for a spinal cord injury has occurred, for example, from a fall from a height, a high-velocity skiing fall, a diving accident, or a blow to the head with loss of responsiveness or altered mental status, initially assume the worst and control the head. If the mechanism is severe, or the patient has signs of a spinal cord injury, immobilize the spine. If the mechanism seems trivial and the patient has no signs of spine injury, you may consider performing a focused spine assessment to gather information to help you decide if immobilizing the spine is necessary.

After a thorough assessment, it is acceptable to consider "clearing" the spine of injury by using a method supported by the Wilderness Medical Society and other pre-hospital medicine experts to rule out spine injury. Without this protocol, we would unnecessarily immobilize all patients with insignificant mechanisms for injury. As with all wilderness protocols, support from a physician advisor is recommended.

Making a decision to not immobilize begins with a thorough patient assessment. Then proceed sequentially through this series of steps:

1. Is the patient reliable? They should be sober, not distracted, able to focus on the assessment, and A+Ox3 or 4.
2. Do they have normal circulation, sensation, and motion in all four extremities?
    * Circulation (warm, pink digits, pedal/radial pulse)
    * Sensation (no numbness, tingling, or other unusual sensations)
    * Motion in all four extremities (unless explainable by another injury)
3. No spine pain or tenderness when the spine is palpated.

If the patient fails any step in this process, or you're uncertain about the results of your exam, immobilize the spine. If at any time you're uncomfortable with this process, you can choose a conservative plan and immobilize the patient.

PATIENT PACKAGING POINTS

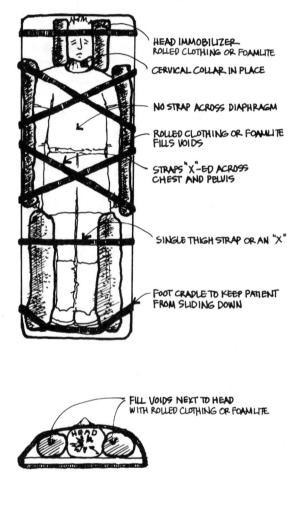

HEAD IMMOBILIZER
ROLLED CLOTHING OR FOAMLITE

CERVICAL COLLAR IN PLACE

NO STRAP ACROSS DIAPHRAGM

ROLLED CLOTHING OR FOAMLITE
FILLS VOIDS

STRAPS "X"-ED ACROSS
CHEST AND PELVIS

SINGLE THIGH STRAP OR AN "X"

FOOT CRADLE TO KEEP PATIENT
FROM SLIDING DOWN

FILL VOIDS NEXT TO HEAD
WITH ROLLED CLOTHING OR FOAMLITE

HEAD

INSERT 1"-2" OF SOFT MATERIAL
TO SUPPORT LOWER BACK and KNEES
FOR PATIENT COMFORT

FINAL THOUGHTS

Airway maintenance, cervical spine precautions, and patient assessment are important treatments for patients with brain and spine injuries, but they are only stopgap measures. A quarter of all brain and spine injuries result in death or permanent disability. The cost of treating a serious brain injury is staggering. In urban settings, first aid for brain or spine injuries includes rapid transport to neurological care—an impossibility in a wilderness setting.

Prevention is the best treatment: Wear a helmet! Be careful out there.

Evacuation Guidelines
- Evacuate if the patient has:
    - —A loss of responsiveness, even if he recovers to A+Ox3 or 4.
    - —Headache, n/v, irritability, or other s/s of mild head injury without loss of responsiveness and is not improving after 24 hours.
- Rapidly evacuate if the patient has:
    - —Distinct changes in mental status (disoriented, irritable, combative).
    - —Persistent vomiting, lethargy, excessive sleepiness, seizures, worsening headache, vision disturbances.
    - —Signs of skull fracture.
- Evacuate any patient with possible spinal cord injury.

FRACTURES AND DISLOCATIONS

INTRODUCTION

As recently as 100 years ago, a fractured femur was a deadly injury. Broken bone ends often did not heal properly. Open fractures frequently became infected, and amputation was a common unpleasant consequence. Modern emergency medicine, especially assessment and splinting in the field, has reduced these complications.

Fractures and dislocations are infrequent at NOLS, making up less than 7 percent of our field injury incidents. Among the general public, however, fractures and dislocations make up as much as 20 percent of reported wilderness injuries. NOLS instructors have cared for femur fractures in the remote backcountry of Yellowstone Park in the winter and at 16,000 feet on Denali. They've expertly splinted uncomplicated wrist fractures and walked patients 20 miles out of the wilderness. They've accurately diagnosed a complicated elbow fracture requiring an urgent helicopter evacuation.

THE SKELETAL SYSTEM

A bony skeleton shapes the body. From this scaffolding hang the soft tissues: the vital organs, blood vessels, muscles, fat, and skin. The skeleton is strong to support and protect internal organs, flexible to withstand stress, and jointed to allow for movement.

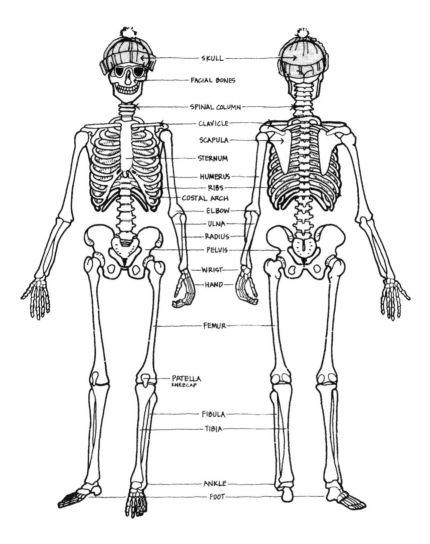

Bone is living tissue combined with nonliving intracellular components. The nonliving components contain calcium and make bone rigid. Bones are connected by ligaments and connective tissue. An adult has 206 bones, ranging in size from the femur, or thigh bone—the largest—to the tiny ossicles of the inner ear.

The skeleton has axial and appendicular components. The axial bones are the pelvis, spinal column, ribs, and skull. Injuries to these structures—except for pelvic fractures—are discussed in the chest and head injury chapters. This chapter covers injuries to the appendicular skeleton: the arms and legs.

The upper extremity consists of the scapula, or shoulder blade; the clavicle, or collarbone; the upper arm bone, or humerus; two bones in the forearm, the radius on the thumb side and the ulna on the little finger side; and 22 bones in the wrist and fingers.

The lower extremity consists of the pelvis; the thighbone, or femur; a small bone in front of the knee, the patella; two bones in the lower leg, the tibia and fibula; and 26 bones in the ankle and foot.

Bones connect at joints. Some joints are fixed; others allow movement. Joints are held together by ligaments, connective tissue, and muscle. Joint surfaces are covered with cartilage to reduce friction, and lubricated with joint fluid for smooth movement.

FRACTURES AND DISLOCATIONS

A fracture is a break in a bone. Fractures can be open or closed. With open fractures, the skin is broken, exposing the bone to contamination. Closed fractures are covered with intact muscle and skin.

Fractures can also be described as transverse, spiral, oblique, or crushed, referring to the type of fracture. This information is usually obtained from an X-ray and has little effect on first aid.

Fractures, in addition to causing pain, loss of function, and swelling, can be complicated by infection and damage to blood

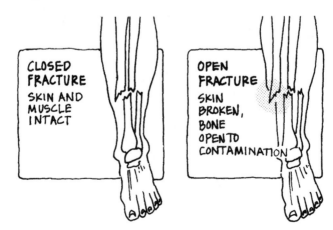

vessels and nerves. Fractured bone ends can pinch or sever blood vessels, blocking circulation or causing bleeding. Fractures of large, long bones, such as the femur or pelvis, are often accompanied by blood loss that can cause life-threatening shock. Infection is a potentially severe complication of an open fracture.

A dislocation is the displacement of a bone end from its normal position at a joint. Dislocations damage the supporting structures at the joint. Blood vessels and nerves can be disrupted. The ball-and-socket joint of the shoulder is a common site for dislocation. Elbow, finger, and ankle dislocations are also possible. Less common are dislocations to the wrist, hip, and knee. Fractures and dislocations can occur together.

Signs and Symptoms of Fractures and Dislocations

Signs and symptoms of fractures or dislocations include pain and tenderness; crepitus, a grating sound produced by bone ends rubbing together (also a sign of instability and unnatural movement at the fracture site); swelling and discoloration, indicating that fluids are pooling in the damaged tissue; deformity of a limb or joint; and loss of function. Dislocations cause loss of function at a joint; fractures cause loss of function to a limb.

Assessment of Fractures and Dislocations

Humans are bilaterally symmetrical animals, one side is the mirror image of the other. Comparing an injured with an uninjured

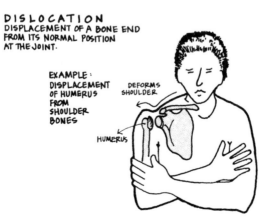

DISLOCATION
DISPLACEMENT OF A BONE END FROM ITS NORMAL POSITION AT THE JOINT.

EXAMPLE: DISPLACEMENT OF HUMERUS FROM SHOULDER BONES

DEFORMS SHOULDER

HUMERUS

Signs and Symptoms of Fractures and Dislocations

- Pain and point tenderness
- Crepitus
- Swelling and discoloration
- Deformity
- Loss of function or range of motion at a joint (dislocation)
- Loss of function at a bone (fracture)
- Altered circulation, sensation, and movement (CSM)

limb can reveal a subtle angulation or deformity. The mechanism of injury also provides a clue to the extent and location of the injury. Particularly violent incidents, such as falls from a height or direct blows to a joint, are common fracture mechanisms in the outdoors.

Look at the limb for deformity, swelling, or discoloration. Open zippers or remove clothing to see the injury if necessary. Feel the limb for localized tenderness, abnormal bumps or protrusions, and swelling.

Assess for circulation, sensation, and movement (CSM). Impaired circulation may also be evidenced by cold, gray, or cyanotic extremities. Good circulation is indicated by pink and warm fingers and toes or the presence of the radial pulse at the wrist or the pedal pulse in the foot.

Assess sensation and movement by asking the patient to move fingers or toes. Test for reaction to touch or pain. Nerve damage maybe be revealed by loss of strength, inability to move the extremity, numbness, or tingling. A blocked artery with loss of distal circulation is an emergency. After several hours, serious damage may result.

Assessment of Fractures and Dislocations

- Assess the bone or joint.
- Remove clothing; visualize the injury.
- Look for deformity, swelling, discoloration.
- Feel for tenderness, deformity, swelling.
- Assess circulation, sensation, and movement (CSM).

Compartment Syndrome

Compartment syndrome involves increased pressure in a muscle compartment secondary to fractures, crush injury, burns, or other trauma or repetitive activities, such as running. Compartment syndrome is most common in the lower leg and forearm, although it can also occur in the hand, foot, thigh, and upper arm.

Signs and Symptoms. Signs and symptoms of compartment syndrome include pain, pallor, pulse-less, and pressure. Pain in the injured extremity is out of proportion to the injury or stimulated by stretching or movement. The skin is pale or cyanotic. The distal pulse may be diminished or absent. The muscle may feel tight or full.

Treatment. Assess all extremity injuries for compartment syndrome. Acute compartment syndrome is a surgical emergency. There is no effective nonsurgical treatment. Evacuate.

Treatment of Fractures and Dislocations

Treat fractures and dislocations by immobilizing the injury. Immobilization prevents movement of bones, reduces pain and swelling and the possibility of further injury, prevents a closed fracture from becoming an open fracture, and helps reduce disability.

Immobilize the Injury. Any time there is loss of function to a limb or joint, the injury should be immobilized in a splint. If it is not clear whether the injury is a sprain or a fracture, immobilize. It is better to splint a sprain than to fail to immobilize a fracture. Immobilize the bones above and below a dislocated joint, and immobilize the joints above and below a fractured bone.

Clean and Dress Wounds. Clean and dress all wounds before splinting. Treat open fractures as contaminated soft tissue injuries. Irrigate, but do not scrub, exposed bone ends and keep them moist with a dressing soaked in disinfected water. An infected fracture is a serious problem that can result in long-term complications.

Splint Before Moving. Splint the injury before moving the patient. A quick splint fashioned from a foamlite sleeping pad can stabilize the injury if you must move the patient off dangerous terrain or to drier, warmer conditions. Strap an injured arm to the body. Tie injured legs together.

Remove Jewelry, Watches, and Tight Clothing. Remove jewelry and watches and loosen clothing that might compromise circulation should swelling occur. If you are managing a splint in cold weather, hot water bottles or chemical heat packs tucked into the splint can provide warmth.

Treatment of Fractures and Dislocations

- Immobilize the injury.
  - —Bones above and below dislocations.
  - —Joints above and below fractures.
- Clean and dress wounds.
- Remove jewelry, watches, and tight clothing.
- Rest, ice, compression, and elevation (RICE) therapy.
- Assess circulation, temperature, and sensation before and after splinting.
- Assess for other injuries.
- Treat for shock.

Elevate to Reduce Swelling. Elevate the injured limb a little (4 to 6 inches) to reduce swelling. RICE treatment, which is discussed in chapter 6 ("Athletic Injuries"), may reduce pain and swelling and is appropriate for splinted fractures and immobilized dislocations. In warm environments where hypothermia and frostbite are not concerns, cold packs or ice or snow encased in a plastic bag and wrapped with a sock, or even a shirt soaked in cold water, may help reduce pain and swelling.

Assess Circulation, Sensation, and Movement. Before and after the splint is applied, assess circulation, sensation, and movement (CSM) to fingers or toes. Repeat this assessment periodically during transport as well.

Assess for Other Injuries. A fracture or dislocation warrants a full patient assessment for other injuries as well.

Treat for Shock. A fracture in and of itself does not cause shock. Damage to nearby tissues, organs, and blood vessels, however, may be a life-threatening problem. Splinting is the basic treatment for shock because it reduces pain and continued injury. Be especially alert for shock with femur and pelvic fractures, multiple fractures, and open fractures.

Angulated Fractures, Dislocations, and Traction-in-Line

Years ago, in basic first aid, we learned to splint fractures and dislocations in the position in which they were found. We were concerned that moving bones to straighten bent extremities would

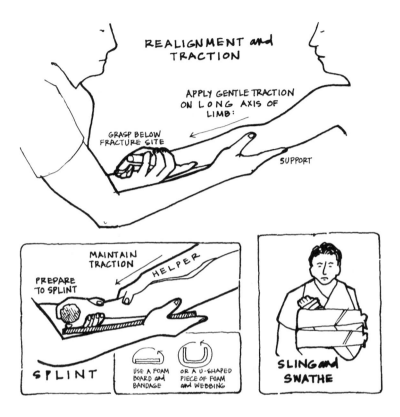

REALIGNMENT and TRACTION

APPLY GENTLE TRACTION ON LONG AXIS OF LIMB:

GRASP BELOW FRACTURE SITE

SUPPORT

MAINTAIN TRACTION

HELPER

PREPARE TO SPLINT

SPLINT

USE A FOAM BOARD and BANDAGE

OR A U-SHAPED PIECE OF FOAM and WEBBING

SLING and SWATHE

injure blood vessels and nerves. In practice, however, we found that gentle traction and straightening of any fracture reduces pain and makes splints more stable.

Medical opinion now favors straightening with gentle traction-in-line femur fractures, fractures that are difficult to splint or transport due to angulation, and any fracture or dislocation with impaired distal circulation, sensation, or movement. The current wisdom is that the danger of muscle, nerve, or blood vessel injury from gentle traction-in-line is less than the damage, discomfort, and pain from an injury splinted in an awkward position for long periods.

To straighten a fracture, apply gentle traction-in-line and re-align the bone ends. To do this, grasp the limb below the fracture site while another person supports the limb. Align the limb with a gentle pull applied on the long axis of the bone. If resistance or pain occurs, stop and splint in the deformed position.

Dislocations. Consensus opinion in wilderness medicine supports reducing dislocations in the field if prompt transport is not possible or if circulation is impaired. The first responder should use judgment and discretion when transport to a medical facility is possible within a few hours. Early reduction decreases pain; is easier if done before swelling, stiffness, and muscle spasms develop; makes immobilization and transportation easier; and reduces risks of long-term circulation and nerve injury.

The scope of practice for a wilderness first responder includes use of traction-in-line to reduce anterior shoulder, patella, and finger/toe dislocations. These tend to be amenable to field reduction with low risk of harm to the patient. Dislocations of the elbow, wrist, knee, ankle, and hip can be complex injuries and unless CSM is complicated, it is recommended that these be immobilized as found and promptly evacuated.

Dislocations are relocated with a variety of traction-in-line techniques, depending on the location of the injury. We recommend that you contact a physician or a reputable wilderness medical program for advice and training on specific relocation techniques.

SPLINTING

In the wilderness, improvised splints are the rule, and they may remain in place for days. Splints should pad, support, and immobilize the limb and insulate the extremity from cold. They should be lightweight to make transporting the patient easier and allow access to feet or hands to check circulation. There are many commercial splints on the market, but in the backcountry, two commonly available items easily meet these specifications. They are the foamlite pad used for insulation under sleeping bags, and the triangular bandage.

Basic Splinting Techniques

Two basic splinting techniques cover most first aid situations. One is to make a foamlite tube to splint an arm or leg. The other

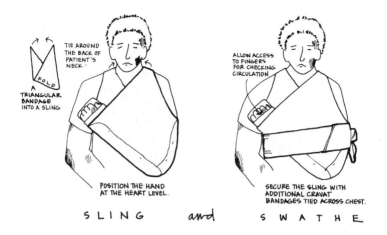

TIE AROUND THE BACK OF PATIENT'S NECK :

FOLD A TRIANGULAR BANDAGE INTO A SLING

POSITION THE HAND AT THE HEART LEVEL.

ALLOW ACCESS TO FINGERS FOR CHECKING CIRCULATION

SECURE THE SLING WITH ADDITIONAL CRAVAT BANDAGES TIED ACROSS CHEST.

S L I N G   and   S W A T H E

is to fashion a sling and swathe to immobilize injuries to the upper extremities.

Foamlite Tube. To make a foamlite tube, roll the foam sleeping pad into a U-shaped tube and trim to fit the limb. Secure with cravats (triangular bandages), elastic bandages, bandannas, sling webbing, or tape. To make this supportive and comfortable, generously pad and firmly (but not tightly) compress it around the limb.

Sling and Swathe. The sling and swathe immobilizes arm, shoulder, and collarbone injuries using two triangular bandages, fabric strips, bandannas, or cravats.

First clean and dress any open wound. Then use soft material such as a pile jacket to pad the injury. Add a firm supporting layer outside the soft padding. Often this is a foamlite pad, Crazy Creek chair, or Therm-A-Rest pad. Sticks, tent poles, or the stays in soft packs can provide additional support. Secure with tape, webbing, or cord. Support the foot or hand, but provide access to fingers and toes to assess for CSM. Upper extremity injuries are often further supported with a sling and swathe.

Specific Splinting Techniques

Hand. The hand and fingers should be splinted in the "position of function": the position of the hand when holding a glass of water. Fingers can also be "buddy-taped" to each other to reduce range of motion yet still allow some degree of function. If the injury is confined to the fingers, the wrist need not be splinted. If the injury involves the bones at the base of the fingers, splint the wrist as well.

Wrist and Forearm. Splint injuries to the wrist and forearm with a foamlite stabilizer or a sling and swathe. Elevating the hand above the level of the heart may help reduce swelling and pain.

Elbow. An elbow dislocation is often a complicated and painful injury. Several nerves and arteries pass around the complex elbow joint and may be damaged by displaced bone ends. The simplest splint for the elbow is the sling and swathe. Splint this injury in the position in which you find it. If the elbow is at an awkward angle, a sling and swathe will not work well. Try a foamlite pad stabilized with a tent pole or the stay from a soft pack bent to the angle of the joint. If possible, bandage the whole arm to the trunk for greater stability.

Upper Arm. The radial nerve and brachial artery lie close to the humerus and can be injured by a fracture. Damage to the artery is most common with elbow dislocations. Damage to the nerve is most common with midshaft fractures. Check the pulse at the wrist. The ability to bend back the hand tests the radial nerve. The humerus can be splinted with a combination of a foamlite splint and sling and swathe. Wrap foamlite on the inside of the arm, over the elbow, and up the outside of the arm for added stability. The patient may be more comfortable if the sling and foamlite cup the elbow without putting pressure on the humerus.

Shoulder. The humerus fits into a shallow socket in the scapula, forming the shoulder joint and allowing for a wide range of motion (ROM). This ROM makes the joint susceptible to injury. Most dislocations are anterior, with the head of the humerus displaced out of the socket toward the chest.

The signs of dislocation are drooping shoulder, a depression on the front of the shoulder, and loss of function or ROM at the joint. A sling and swathe provide a simple and effective splint. If the shoulder is immobile at an awkward angle,

---

Qualities of a Good Splint

- Rigid; supports the injury
- Pads the injury
- Insulates from cold
- Lightweight
- Offers access to distal circulation

WRIST SPLINT

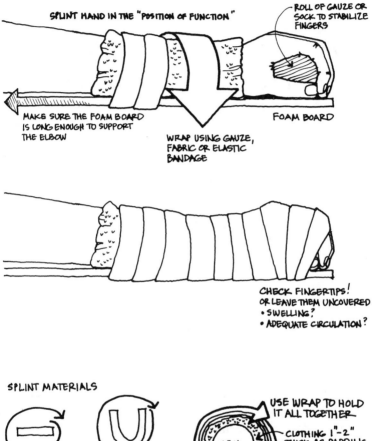

SPLINT HAND IN THE "POSITION OF FUNCTION"

ROLL OF GAUZE OR SOCK TO STABILIZE FINGERS

MAKE SURE THE FOAM BOARD IS LONG ENOUGH TO SUPPORT THE ELBOW

FOAM BOARD

WRAP USING GAUZE, FABRIC OR ELASTIC BANDAGE

CHECK FINGERTIPS!
OR LEAVE THEM UNCOVERED
• SWELLING?
• ADEQUATE CIRCULATION?

SPLINT MATERIALS

USE A FOAM BOARD and WRAP

OR A U-SHAPED PIECE OF FOAM AND WEBBING

USE WRAP TO HOLD IT ALL TOGETHER

CLOTHING 1"-2" THICK AS PADDING

ARM

FOAM BOARD

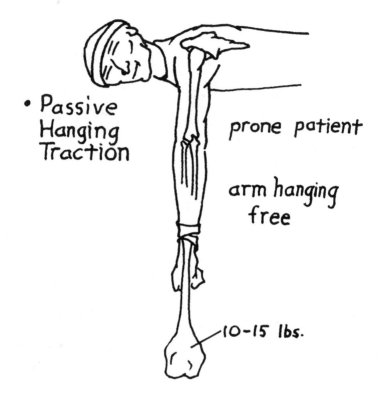

• Passive Hanging Traction

prone patient

arm hanging free

10-15 lbs.

padding may be necessary to support the arm away from the chest.

One technique you can use to attempt to reduce an anterior shoulder dislocation is passive hanging arm traction. The patient is positioned prone with their dislocated arm hanging loosely. The technique is passive and may work with the weight of the arm, or ten to fifteen pounds of weight on the wrist may help relax the muscles and allow the shoulder to relocate.

Collarbone. The clavicle acts as a strut, propping the shoulder. It can be fractured by a direct blow to the shoulder or by a blow transmitted up an extended arm. A broken collarbone is a common mountain biking injury. Deformity and tenderness can often be found by feeling the entire clavicle from sternum to shoulder. Typically, a patient with an injured clavicle is unable to use the arm on the injured side. Splint with a sling and swathe, immobilizing the shoulder and arm.

Pelvis. The pelvis is a bowl-shaped structure consisting of three bones fused with the sacrum, the lower portion of the vertebral column. The upper part of the femur meets the pelvis at a shallow socket and forms the hip joint.

A broken pelvis is a serious injury. It takes considerable force to break a pelvis; such force can cause associated internal injuries, including rupture of the bladder and blood loss. Treat this patient as if he or she has a back injury, and immobilize the trunk and legs. A backboard, Stokes litter, or improvised litter is necessary to immobilize and carry the patient. A garment or piece of fabric wrapped supportively around the pelvis at the level of the hips may help stabilize the pelvis.

Femur and Hip. A dislocated hip is usually the result of a high-velocity mechanism, such as a fall from height. A leg with a dislocated hip is generally shortened, with the foot and knee turned in. If the hip is dislocated for more than a few hours, the blood supply to the head of the femur can be compromised, and permanent damage to the bone can occur. Splint hip fractures or dislocations with a U-shaped foamlite tube, immobilizing the entire leg.

Muscles surrounding the fracture of long bones may contract, causing the bone ends to override. This increases pain and soft tissue damage, as well as increasing the possibility of artery and nerve injury. Spasm of the large thigh muscles is of special concern in fractures of the femur. A femur fracture can bleed into the surrounding tissues, causing life-threatening shock. The leg may appear shortened and the thigh swollen.

Traction Splints. A traction splint is a potential treatment for a midshaft femur fracture. Fractures close to the knee or the hip, or femur fractures without muscle spasm, are often splinted with a fixation splint. Traction splints place tension on the muscles surrounding a midshaft fracture, and may help reduce pain. Traction splints for femur fractures in the wilderness are a challenge to improvise, and the traction straps require constant attention to make sure they are not causing reduced blood flow to the foot.

Before you begin constructing the traction splint, splint the injury with a full-leg foamlite splint. The leg splint will provide support, insulation, and padding. Follow this by applying padding at the ankle. Ideally, you can promptly provide traction-in-line for the thigh and hold it while you are preparing the traction splint. This is not always practical, however, and you may need to apply a fixation splint, construct your traction splint, then apply traction.

1. To prepare for applying traction, attach traction straps over the boot or padded ankle. Fold two cravats into long, narrow bandages. Fold lengthwise, and pass one over and one behind the ankle, making sure the ends of each bandage are facing in opposite directions. Now pull the ends of each bandage through the loop in the other bandage. The bandages should fit snugly and flat against the ankle. The toes should remain visible or at least accessible for assessing blood flow and nerve function.
2. To construct the traction splint, place a ski pole, tent pole, or any polelike object a foot longer than the leg against the outside of the leg. Anchor the pole using a well-padded strap over the thigh at the hip.
3. Apply traction on the thigh by pulling the traction straps. Maintain traction by securing the traction straps to the end of the pole. Tie the traction splint to the leg splint.

Knee. Most knee injuries can be wrapped with an Ace bandage, taped, or stabilized with a foamlite splint in such a way that the patient can walk out without further damage. A grossly unstable knee with major ligament rupture is accompanied by severe pain, inability to move the joint or bear weight, swelling, and obvious deformity. This injury requires a simple splint and a litter evacuation. In some cases, it may be difficult to tell if the femur, the tibia, or the knee is injured. Assume the worst and splint the femur.

Lower Leg. The lower ends of the tibia and fibula are the prominent knobs on the sides of the ankle. The thin layers of skin over the tibia make open fractures common. Splint both the knee and the ankle in a roll of foamlite.

Ankle. It can be difficult to differentiate between a fracture and a sprain to the ankle. The injury can be immobilized with a

TRACTION

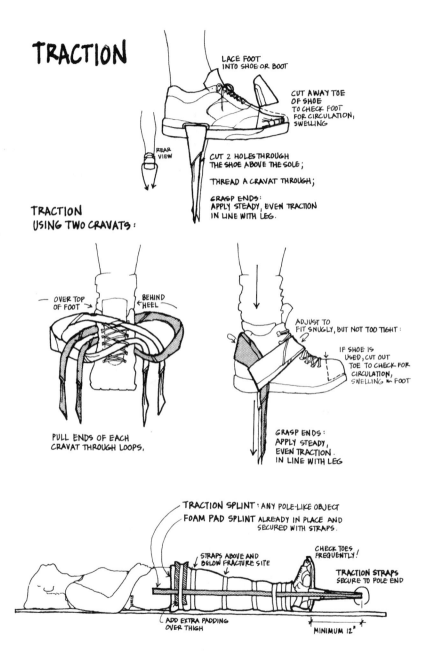

LACE FOOT
INTO SHOE OR BOOT

CUT AWAY TOE
OF SHOE
TO CHECK FOOT
FOR CIRCULATION,
SWELLING

REAR
VIEW

CUT 2 HOLES THROUGH
THE SHOE ABOVE THE SOLE;

THREAD A CRAVAT THROUGH;

GRASP ENDS:
APPLY STEADY, EVEN TRACTION
IN LINE WITH LEG.

TRACTION
USING TWO CRAVATS:

OVER TOP
OF FOOT

BEHIND
HEEL

PULL ENDS OF EACH
CRAVAT THROUGH LOOPS.

ADJUST TO
FIT SNUGLY, BUT NOT TOO TIGHT:

IF SHOE IS
USED, CUT OUT
TOE TO CHECK FOR
CIRCULATION,
SWELLING IN FOOT

GRASP ENDS:
APPLY STEADY,
EVEN TRACTION.
IN LINE WITH LEG

TRACTION SPLINT: ANY POLE-LIKE OBJECT
FOAM PAD SPLINT ALREADY IN PLACE AND
SECURED WITH STRAPS.

STRAPS ABOVE AND
BELOW FRACTURE SITE

CHECK TOES
FREQUENTLY!

TRACTION STRAPS
SECURE TO POLE END

ADD EXTRA PADDING
OVER THIGH

MINIMUM 12"

SIMPLE LEG SPLINT

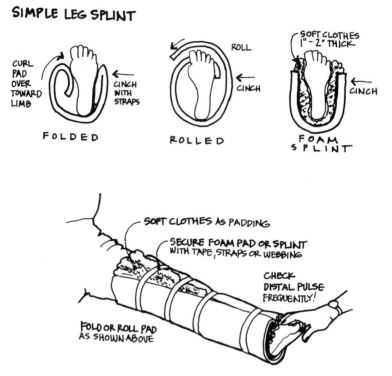

stirrup of foamlite and wrapped with clothing for insulation and padding. Knee and ankle injuries are also addressed in chapter 6 ("Athletic Injuries").

FINAL THOUGHTS

In NOLS' experience, fractures and dislocations are not common in wilderness activities, but they do occur, and the first responder should be prepared. A careful assessment, traction-in-line, immobilization, and RICE are the cornerstones of our treatment. Most of us, conscious of weight and bulk when we travel in the wilderness, don't carry prepared commercial splints. We know that we can create what we need from materials at hand such as clothing, sleeping pads, packs, stays, tent poles, bandannas, and natural materials such as sticks. Practice improvising splints from the material you commonly have with you in the wilderness.

Evacuation Guidelines
- Evacuate all musculoskeletal injuries showing loss of function, unreducible dislocations, and any first time dislocation.
- Rapidly evacuate all open fractures and any musculoskeletal injury with altered CSM.

CHAPTER 6 | ATHLETIC INJURIES

INTRODUCTION

Living and traveling in the wilderness, carrying a pack, hiking long distances, climbing, and paddling can all cause sprains, strains, and tendinitis. Athletic injuries account for 50 percent of injuries on NOLS courses and are a frequent cause of evacuations.

Sprains, or injuries to ligaments, are categorized as grades one, two, or three. With a grade one injury, ligament fibers are stretched but not torn. A partly torn or badly stretched ligament is a grade two injury. Completely torn ligaments are grade three injuries. Strains are injuries to muscles and tendons. A muscle stretched too far is commonly referred to as a "pull." A muscle or tendon with torn fibers is a "tear." A tendon irritated from overuse can become a tendinitis.

When faced with an athletic injury, the first responder in the wilderness has to choose between treating the injury in the field—possibly altering the expedition route and timetable to accommodate the patient's loss of mobility—or evacuation.

We don't try to diagnose the injury or grade the sprain or the strain. We decide if an injury is usable or not. If usable, we use RICE therapy and may use tape or a brace for support. If unusable, we immobilize and evacuate.

The most common athletic injuries on NOLS courses are ankle and knee sprains, Achilles tendinitis, and forearm tendinitis.

Common Causes of Athletic Injury on NOLS Courses

- Playing games such as hug tag and hacky sack.
- Tripping while walking in camp.
- Stepping over logs.
- Crossing streams, including shallow rock hops.
- Putting on a backpack.
- Lifting a kayak or raft.
- Falling or misstepping while hiking with a pack (on any terrain).
- Falling while skiing with a pack.
- Shoveling snow.
- Bending over to pick up firewood.

GENERAL TREATMENT FOR ATHLETIC INJURIES (RICE)

Athletic injuries are generally treated with RICE: rest, ice, compression, and elevation. Gently rub the injured area with ice, wrapped in fabric to prevent frostbite, for 20 to 40 minutes every 2 to 4 hours for the first 24 to 48 hours, then allow it to passively warm. (These times are guidelines, not absolutes.) Cooling is thought to decrease nerve conduction and pain, constrict blood vessels, and limit the inflammatory process. If you don't have ice, use the coolest water available—sometimes this is simply a bandanna soaked in cool mountain water.

Compression with an Ace bandage helps reduce swelling. Care must be taken when applying the wrap not to exert pressure on an injury that swells dramatically or to cut off blood flow to the fingers or toes.

Elevating the injury above the level of the heart reduces swelling. Nonprescription pain medications such as acetaminophen and ibuprofen may help as well.

Assessment for Athletic Injuries

A thorough assessment includes an evaluation of the mechanism of injury, as well as the signs and symptoms. Knowing the mecha-

General Treatment for Athletic Injuries (RICE)

- Rest: allows time for healing.
- Ice: 20 to 40 minutes every 2 to 4 hours for 24 to 48 hours.
- Compression: elastic bandage to reduce swelling.
- Elevation: reduces swelling.

Signs and Symptoms of Sprains

- Swelling and discoloration
- Pain or tenderness
- Instability and/or loss of range of motion
- Inability to bear weight

nism helps you determine whether the occurrence was sudden and traumatic, indicating a sprain, or whether it was progressive, suggesting an overuse injury.

Signs and symptoms of a sprain include swelling, pain, and discoloration. Point tenderness and obvious deformity suggest a fracture. Ask the patient to try to move the joint through its full range of motion. Painless movement is a good sign. If the patient is able to use or bear weight on the affected limb, and pain and swelling are not severe, he or she may be treated in the field.

Severe pain, the sound of a pop at the time of injury, immediate swelling, and inability to use the joint are signs of a serious sprain, possibly a fracture. This injury should be immobilized and the patient evacuated from the field.

Ankle Sprains

Uneven ground, whether boulder fields in the backcountry or broken pavement in the city, contributes to the likelihood of ankle sprains. Of all ankle sprains, 85 percent are inversion injuries—those in which the foot turns in to the midline of the body and the

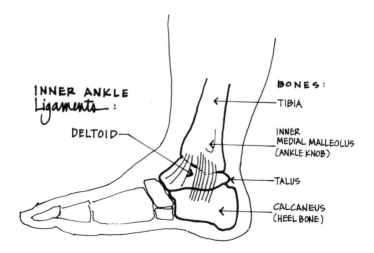

ankle turns outward. Inversion injuries usually sprain one or more of the ligaments on the outside of the ankle.

Ankle Anatomy. The bones, ligaments, and tendons of the ankle and foot absorb stress and pressure generated by both body weight and activity. They also allow for flexibility and accommodate surface irregularities so that we don't lose our balance.

Bones. The lower leg bones are the tibia and the fibula. The large bumps on either side of the ankle are the lower ends of these bones—the fibula on the outside, and the tibia on the inside. Immediately under the tibia and fibula lies the talus bone, which sits atop the calcaneus (heel bone). The talus and calcaneus act as a rocker for front-to-back flexibility of the ankle. Without them, we would walk stiff-legged.

In front of the calcaneus lie two smaller bones, the navicular (inside) and the cuboid (outside). They attach to three small bones called the cuneiforms. Anterior to the cuneiforms are five metatarsals, which in turn articulate with the phalanges (toe bones).

Ligaments. Due to the number of bones in the foot, ligaments are many and complex. For simplicity, think of there being a ligament on every exterior surface of every bone, attaching to the adjacent articulating bone.

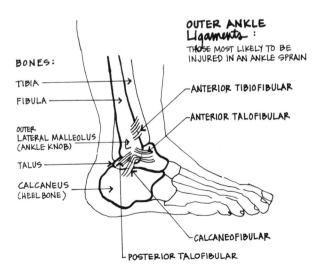

BONES:

TIBIA

FIBULA

OUTER LATERAL MALLEOLUS (ANKLE KNOB)

TALUS

CALCANEUS (HEEL BONE)

OUTER ANKLE Ligaments :
THOSE MOST LIKELY TO BE INJURED IN AN ANKLE SPRAIN

ANTERIOR TIBIOFIBULAR

ANTERIOR TALOFIBULAR

CALCANEOFIBULAR

POSTERIOR TALOFIBULAR

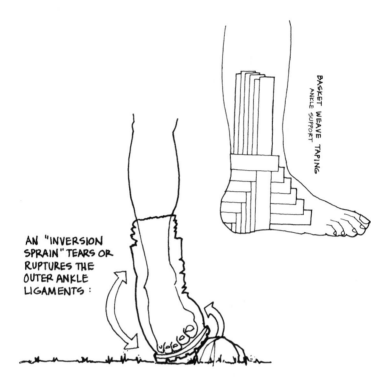

AN "INVERSION SPRAIN" TEARS OR RUPTURES THE OUTER ANKLE LIGAMENTS :

BASKET WEAVE TAPING ANKLE SUPPORT

There are four ligaments commonly associated with ankle sprains. On the inside of the ankle is the large, fan-shaped deltoid ligament joining the talus, calcaneus, and several of the smaller foot bones to the tibia. Rolling the ankle inward, an eversion sprain, stresses the deltoid ligament. Spraining the deltoid requires considerable force, and due to its size and strength, it is seldom injured. In fact, this ligament is so strong that if a bad twist occurs, it frequently pulls fragments of bone off at its attachment points, causing an avulsion fracture.

On the outside, usually the weaker aspect, three ligaments attach from the fibula to the talus and the calcaneus. Together these three ligaments protect the ankle from turning to the outside.

Muscles and Tendons. Muscles in the lower leg use long tendons to act on the ankle and foot. The calf muscles—the gastrocnemius and soleus—shorten to point the toes. These muscles taper into the largest tendon, the Achilles, which attaches to the back of the calcaneus.

Treatment of Ankle Sprains
• RICE
• Taping for support

Treatment of Ankle Sprains. Sprains should have the standard treatment of rest, ice, compression, and elevation to limit swelling and pain. If a severe sprain or a fracture is suspected, immobilize the ankle. Treating a usable sprain with RICE for the first 24 to 48 hours and letting it rest for a few days may allow a patient to stay in the mountains rather than cut the trip short. A simple method for providing ankle support is to tape the ankle using the basket weave.

Knee Pain

Pain in the knee from overuse can be treated by ceasing the activity causing the discomfort and controlling pain and swelling with RICE. In the event of a traumatic injury resulting in an unstable knee, splint and evacuate. If the injury is stable and the patient can bear weight, use RICE to control pain and swelling. If the patient can walk without undue pain, wrap the knee with foamlite for support.

TENDINITIS

A tendon is the fibrous cord by which a muscle is attached to a bone. Its construction is similar to that of kernmantle rope, with an outer sheath of tissue enclosing a core of fibers. Some tendons, such as those to the fingers, are long. The activating muscles are in the forearm, but the tendons stretch from the forearm across the wrist to each finger. These tendons are surrounded by a lubricating sheath to assist their movement.

Tendinitis is inflammation of a tendon. When the sheath and the tendon become inflamed, the sheath becomes rough, movement is restricted and painful, and the patient feels a grating of the tendon inside the sheath. Fibers can be torn or, more commonly, irritation from overuse or infection can inflame the sheath, causing pain when the tendon moves. There may be little pain when the tendon is at rest.

Signs and Symptoms of Tendinitis

- Redness
- Warmth
- Crepitus
- Localized pain

Tendons are poorly supplied with blood, so they heal slowly. Tendons are well supplied with nerves, however, which means that an injury may be painful. Tendons can be injured by sudden overloading, but are more frequently injured through overuse. Factors contributing to tendinitis include poor technique, poor equipment, unhealed prior injury, and cool and tight muscles.

Assessment for Tendinitis

Tendinitis, in contrast to ankle sprains, is a progressive overuse injury, not a traumatic injury. Common sites for tendinitis are the Achilles tendon and the tendons of the forearm. The Achilles, the largest tendon in the body, may fatigue and become inflamed during or following lengthy hikes, especially with significant elevation gain. Boots that break down and place pressure on the tendon can provide enough irritation in one day to initiate inflammation.

Canoeists and kayakers may experience forearm tendinitis. Poor technique and inadequate strength and flexibility contribute to the injury. Similar tendinitis comes with repetitive use of ski poles, ice axes, and ice climbing tools.

Tendinitis may also occur on the front of the foot, usually caused by tightly laced boots or stiff mountaineering boots. The tendons extending the toes become irritated and inflamed. Tendinitis causes swelling, redness, warmth, pain to the touch (or pinch), painful movement, and sounds of friction or grinding (crepitus).

Treatment of Achilles Tendinitis

- RICE
- Heel lifts
- Pads on ankle to protect the tendon

Treatment of Forearm Tendinitis

- RICE
- Taping wrist to limit range of motion

Treatment of Tendinitis

Treat tendinitis with RICE: rest, ice, compression, and elevation. It may be necessary to cease the aggravating activity until the inflammation subsides. Prevent or ease tendinitis of anterior muscles by varying boot

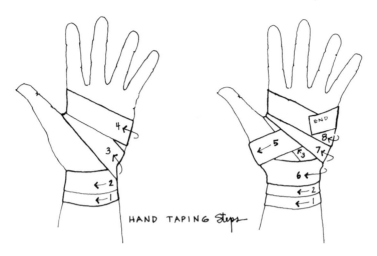

HAND TAPING *Steps*

lacing. Lace boots more loosely when hiking and more tightly when climbing.

Achilles Tendinitis. To relieve stretch on the Achilles tendon, provide a heel lift. To relieve direct pressure from the boot, place a 6-inch by 1-inch strip of foamlite padding on either side of the Achilles tendon. The placement should take the pressure off without touching the Achilles.

Forearm Tendinitis. Forearm tendinitis is primarily associated with the repetitive motion of paddling. Pay close attention to proper paddling technique. Keep a relaxed, open grip on the paddle. On the forward stroke, keep the wrist in line with the forearm during the pull and push, and avoid crossing the upper arm over the midline of the body.

Other paddling techniques that may help prevent forearm tendinitis include keeping the thumb on the same side of the paddle as the fingers and switching a feathered paddle for an unfeathered paddle. The feathered paddle requires a wrist movement that can sometimes aggravate tendinitis.

Tendinitis of the forearm is treated with RICE. Also, the wrist can be taped to limit movement that aggravates the condition.

MUSCLE STRAINS

Muscles can be stretched and torn from overuse or overexertion. Initial treatment is RICE, followed by heat, massage, and gentle stretching. Radiating muscle pain, strong pain at rest, pain secondary to an illness, or pain from a severe trauma mechanism is a reason to evacuate the patient for evaluation by a physician.

FINAL THOUGHTS

RICE can make the patient more comfortable by reducing pain and swelling. It's not clear if RICE speeds healing any faster than rest and patience. Most athletic injuries—sprains, strains, and tendinitis—will take weeks to heal, and this time of reduced activity can impact ability to travel on a wilderness expedition. Prevention is the key.

Errors in technique and inadequate muscular conditioning or warm-up produce injury. Overuse of muscles and joints (when there is no single traumatic event as the cause of injury) generates many of the sprains and strains on NOLS courses.

Jerky movements, excessive force, or an unnecessarily tight grip on the paddle while kayaking contribute to forearm tendinitis. Performing the athletic movements required for difficult rock climbs without warming up or paying attention to balance and form can cause injury. Even the seemingly simple actions of lifting a backpack or boat, stepping over logs, and wading in cold mountain streams can be dangerous.

Steep terrain and wet conditions contribute to injuries. Slippery conditions make it harder to balance and can cause falls. Falls that occur in camp and while hiking are the cause of many athletic injuries. Surprisingly, injuries are just as likely to occur when backcountry travelers are wearing packs as when they are not. Possibly this is because people are more attentive to technique when hiking or skiing with a pack.

You are more likely to be injured when you are tired, cold, dehydrated, rushed, or ill. You're not thinking as clearly, and your muscles are less flexible and responsive. Injuries happen more frequently in late morning and late afternoon, when dehydration and fatigue reduce awareness and increase clumsiness. Shifting from a three-meal-a-day schedule to breakfast and dinner plus three or four light snacks during the day helps keep your food supply constant.

Haste, often the result of unrealistic timetables, is frequently implicated in accidents. Try to negotiate the more difficult terrain in the morning, when you are fresh. Take rest breaks before difficult sections of a hike or paddle. Stop at the base of the pass, the near side of the river, or the beginning of the boulder field. Drink, eat, and stretch tight muscles. Check equipment for loose gaiters that may trip you and for poorly balanced backpacks.

The sustained activity of life in the wilderness and the need for sudden bursts of power when paddling, skiing, or climbing necessitate physical conditioning prior to a wilderness expedition. A regimen of endurance, flexibility, and muscle strength training will help prevent injuries and promote safety and enjoyment of wilderness activity.

Evacuation Guidelines
- Evacuation decisions on athletic injuries are usually based on practical considerations—continued pain, an injury that does not heal, or inability to travel.

CHAPTER 7 | SOFT TISSUE INJURIES

INTRODUCTION

Outside the wilderness, we give little thought to the consequences of soft tissue injuries. Our lives are not disrupted by small wounds, and infection is an unusual aftermath. On NOLS courses, however, backcountry travelers take falls while carrying packs and experience lacerations while preparing meals or walking or swimming barefoot. On an expedition, even relatively minor injuries can have serious consequences. Cut or blistered feet can result in litter evacuations, and hand wounds can end climbing trips. Infection is a real and ever-present risk.

Responding with the proper first aid is essential to expedition members' health and safety. Soft tissue wounds account for 30 percent of injuries on NOLS courses, but only a small number of these become infected. In addition to controlling bleeding, first aid for soft tissue injuries in the wilderness includes cleaning the wound, monitoring for signs of infection, and making decisions about when to evacuate.

SKIN

The skin is the single largest organ of the body. It protects the internal organs by providing a watertight shell that keeps fluids in and bacteria out. The skin helps regulate body temperature by

LAYERS OF THE SKIN:

SWEAT
GLAND

SEBACEOUS
GLAND

HAIR
FOLLICLE

BLOOD
VESSELS

LAYERS OF THE SKIN:

EPIDERMIS

DERMIS

SUBCUTANEOUS
TISSUE (MOSTLY FAT)

MUSCLE

providing a means of heat dissipation. Sweat glands produce sweat, which evaporates, cooling the body. Nerves near the skin's surface send messages to the brain about heat, cold, pressure, pain, and body position.

The skin is composed of three layers. The innermost layer is subcutaneous tissue, which consists mostly of fat. This layer is an insulator for the body and a reservoir for energy. Beneath the subcutaneous tissue lies muscle.

The second layer is the dermis, which contains sweat glands, sebaceous glands, hair follicles, nerves, and blood vessels. Sweat glands are found on all body surfaces, with most on the palms of the hands and soles of the feet. Sweat glands secrete .5 to 1 liter of sweat per day, and can produce up to 1 liter per hour during strenuous exercise. The sebaceous glands produce sebum (oil) and lie next to the hair follicles. Sebum waterproofs the skin and keeps the hair supple. Blood vessels in the dermis provide nutrients and oxygen to each cell and remove waste products such as carbon dioxide.

The outermost layer of the skin is the epidermis. The epidermis is made up primarily of dead cells held together by sebum. These dead cells continually slough off and are replaced by more dead cells.

Soft tissue injuries are classified as open or closed. With closed injuries, the skin remains intact; open injuries involve a break in the skin's surface.

CLOSED WOUNDS

Closed injuries include contusions (bruises) and hematomas. With both, the tissue and blood vessels beneath the epidermis are damaged. Swelling and discoloration occur because blood and plasma leak out of the damaged blood vessels. With contusions, blood is dispersed within the tissues. Hematomas contain a pool of blood—as much as a pint surrounding a major bone fracture. Depending on the amount of blood dispersed, reabsorption can take from 12 hours to several days. In some cases, the blood may have to be drained by a physician to enhance healing.

Treatment for Closed Wounds

A memory aid for treating closed injuries is RICE: rest, ice, compression, and elevation.

Rest. Rest decreases bleeding by allowing clots to form. In the event of a large or deep bruise, extremities can be splinted to decrease motion that may cause newly-formed clots to break away and bleeding to continue. See chapter 5 ("Fractures and Dislocations").

Ice. Ice causes the blood vessels to constrict, decreasing bleeding. Never apply ice directly to bare skin, as this can cause frostbite. Instead, wrap the ice in fabric of a towel-like thickness before applying to the skin. Ice the wound for 20 to 40 minutes every 2 to 4 hours for the first 24 to 48 hours, then allow the area to passively warm.

Compression. Apply manual pressure or a pressure dressing. When applying a pressure dressing, wrap it snugly enough to stop bleeding but not so tightly that the blood supply is shut off. Check by feeling for a pulse distal to the injured site.

Elevation. Elevate the injury above the level of the heart. Elevation reduces bleeding and swelling by decreasing the blood flow to the injury.

Treatment for Closed Injuries: RICE

- Rest
- Ice 20 to 40 minutes every 2 to 4 hours
- Compression to reduce swelling and bleeding
- Elevate above heart level

OPEN WOUNDS

Open injuries include abrasions, lacerations, puncture wounds, and major traumatic injuries—avulsions, amputations, and crushing wounds.

Abrasions. Abrasions occur when the epidermis and part of the dermis are rubbed off. These injuries are commonly called "road rash" or "rug burns." They usually bleed very little but are painful and may be contaminated with debris.

Abrasions heal more quickly if treated with ointment and covered with a semiocclusive or occlusive dressing.

Lacerations. Lacerations are cuts produced by sharp objects. The cut may penetrate all the layers of the skin, and the edges may be straight or jagged. If long and deep enough to cause the skin to gap more than ½ inch (1 cm), lacerations may require sutures. Sutures, a task for a physician, are also indicated if the cut is on the face or hands or over a joint, or if it severs a tendon, ligament, or blood vessel. Tendons and ligaments must be sutured together to heal properly. Lacerations on the hands or over a joint may be sutured to prevent the wound from being continually pulled apart by movement. Lacerations on the face are usually sutured to decrease scarring.

Puncture Wounds. Puncture wounds are caused by pointed objects. Although the skin around a puncture wound remains closed and there is little external bleeding, the object may have penetrated an artery or organ, causing internal bleeding.

If an impaled object is through the cheek and causing an airway obstruction, it must be removed to allow the patient to breathe. As well, if the object prevents transport, cannot be stabilized, or prevents bleeding control, it may need to be removed.

OPEN INJURIES

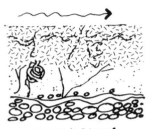

ABRASION
EPIDERMIS / DERMIS
RUBBED OFF.

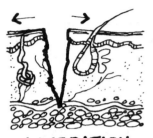

LACERATION
CUTS PRODUCED BY
SHARP OBJECTS.
EDGES CAN BE CLEAN
OR RAGGED.

AVULSION
THE TEARING OFF OF A
FLAP OF SKIN OR ENTIRE
LIMB.

PUNCTURE
POINTED OBJECT
PENETRATES SKIN AND
POSSIBLY AN UNDERLYING
ORGAN OR ARTERY.

Otherwise, leave the impalement in place. Removing the object may cause more soft tissue injury and increase bleeding by releasing pressure on compressed blood vessels.

Tetanus is a rare but serious complication. Although tetanus may be more likely to occur in a farm or ranch environment than on a "clean" mountainside, it is a good idea to make sure your tetanus booster is up-to-date before you take off into the backcountry. Tetanus boosters should be given at least every 10 years.

Major Traumatic Injuries. Major traumatic injuries include avulsions, amputations, and crushing injuries.

Avulsion. An avulsion is a "tearing off" that can range in severity from a small skin flap to the near amputation of an entire limb. Skin tends to separate along anatomical planes, such as between subcutaneous tissue and muscle.

To treat a small to moderate-sized avulsion, clean the skin flap and reposition it over the wound. If the area avulsed is larger than 2 inches in diameter, a skin graft may be required for the wound to heal properly.

Amputation. Amputation is the complete severance of a part or extremity. If blood vessels are partially torn, they cannot constrict, and bleeding may be massive. In contrast, the stump of a cleanly severed extremity may not bleed profusely because the severed blood vessels respond by retracting and constricting. If elevation and direct pressure do not stop the stump from bleeding, a tourniquet may be necessary.

After treating the patient, rinse the amputated body part with clean water; wrap it in moist, sterile gauze; and place it in a plastic bag. Then place the bag in cold water or on ice. Do not bury the part in ice, as this may cause cold injury. Make certain that the wrapped part accompanies the patient to the hospital. Reattachment may be possible if you can get to a hospital quickly.

Crushing Injuries. Crushing injuries can cause extensive damage to underlying tissue and bones, and large areas may be lacerated and avulsed. Always consider what underlying body parts may be damaged, and always conduct a focused exam to find out if any bones have been fractured or if an internal organ has been crushed.

Treatment for Open Wounds

The principles for treating open wounds are to control bleeding, clean and dress the wound, and monitor for infection.

Control Bleeding. Controlling bleeding is the first priority when treating open wounds. Death can come quickly to a patient with a tear in a major blood vessel. There are four methods for controlling bleed-

Controlling Bleeding

- Direct pressure
- Elevation
- Pressure dressings
- Tourniquets

ing. The most effective—direct pressure and elevation—will stop most bleeding when used in combination. Pressure dressings and tourniquets are also used.

Direct Pressure. The best method for controlling bleeding is to apply pressure over the wound site. Using your hand and a piece of wadded fabric—preferably sterile gauze—apply direct pressure to the wound. Be sure to wear rubber or latex gloves or place your hand in a plastic bag. If the wound is large, you may need to pack it with gauze before applying pressure. If a dressing becomes soaked with blood, leave it in place and apply additional dressings. Removing the dressing disturbs the blood clots that are forming.

Elevation. As with closed injuries, the combination of splinting, a pressure dressing, and elevation will help decrease the bleeding. Direct pressure and elevation control almost all bleeding. In fact, it is unusual for a wound to require the first responder to utilize a tourniquet.

Pressure Dressings. A bulky dressing, firmly secured with roller gauze, Ace wrap, or a strip of cloth or cravat can provide pressure on the wound and free your hands for other tasks. Check the CSMs to make sure you have not inadvertantly made a tourniquet.

Tourniquets. Tourniquets are rarely needed outside a combat situation. Apply a tourniquet only as a last resort, when no other

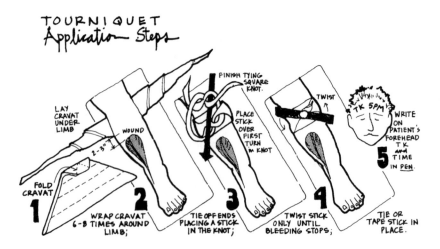

TOURNIQUET
Application Steps

1 FOLD CRAVAT / LAY CRAVAT UNDER LIMB

2 WRAP CRAVAT 6-8 TIMES AROUND LIMB; WOUND

3 TIE OFF ENDS PLACING A STICK IN THE KNOT; PLACE STICK OVER FIRST TURN in KNOT / FINISH TYING SQUARE KNOT.

4 TWIST STICK ONLY UNTIL BLEEDING STOPS; TWIST

5 TIE OR TAPE STICK IN PLACE. TK 5PM WRITE ON PATIENT'S FOREHEAD T K AND TIME IN PEN.

How to Apply a Tourniquet

1. Once you've determined that a tourniquet is necessary, apply it as close to the injury as possible, between the wound and the heart. Use a bandage that is 3 to 4 inches wide and 6 to 8 layers thick. Never use wire, rope, or any material that will cut the skin.
2. Wrap the bandage snugly around the extremity several times, then tie an overhand knot.
3. Place a small stick or similar object on the knot, and tie another overhand knot over the stick.
4. Twist the stick until the bandage becomes tight enough to stop the bleeding. Tie the ends of the bandage around the extremity to keep the twists from unraveling.
5. Using a pen, write "TK" on the patient's forehead and the time the tourniquet was applied. Once it is in place, do not remove the tourniquet. It should remain in place until the patient arrives at the emergency room.
6. There are ongoing arguments about tourniquet release in wilderness medicine. Definitive statements are likely to remain elusive. Check with your physician advisor about this issue.

method will stop the bleeding. Tourniquets completely stop the blood flow and are intended to save the life at the risk of the limb. If the tourniquet is left on for more than a few hours, there is a chance that the tissue distal to the tourniquet will be damaged.

Clean the Wound. Consider any wound, even a minor finger cut or a blister, as potentially infected. On wilderness expeditions wound cleaning is a priority. When you clean a wound, eliminate as much potentially infectious bacteria and debris as possible without further damaging the skin.

Wash Your Hands and Put on Gloves. Wash your hands. Use soap and water to prevent contamination of the wound. Put on rubber or latex gloves.

Scrub and Irrigate the Wound. Scrub the skin around the wound, being careful not to flush debris into the wound. Clip long hair, but don't shave the skin. Then irrigate an open wound with water that has been disinfected with chlorination or iodination, filtering, or water that has been boiled and cooled. Many wounds can be cleaned simply by irrigating with clean water. If

Cleaning Wounds

- Wash your hands with soap and water.
- Put on rubber or latex gloves.
- Scrub and irrigate the wound.
  —Scrub the area around the wound.
  —Use sterilized tweezers to remove debris.
  —Use pressure irrigation.
- Rinse thoroughly with disinfected water.
- Dress and bandage the wound.
- Check circulation, sensation, and movement.

the wound is obviously dirty or contaminated, a 1 percent povidone-iodine (usually one part 10 percent povidone-iodine diluted with 10 parts water to approximate the color of dark tea) is a suitable irrigation solution. Medical science tells us that the volume of water is the most important factor in cleaning the wound. At NOLS, we carry 35cc syringes in the first aid kit for pressure-irrigating wounds. Remove large pieces of debris with tweezers that have been boiled or cleaned with povidone-iodine.

Rinse with Disinfected Water. After cleaning the wound, rinse off the solution with liberal amounts of disinfected water. See chapter 22 ("Hygiene and Water Disinfection"). Check for further bleeding—you may need to apply direct pressure again if blood clots were broken loose during the cleaning process.

Dress and Bandage the Wound. Dressings are sterile gauze placed directly over the wound; bandages hold the dressing in place. Both come in many shapes and sizes. Semiocclusive (Telfa) or occlusive (Second Skin, Opsite, Tegaderm) dressings promote healing by keeping the area moist. Ointments (such as Polysporin or Bacitracin) serve the same purpose. Dry dressings that adhere to the wound impede the healing process.

Next, apply an antibiotic ointment. The ointment should be applied to the dressing rather than directly to the wound. Apply the bandage neatly and in such a way that blood flow distal to the injured area is not impaired. After applying the bandage, check CSMs distal to the injury.

Do not close wound edges until the wound has been thoroughly cleaned. Generally, the edges of a small wound will come together on their own. If the skin is stretched apart, butterfly bandages or Steri-strips can hold the edges together. If the injury is over a joint, the extremity may require splinting to prevent the edges from pulling apart. Highly contaminated wounds should be packed open.

Physicians don't agree on how long a wound can be kept open until it is stitched. A wound that will not close on its own or with a bandage can usually be stitched even a day or two later. The need to use sutures to close a wound does not, by itself, create an emergency. Reasons to expedite an evacuation for an open wound include obvious dirt or contamination; animal bites; wounds that open joint spaces; established infection; wounds from a crushing mechanism; any laceration to a cosmetic area, especially the face; wounds with a lot of dead tissue on the edges or in the wound itself; and wounds that obviously need surgical care, such as open fractures and very deep, gaping lacerations.

Animal bites are a concern for infection because of the bacterial flora in animal mouths and the crushing, penetrating, and tearing mechanism of the wounds. In North America, wild animal attacks, while dramatic and often highlighted in the press, are unusual.

After the Bandage Is Applied. Check circulation, sensation, and movement of the body part distal to the injury. Can the patient tell you where you are touching? Can he or she flex and extend the extremity? Is the area distal to the injury pink and warm, indicating good blood perfusion? Any negative answers to these questions may indicate nerve, artery, or tendon damage that will require evacuating the patient.

Dressings should be changed daily and the injured area checked for signs of infection.

Signs and Symptoms of Infections

MILD/MODERATE INFECTIONS
- Redness and swelling
- Pus, heat, pain

SERIOUS INFECTIONS
- Red streaks radiating from the wound
- Fever and chills
- Swollen lymph nodes

KEY POINTS
- A very high level of suspicion for infection needs to be maintained for any soft tissue problem.
- Any area of redness should be watched closely during the first 18 to 36 hours.
- Always think, "Is this an infection?"
- Oral antibiotics should be started early.
- Additional measures including applied heat and elevation/immobilization are important.

Infection

The newspapers and television media occasionally tell dramatic tales of aggressive and resistant wound infections and "flesh-eating bacteria." But on a daily basis outside the wilderness, we give little thought to the potential for wounds to be contaminated and colonized by bacteria. Before modern medicine understood infection and practiced clean wound care, infections were common and dangerous. In some environments, such as the tropics, they remain quite common and serious. In the wilderness we have less than ideal circumstances for cleaning wounds, but our efforts are essential in preventing wound infection.

Assessment for Infection. Redness, swelling, pus, heat, and pain at the site; faint red streaks radiating from the site; fever; chills; and swollen lymph nodes are all signs of infection.

It may be difficult to decide if local swelling, without an obvious wound, is due to a muscle strain, bug bite, or infection. The possibility of a deep infection is a concern. History may help rule out the muscle strain.

The four cardinal signs of a soft tissue infection are redness, swelling, warmth, and local pain. The progression in a wound to increased pain, warmth, increased soft tissue swelling, and expansion of redness over 18 to 24 hours suggests infection. Drawing a circle around the swollen area with a pen will help you determine if the infection is spreading or resolving.

Treatment for Infected Wounds

- Soak in warm antiseptic solution.
- Pull wound edges apart and clean wound.

Treatment of Infection. An infection that is localized to the site of the injury can be treated in the field. If the edges of the wound are closed, pull them apart and soak the area in warm antiseptic solution or warm water for 20 to 30 minutes three to four times a day. If the infection starts to spread—as evidenced by fever, chills, swollen lymph nodes, or faint red streaks radiating from the site—or if the wound cannot be opened to drain, evacuate the patient. If you have oral antibiotics and a protocol for their use, start them early in suspected wound infections.

Blisters

Blisters—a common backcountry occurrence—can be debilitating. Blisters are caused by friction and occur in areas where the epidermis is thick and tough enough to resist abrasion. At first there is a red, sore area called a "hot spot." If the friction continues, the epidermis separates and fluid enters the space, causing a blister.

The First Step: Prevention. Prevent blisters by making sure boots fit properly, wearing two pairs of socks to decrease friction on the skin, checking feet frequently at rest breaks, and stopping at the first sign of rubbing. Apply a solid piece of moleskin or athletic tape to areas that you suspect may cause problems.

Hot Spots. Cut a doughnut-shaped piece of moleskin and center it over the hot spot as a buffer against further rubbing.

Small Blisters. If a small blister has already developed, cut a doughnut-shaped piece of molefoam and center it over the blister. The doughnut "hole" prevents the adhesive from sticking to the tender blister and ripping it away when the molefoam is changed.

Larger Blisters. If the blister is nickel-sized or larger, drain it. Begin by carefully washing your hands and putting on rubber or latex gloves. Clean the area around the blister to decrease the risk of infection. Use a needle that has been soaked in an antiseptic solution such as povidone-iodine or has been heated until it glows red, then cooled. Insert the needle at the base of the blister, allowing the fluid to drain from the pinprick. After draining the blister, apply an antibiotic ointment and cover the area with gauze. As with an intact blister, center a doughnut-shaped piece of molefoam over the drained blister and gauze. Follow up by checking the blister every day for signs of infection.

FINAL THOUGHTS

NOLS has had great success in reducing the number of people who need to be evacuated for preventable wound infections by focusing on initial wound cleaning, good dressing and bandaging, and recognition and early intervention for infections. It's these simple skills that are at the core of wilderness medicine.

Evacuation Guidelines
- Evacuate an infection without improvement within 12 to 24 hours, or with signs or symptoms of serious/systemic infection.
- Evacuate any patient with a wound that cannot be closed in the field.
- Rapidly evacuate a wound that is heavily contaminated, opens a joint space, involves underlying tendons or ligaments, was caused by an animal bite, is on the face, has an impaled/imbedded object, was caused by a crushing mechanism, or shows evidence of serious infection.

BURNS

INTRODUCTION

In the wilderness the obvious mechanisms for a burn are the sun, stoves, lanterns, and fires. Improper stove use has caused stoves to flare or pressure caps to release and flame, burning unwary cooks, but the most common cause of a burn on a NOLS course, other than a sunburn, is a scald from spilled hot water.

Minor burns may be no more than a trivial nuisance, yet they represent a potential site of infection. Burns of joints, feet, hands, face, and genitalia, however, can impair these complex structures. A large burn causes significant loss of fluid and may rapidly cause shock.

TYPES OF BURNS

There are four types of burns: thermal, chemical, radiation, and electrical.

Thermal Burns

Thermal burns are caused by flames, flashes of heat (as in explosions), hot liquids, or contact with hot objects. The degree of associated tissue death depends on the intensity of the heat and the length of exposure. Water at 140°F (59°C) will burn skin in 5 seconds; water at 120°F (48°C) in 5 minutes.

Chemical Burns

Chemical burns are caused by contact with alkalis, acids, or corrosive material. Backcountry chemical burns are rare, but burns from leaking batteries, carbide lamps, or spilled gas are a possibility.

Radiation and Electrical Burns

Electrical burns in the wilderness are caused by lightning. The most common burn in the wilderness is a radiation burn, or sunburn.

ASSESSMENT OF BURNS

The assessment of a burn includes the depth and extent of the injury.

Depth of the Burn

Burns are classified by the depth of the injury as superficial, partial-thickness, and full-thickness.

Superficial. These burns injure only the epidermis. A superficial burn is red and painful and blanches white with pressure. There are no blisters, and the wound can be painful. The area heals in 4 or 5 days with the epidermis peeling.

Partial-Thickness. Deeper burns injure both the epidermis and the dermis and can be painful. The skin appears red, mottled, wet, and blistered and blanches white with pressure. Blisters can develop quickly after the injury or may take as long as 24 hours to form. The burn takes from 5 to 25 days to heal, and longer if it becomes infected.

Full-Thickness. These burns penetrate deep and injure the epidermis, dermis, and subcutaneous tissue. The skin appears leathery, charred, pearl gray, and dry (or white and firm if it's a thermal burn). The area is sunken and has a burned odor. The skin does not blanch and is not painful because blood vessels and nerve endings are destroyed. Painful first- or second-degree burns may surround the third-degree area. Full-thickness burns destroy the dermis and, if large, require skin grafts to heal.

Extent of the Burn: The Rule of Palms

The extent of burns can be determined by the rule of palms. The patient's palm and fingers when held together represents 1 per-

ASSESSMENT of BURNS:

SUPERFICIAL
EPIDERMIS ONLY BURNED
- SKIN RED, PAINFUL

PARTIAL THICKNESS
EPIDERMIS AND DERMIS BURNED
- SKIN BLISTERED (MAY TAKE 24 HOURS +)
- RED, MOTTLED, WET, PAINFUL

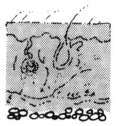

FULL THICKNESS
EPIDERMIS, DERMIS AND SUBCUTANEOUS TISSUE BURNED
- LEATHERY, DRY, CHARRED
- PEARLY GRAY in COLOR

cent of his or her body surface area. Using the palm as a size indicator, estimate the percentage of body area involved.

Location of the Burn

Burns to the face and neck are dangerous due to potential airway problems as well as cosmetic concerns. Burns to the hands and feet are worrisome due to possible loss of function. Burns to the genitals are serious for obvious reasons. Circumferential burns of extremities can produce a constriction that impairs circulation.

TREATMENT FOR THERMAL BURNS

Thermal, electrical, radiation, and chemical burns are all treated essentially the same way. First, the source of the burn must be eliminated. Then, the airway should be checked. The burn itself is cooled, assessed, cleaned, and dressed.

Put Out the Fire. "Stop, drop, and roll" is the sequence to follow if someone catches on fire. Stop the person from running. Make him or her drop to the ground and roll, or roll the person in a sleeping bag or jacket to put out the flames.

Quickly remove the patient's clothing and any jewelry. These retain heat and cause continued burning. Hot water spilled on legs clothed in polypropylene or wool can cause serious burns, as can water spilled into boots, because the boot and sock retain and concentrate the heat.

Check the Airway. Inhalation burns are life-threatening and must be recognized early.

Cool the Burn. Smaller burns can be cooled by pouring cool water (not ice-cold) or applying cool, wet cloths on the burned site. Avoid hypothermia. Never put ice directly on the site, as it may cause frostbite. Ice also causes blood vessels to constrict, which deprives the burned area of blood and thus oxygen and nutrients.

Assess the Depth and Extent of the Burn. Most burns are combinations of partial and superficial injuries. Assess the surface area of each burn type using the rule of palms.

Clean and Dress the Burn. Clean the burn with cool, clean water and apply antibiotic ointment. Embers or smoldering clothing on the surface should be removed; do not attempt to remove melted material from the skin. Moist dressings are fine for small burns (less than 3 percent of the body surface area). Use dry dressings on extensive burns. Change the dressing once a day, and monitor the site for signs of infection. Blisters should be kept intact. If they do rupture, gently wash them with antiseptic soap and water, rinse well, pat dry and cover with sterile gauze.

TREATMENT FOR INHALATION BURNS

Inhalation burns are caused by breathing hot air or gases and/or particles. The cilia (hairlike structures lining the upper airways) and mucous membranes lining the respiratory tract may be destroyed instantly. The mucous membranes swell, and fluid leaks into the lungs. The body is unable to expel mucus because the cilia are damaged. Mucus collects in the upper airway, decreasing carbon dioxide and oxygen exchange. Oxygenation is impaired when carbon monoxide from burning material competes with oxygen for binding sites on red blood cells.

If you suspect an inhalation burn, check the mouth, nose, and throat for signs of soot, redness, or swelling. Are the facial hairs or nasal hairs singed? Check for signs of respiratory distress, such as coughing or noisy, rapid breaths.

Inhalation burns always require that the patient be evacuated to a medical facility. Signs and symptoms of respiratory distress may not become apparent for 24 to 48 hours.

TREATMENT FOR CHEMICAL BURNS

Flush chemical burns with any available water for a minimum of 20 minutes. Brush off any dry chemical before rinsing the burn. Remove clothing, jewelry, and contact lenses, as these may retain the chemical and continue to burn the victim.

Speed is important. The longer a chemical stays on the body, the more damage it causes. Looking for specific antidotes wastes time. Use plain water to flush, then wash the burn with mild soap and water.

Rinse a chemically burned eye with water for at least 20 minutes. After flushing the affected eye, cover it with a moist dressing. After 20 to 30 minutes, remove the dressing. If the patient complains of changes in vision, reapply the dressing and evacuate.

TREATMENT FOR RADIATION BURNS

Most skin damage is caused by short wavelengths of ultraviolet radiation (UVA and UVB). UVB causes more sunburn than UVA, but both wavelengths damage skin. The only known beneficial effect of solar radiation on skin is in the metabolism of vitamin D. Long-term exposure to the sun increases your risk of skin cancer.

Two-thirds of ultraviolet radiation is received during the hours of 10:00 a.m. to 2:00 p.m. At high altitude, the thin atmos-

---

Treatment for Burns

- Remove the source of the burn:
  —For thermal burns, stop, drop, roll.
  —For dry chemical burns, brush off dry chemicals.
  —For wet chemical burns, flush with water for 20 minutes.
- Remove clothing and jewelry.
- Assess the airway.
- Cool the burn.
- Assess the depth and extent of the burn.
- Clean the burn.
- Apply a dressing.

---

phere filters out less ultraviolet radiation, and the skin is damaged more quickly. Snowfields reflect 70 to 85 percent of the ultraviolet radiation. Water reflects 2 percent when the sun is directly overhead, and more when the sun is lower. Grass reflects 1 to 2 percent. Mountaineering at high altitudes, especially on snow, increases the risk of sun-related problems. Clouds filter out infrared heat radiation, and your skin feels cooler, but ultraviolet radiation still passes through and the risk of sun exposure still exists.

Sunburn

People with fair skin, usually blonds and redheads, are susceptible to burning. Darker skin contains more of the protective pigment melanin, but does not eliminate the chance of sunburn or provide protection against the cumulative effects of sun exposure.

Unprotected skin can receive superficial or partial-thickness burns from the sun. Fever blisters or cold sores often follow sunburn of the lips. These are herpes simplex (viral) infections and can be quite painful. A patient with extensive sunburn may complain of chills, fever, or headache.

Phototoxic Reactions. A phototoxic reaction is an abnormally severe sunburn related to the ingestion of a drug, plant, or chemical or the application of a drug, plant, or chemical to the skin. Certain drugs, such as sulfonamides (Bactrim, Septra), tetracyclines (Vibramycin), oral diabetic agents, and tranquilizers (Thorazine, Compazine, Phenergan, Sparine), increase the skin's sensitivity to sunlight.

Treatment of Sunburned Skin. Cool, wet dressings will relieve some of the pain. Aspirin, ibuprofen, or related nonsteroidal anti-inflammatory drugs are recommended. Anesthetic sprays and ointments may relieve the pain but increase the risk of a phototoxic reaction.

Prevention with Sunscreens. Exposure to the sun in small doses promotes tanning, which protects the skin from burns. Unfortunately, degenerative changes still occur in the skin, so it is best to use sunscreens or sunblocks and to wear broad-brimmed hats, long-sleeve shirts, and long pants.

Sunscreens are rated by their sun protection factor (SPF). The SPF number is a guideline for the length of time a person wearing the sunscreen can spend in the sun. SPF is based on the minimal "erythemal dose," or the length of time before the exposed skin becomes red. For example, a person without sunscreen may be able to spend 30 minutes safely in the sun. Applying a sunscreen with an SPF of 10 should allow the same person to spend 10 times as long in the sun, or 300 minutes, before the skin turns red. This system assumes that the sunscreen is not washed off by water or sweat and is used in adequate amounts.

Creams that completely block ultraviolet radiation (zinc oxide, A-Fil, red veterinarian petrolatum) are good for areas that are easily burned, such as the nose, ears, and lips. Use a sunscreen that guards against both UVB and UVA radiation—the label should explain the coverage of the sunscreen. Most people do not apply enough sunscreen and do not apply it often enough. Sunscreens should be applied on cloudy or overcast days as well as on sunny ones. The ultraviolet radiation that penetrates cloud cover is often great enough to burn the skin. Sunscreens work better if applied when the skin is warm and allowed to soak in half an hour before sun exposure. It's a good habit to apply sunscreen well before you are exposed.

Tips for Preventing Sun-Related Injury: Don't Sunburn!

1. Apply sunscreen 30 minutes before going out, and reapply it frequently.
2. Apply sunblock to your lips, nose, and other sensitive areas.
3. Wear a hat with a brim.
4. Wear sunglasses with 100 percent UV protection, even on cloudy days.
5. Minimize sun exposure between 10 A.M. and 2 P.M.
6. Wear a long-sleeve shirt and pants.
7. Examine your skin, and see a physician if you notice a mole changing shape, color, or size or if you have a "sore" that won't heal.

Sun Bumps

The itching, red blistered rash we know as "sun bumps" has a real medical name—polymorphous light eruption (PMLE). PMLEs are unusual reactions to light that, as far as can be determined, are not associated with other disease or drugs.

Sunlight in general and UVA specifically is thought of as the causative factor in PMLE, although the overall natural history of the eruption is probably intertwined with skin type, diet, sun exposure, altitude, sensitizing cosmetics, sun cream use, and other factors. It's more common in people from northern climates and affects at least 10 percent of the population (21 percent in Sweden). It's reported 3 to 4 times more in women than men. PMLE typically occurs in spring following ultraviolet radiation exposure reflected from snow. Human skin adapts to UV exposure with time—the hardening phenomenon. This may explain the reduced incidence of PMLE during the summer.

Medical experts say that 30 minutes to several hours of exposure are required to trigger the eruption, which will subside over 1 to 7 days without scarring.

Signs and Symptoms. As the name implies, these eruptions come in different forms. Medically they are described as papules (a raised lesion on the skin) and papulovesicles (small blisters) that can coalesce into plaques and erythema multiforme–like lesions (red or pink raised rash). They can itch miserably and sometimes cause stinging sensations and pain.

Treatment. Short-term management treats symptoms, the prime one being itching. Antihistamines and topical steroid creams are recommended, but really don't work all that well. Unfortunately the reaction seems to run its course, despite our efforts to shorten the discomfort.

Prevention includes wearing protective clothing, using sun block, and ensuring gradual exposure to the sun. We know this does not work for everyone, and the medical literature agrees. There are a variety of drugs that are used for people with recurrent reactions, none of which seen to be particularly effective.

A related condition to PMLE is phytophotodermatitis (PPD), a reaction from exposure to certain plants along with subsequent exposure to sunlight.

PPD can occur through ingestion of the plant or, more commonly, through topical contact. Common plants implicated include celery, giant hogweed, parsnip, fennel, parsley, lime, lemon, rue, fig, mustard, scurf pea, and chrysanthemums. Plant oils in perfumes are also implicated in these reactions.

This can look like PMLE with initial burning pain and a raised, red rash, followed by blistering.

Treat mild reactions with cool wet dressings, topical steroid creams, and nonsteroidal anti-inflammatory drugs (NSAIDs). Severe reactions may require systemic steroids.

Snow Blindness

Burning of the cornea and conjunctiva by the sun is called snow blindness. Affected people aren't actually blind, but they're reluctant to open their eyes because of the pain. The eyes feel dry, as if they are full of sand. Moving, blinking, or opening the eyes is painful. The eyes are red and tear excessively. This can happen with as little as an hour exposure to bright sunlight. Symptoms may not develop for 8 to 12 hours after the eyes have been exposed to the sun.

Treatment. Snow blindness heals spontaneously in several days. Cold compresses, pain medication, and a dark environment relieve the pain. Don't rub the eyes or put anesthetics in the eyes. These can damage the cornea.

Sunglasses, especially those with side blinders, decrease the ultraviolet radiation received by the eyes and prevent snow blindness. If you lose your sunglasses, make temporary ones from two pieces of cardboard with slits cut in them to see through. Wear sunglasses on cloudy or overcast days as well as sunny days.

FINAL THOUGHTS

The American Burn Association and the American College of Surgeons classify burns by depth and extent. They recommend that burns greater than 10 percent of the body surface area be treated at a burn center. We often evacuate smaller burns due to patient discomfort, worry of infection, inadequate amounts of first aid materials to handle the daily dressing changes, and inability to use the injured body part.

A patient with burns of the face may also have inhalation burns. Partial- and full-thickness burns of the hands and feet may require special treatment to preserve function, and burns of the groin may produce enough swelling to prevent urination. Burns completely encircling a limb may cut off circulation. Burns, like other soft tissue wounds, must be kept clean to reduce the risk of infection.

Burns are serious injuries, more easily prevented than treated. Keep safety in mind at all times, especially when around fires and stoves.

Clothing is portable shade and a simple sunburn prevention method. A brimmed hat shades the face and neck. Long-sleeve shirts and pants protect skin from the sun. Develop the habit of putting on sunscreen early and often.

Evacuation Guidelines

Evacuate all full-thickness burns. Consider evacuating partial thickness burns, especially to the hands, feet, face, armpits, or groin for pain management and wound care.

- Rapidly evacuate any patient with partial- or full-thickness burns covering more than 10 percent total body surface area (TBSA); any patient with partial- or full-thickness circumferential burns, and any patient with signs and symptoms of airway burns.

ENVIRONMENTAL INJURIES

The wilderness environment that gives us so much enjoyment can also threaten our health with heat and cold, dangerous creatures and plants, altitude, and lightning. NOLS incident data shows that sound leadership and outdoor skill keeps us healthy in the wilderness. This section discusses treatment principles to guide our first aid for heat challenges, frostbite, hypothermia, altitude illness, submersion, and unwanted interactions with noxious animals, insects, and plants. The experienced outdoor leader knows it is easier to stay warm than to warm the hypothermic patient, easier to stay cool than to treat heatstroke in the field, easier to avoid snakebite than to deal with an envenomation. In this vein, the discussions of these topics share tips for the most important first aid skill, prevention.

COLD INJURIES

INTRODUCTION

On a snowy subzero morning in early November, after 2 days of searching, a lost hunter was found in the Wind River Mountains south of Lander, Wyoming. His nose, hands, feet, and stomach were severely frostbitten, and he showed limited signs of life. After several hours of evacuation by snow litter and four-wheel drive, rescuers delivered him to the emergency room with a rectal temperature of 74°F (23°C).

His ordeal was not over yet. The hypothermia caused his heart to stop, and only after 3 hours of warming and CPR did he begin to recover. His story was presented by the media as one of "miraculous" survival. He was lucky, and he knows it. Today, this man is a strong advocate of hypothermia prevention.

THE PHYSIOLOGY OF TEMPERATURE REGULATION

Humans are warm-blooded animals that maintain a relatively constant internal temperature regardless of the environmental temperature. Human cells, tissues, and organs, and especially the biological catalysts known as enzymes, operate efficiently only within narrow temperature limits. If your temperature rises 2°F above the normal 98.6°F (37°C), you become ill. If it rises 7°F, you become critically ill. If your temperature decreases 2°F, you feel cold. A 7°F decrease puts your life in jeopardy.

Humans are designed to live in tropical climates; our heat loss mechanisms are highly developed. Our insulation mechanisms are less efficient. To adapt structurally to cold, our bodies would have to be covered with thick insulating hair and develop greater reserves of fat. Rather than remaining angular and cylindrical, which promotes heat loss, our body shape would become rounder and shorter to prevent heat loss. This would especially affect our ability to tolerate lower body temperatures and near-freezing temperatures in our fingers and toes.

We gain heat from the chemical potential energy in food and oxygen when we exercise or metabolize food, but this by itself is not sufficient to keep us warm all winter.

As it is, human beings can live in the cold because our intellectual responses enable us to deal effectively with environmental stress. Much of what students learn on NOLS courses is how to live comfortably in extreme environmental conditions by employing skill, disciplined habits, and quality equipment. We compensate for our physical deficiencies with behavioral responses such as eating, drinking, and creating microclimates through the use of clothing, fire, and shelter. The diminished intellectual response evident in early stages of hypothermia, as well as in altitude sickness, heat illness, and dehydration, dangerously impairs our ability to react to the environment.

Mechanisms of Heat Production
The three main physiological means for producing heat are metabolism, exercise, and shivering.

Resting Metabolism. The basal metabolic rate is like a constant internal furnace, liberating heat as a by-product of the biochemical reactions that keep us alive. Metabolism is not an efficient means to convert the energy potential in food into work. As a result, much of the energy from metabolism is lost as heat. Metabolic rate increases slightly when we are exposed to cold for long periods, but not enough to satisfy the body's entire heat requirements in winter conditions. Food is the fuel for metabolism.

Nutritionally sound rations and good cooking skills are critical to health on wilderness expeditions.

Exercise. Exercise is an important method of heat production. Muscles, which make up 50 percent of our body weight, produce 73 percent of the heat generated during work. Short bursts of hard physical effort can generate tremendous amounts of heat, while moderate levels of exercise can be sustained for long periods. This valuable source of heat does have its limitations. Physical conditioning, strength, stamina, and fuel in the form of food and water are necessary to sustain activity.

Shivering. Shivering—a random quivering of muscles—produces heat at a rate 5 times greater than the basal metabolic rate. It is our first defense against cold. Shivering occurs when temperature receptors in the skin and brain sense a decrease in body temperature and trigger the shivering response.

As with all forms of work, the price of shivering is fuel. How long and how effectively we shiver is limited by the amount of carbohydrates stored in muscles and by the amount of water and oxygen available. In order to shiver, we have to pump blood into the muscles. Warm blood flowing close to the surface reduces our natural insulation and increases heat loss.

Shivering also hinders our ability to perform the behavioral tasks necessary to reduce heat loss and increase heat production. It is difficult to zip up your parka, start your stove, or ski to camp during violent shivering. Vigorous physical activity can override the shivering response. If we don't capture the heat produced by vigorous exercise in insulating clothing, we can cool past the point of shivering without experiencing the response.

Mechanisms of Heat Loss

The core of the body contains the organs necessary for survival: the heart, brain, lungs, liver, and kidneys. The shell consists of the muscles, skin, and superficial tissues. The ebb and flow of blood from core to superficial tissues is a constant process. As our temperature rises, blood volume shifts and carries heat to the outer layers of the skin. As we cool, less blood flows to the periphery, preserving heat for the vital organs.

MECHANISMS OF Heat Loss

Our mechanisms for heat loss are so well developed that we lose heat in all but the hottest and most humid conditions. On a warm day, if we did not lose most of the heat our bodies produced, our body temperature would rise. The primary means of heat loss is through the skin. Warm, flushed skin can dispose of heat through conduction, convection, radiation, or evaporation.

The circulatory system controls heat by regulating the volume of blood flowing to the skin and superficial muscles. When we are resting comfortably, only a small percentage of blood flows directly to the skin. During heat stress, however, the blood vessels open up and blood flow to the skin may increase a hundredfold. During cold stress, blood is shunted from the periphery to the core, reducing the heat lost to the environment. Constricted blood vessels can reduce blood flow to the skin by 99 percent.

Conduction. Conduction is the transfer of heat through direct contact between a hot and a cold object. Energy as heat moves from the warmer to the colder object. We lose heat when we lie on cold, wet ground. We gain heat when we lie on a hot beach or rock. The rate of heat transfer is determined by the temperature difference between the two objects, the surface area exposed to the cold surface, and the effectiveness of the insulation between the body and the cold surface. The more efficient the insulation, the less heat is transferred. Warm, still air trapped in clothing is an effective insulator. Water, metal, and snow are good conductors.

We reduce conductive heat loss every night by sleeping with a foam pad between ourselves and the ground. If we wake up cold, we often add insulation between ourselves and the ground before we put on more clothing. Damp cotton conducts heat, so if we're cold and wearing a damp cotton shirt, we'll take it off. On winter expeditions we place extra insoles in our boots, and in camp we stand on foam pads to reduce conduction between our feet and the snow.

Convection. Convective heat transfer occurs when two surfaces, in direct contact, are moving relative to each other. When we're in direct contact with cold moving air or water, heat escapes from the surface of the body by convection. The rate of heat transfer depends on the temperature difference between the warmer and the cooler body, the surface area in contact, and the speed at which the air or water is moving. Moving air (wind chill), besides cooling us directly, strips away the microclimate of air heated by the body. The loss of this insulating layer next to the body further accelerates heat loss.

To discover the cooling power of moving water, place your fingers in a bowl of cold water. Slowly swirl your fingers. The increase in heat loss is immediately perceptible. Immersion in cold water is a profound threat to temperature balance.

Heat is transferred by convection through the body by the blood. As we cool and the body shunts blood away from the skin, the superficial tissues—especially in our fingers and toes—no longer gain heat from the blood, which increases the likelihood of frostbite.

We reduce convective heat loss by wearing wind-resistant clothes, tight-weave nylon jackets and pants, and hoods to protect the vulnerable head and neck.

Radiation. Radiation is the transfer of electromagnetic energy from a hot object to a cold object. With a normal body temperature of 98°F (37°C), humans are often the warmer objects in the environment, and we lose heat through radiation. We receive radiative heat input from fires, from the sun, or from reflection off snow, water, or rocks.

Radiative heat loss makes clear winter nights colder than cloudy nights. Cloud cover reflects much of the earth's radiative heat back to the ground, reducing the severity of the nighttime temperature drop. Reflected, radiated heat waves bouncing off the walls and snowfields of a cirque during bright sunshine increase warmth—and the possibility of sunburn.

When exposed to the environment, the skin acts as a radiator. Higher radiative heat loss occurs from uncovered skin, commonly the hands, face, and head. Clothing reduces radiative heat loss.

Evaporation. When perspiration evaporates from the skin's surface, the change in state from liquid to gas consumes energy from the surface of the skin. Evaporative heat loss accounts for 20 percent of the body's total heat loss in normal conditions—much more when we are under heat stress or working hard. We use this to our advantage to cool ourselves in hot environments.

Sweating accounts for roughly two-thirds of evaporative heat loss. The remaining one-third is lost through breathing. Inhalation humidifies air and warms it to body temperature. During exhalation, evaporation of moisture from the surface of the lungs and airways uses heat and cools the body. The rate and depth of breathing and the humidity of the air determine the amount of heat and moisture lost. The colder and drier the air and the faster the breathing rate, the greater the heat loss.

We reduce evaporative heat loss by controlling our work rate, by using techniques such as the rest step (walking with flat feet, transferring weight slowly and smoothly from one leg to the other) when backpacking, and by avoiding hard breathing and sweating. Sweating in cold environments is to be avoided. It wets insulation and cools the body.

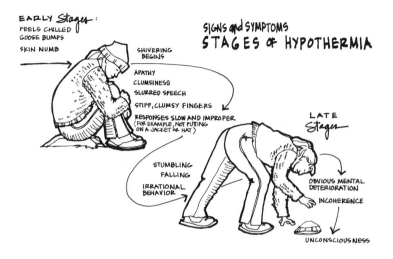

EARLY Stages:
FEELS CHILLED
GOOSE BUMPS
SKIN NUMB

SHIVERING BEGINS

SIGNS and SYMPTOMS
STAGES OF HYPOTHERMIA

APATHY
CLUMSINESS
SLURRED SPEECH
STIFF, CLUMSY FINGERS
RESPONSES SLOW AND IMPROPER
(FOR EXAMPLE, NOT PUTTING ON A JACKET OR HAT)

STUMBLING
FALLING
IRRATIONAL BEHAVIOR

LATE Stages

OBVIOUS MENTAL DETERIORATION
INCOHERENCE
UNCONSCIOUSNESS

HYPOTHERMIA

A constant balance of heat gain and loss is required to maintain a stable body temperature. The adjustments the body makes are designed to keep our vital organs—heart, brain, lungs, kidneys, and liver—within a temperature range in which they operate effectively. If core temperature rises above normal, potentially life-threatening conditions—heatstroke or high fever—develop. When core temperature drops below normal, hypothermia may be the result.

Hypothermia can develop whenever heat loss exceeds heat gain and is as common during the wind, rain, and hail of summer as it is during winter. Immersion in cold water can cause hypothermia. If body temperature drops as low as 80°F (26.4°C), death is likely.

Signs and Symptoms of Hypothermia

As body temperature falls, mental functions decline and the patient loses the ability to respond appropriately to the environment. Responses are slow and/or improper, such as not changing into dry clothes or wearing a rain jacket or hat. Muscular functions deteriorate until the patient is too clumsy to walk or stand. Biochemical processes become slow and deficient as the body cools.

Signs and Symptoms of Hypothermia

MILD HYPOTHERMIA
- Shivering, numb skin with goose bumps.
- Minor impairment of muscular performance: stiff and clumsy fingers.
- Mental deterioration begins: poor decisions, confused and sluggish thinking.

MODERATE HYPOTHERMIA
- Stumbling, apathy, lethargy.
- Obvious mental status changes, irritability, forgetfulness, and complaining.
- Obvious muscular incoordination: stumbling, falling, and clumsy hands.

SEVERE HYPOTHERMIA
- Energy reserves are depleted, shivering may cease.
- Obvious mental deterioration occurs (e.g., incoherence, disorientation, irrational behavior).
- As the body becomes cooler, heart and respiratory rate and blood pressure fall.
- Severe muscular rigidity may occur.
- The pulse may be undetectable, and the patient may appear to have stopped breathing or to have died.

Recognizing Hypothermia (Assessment)

Hypothermia is easily overlooked. In cities, it has been mistaken for alcohol intoxication, stroke, and drug overdose. It may be associated with illnesses such as diabetes and other metabolic disturbances or with the elderly and the homeless. In the wilderness, hypothermia has been confused with fatigue, irritability, dehydration, and mountain sickness.

You can measure the patient's temperature to detect hypothermia. Choose a low-reading hypothermia thermometer for your medical kit; conventional thermometers read only to 94°F (34°C). A rectal temperature is ideal in the field; oral or axillary (armpit) temperatures may not reflect the status of the core organs. Obtaining a rectal temperature on a cold and confused patient, however, can be awkward. Also, undressing the patient to obtain a rectal reading may cause further cooling, is not practical, and is rarely done in the wilderness.

Early signs and symptoms of hypothermia can be difficult to recognize. The patient does not feel well. You may assume that he or she is tired, not hypothermic. Yet this is the stage at which successful warming in the wilderness is possible.

This patient may not be hypothermic; that is, his core temperature may not have dropped significantly. He may only be wet, cold and unhappy, hungry. Regardless, we need to recognize and address this situation early.

Hypothermia in its later stages may be more obvious. The patient is grossly uncoordinated with a clearly altered mental status. This stage of hypothermia is easier to recognize but much harder to treat in the wilderness.

The most important diagnostic tool in the backcountry is the first responder's awareness of the possibility of hypothermia and attention to the patient's mental state. Anyone in a cool or cold environment is at risk for hypothermia. Persons with altered mental status (confused, slurred speech, disoriented) in the outdoors may be hypothermic. Whether you can obtain a temperature or not, if you suspect hypothermia, treat it immediately and aggressively.

Assessment of Hypothermia

MILD TO MODERATE
- Awake
- Shivering
- Able to walk
- Alert (altered mental status possible)

SEVERE
- Altered mental status
- No shivering
- Unable to walk

Treatment of Mild to Moderate Hypothermia
Prevention of hypothermia is simple. Treatment is not. Warming can be a long and complex process that takes hours, and it may

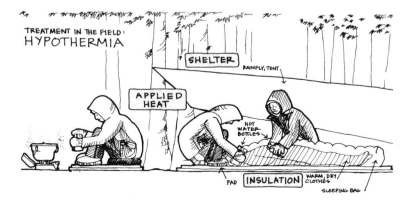

TREATMENT IN THE FIELD:
HYPOTHERMIA

SHELTER — RAINFLY, TENT

APPLIED HEAT

HOT WATER BOTTLES

PAD — INSULATION — WARM, DRY CLOTHES

SLEEPING BAG

be impossible in the backcountry.

A mildly hypothermic patient may be warmed in the field. In the absence of a serious underlying medical condition, the chances for successful warming are good. Although we can't change the weather, we can replace wet clothing with dry, protect the patient from the wind, add layers of insulation, hydrate and feed the patient, and apply heat.

Dry the patients, dress them in warm clothes, get them to move, give them hot drinks, and everything usually works out fine. If a patient is seriously cold, you place him or her in a sleeping bag "hypothermia wrap" with hot water bottles, build a fire, and take other aggressive actions as necessary.

Prevent further heat loss:
- Dress the patient in dry clothing, especially a hat to reduce heat loss from the head and neck. For mild hypothermia, this and a hot drink are often all the treatment that's needed.

Feed and hydrate the patient:
- Warm drinks are a source of heat, fluid, and sugar. The patient must be alert and able to hold the drink and consume it under his or her own power.
- Warm drinks and simple foods, such as candy bars, can be followed by a good meal after the patient is warmed. A fatigued or dehydrated patient is a strong candidate for another episode of hypothermia. Keep the patient insulated and resting until energy and fluid reserves have been replenished. In our experience, it's best to keep the warmed patient in the sleeping bag for a good night's sleep and to give him or her a hot meal and several liters of water.

The hypothermia wrap:
- A sleeping bag in a "hypothermia wrap" is the backcountry's most tried and true warming tool. Place the patient into a sleeping bag with a foam pad underneath. If you have extra sleeping bags, use them.
- Heat packs or hot water bottles may be helpful sources of heat. Apply the hot water bottles to yourself first to make

sure they are not too hot, then wrap these carefully so as
to avoid burning the patient. The first hot water bottle
usually goes into the patient's hands, which they hold on
their chest. This may warm the core, as well as the hands.
The next water bottle goes by their feet, to prevent frostbite.

- This whole package is wrapped "burrito style" in a tarp
  or plastic sheet to insulate from wind and moisture loss.
- If you are without a sleeping bag, dress the patient in dry
  clothes for insulation.
- Fires are an excellent source of heat. Use a space blanket
  as a reflector.

Mild or moderately hypothermic patients who can shiver and
still produce heat warm themselves if their body heat is captured
by warm, dry, windproof insulation.

In our experience, the hypothermia wrap with hot water bottles is a more effective practice than putting another person in the
bag. It can be hard to close a sleeping bag tightly around two people. The warmers are not available for other tasks such as setting
up camp and preparing food. The warmers can quickly become
cold and fatigued. Experts disagree on the amount of heat transferred body to body—some think it's low. The value of a warm
person in the sleeping bag may be to heat the insulation, not to
transfer heat directly to the patient. If this method is used, we recommend that the warmers wear at least a thin layer of clothing.
Feed the warmers to keep their energy levels up. Clothing placed
over the opening of zipped-together sleeping bags helps reduce
heat loss. Placing several sleeping bags over the patient and the
warmers also helps. A humid environment inside the sleeping bag
reduces respiratory heat loss, as does loosely wrapping a scarf or
other article of clothing across the patient's mouth and nose.

Be Persistent: Warming Takes Time. Individuals such as the
hunter described in the introduction have recovered from prolonged, profound hypothermia. Newspaper headlines occasionally describe "frozen" and "dead" people who were successfully
warmed. The adage to remember about hypothermia treatment
is that "the victim is never dead until he is warm and dead."

Treatment of Severe Hypothermia

A severely hypothermic patient produces little or no heat and, in the absence of external heat sources, may cool further. A cold heart is susceptible to abnormal rhythms such as ventricular fibrillation, a random quivering of the heart that fails to pump blood. Jarring or bouncing, almost inevitable in transport from the backcountry, can trigger this rhythm.

In severe hypothermia, there may be complications from an underlying medical condition or trauma and complex disturbances in the body's biochemical balance. For these reasons, a patient with severe hypothermia needs to be transported to a hospital.

Evacuation of a severely hypothermic patient must occur simultaneously with attempts to prevent further cooling. If you do not apply heat to the patient during transport, further cooling is almost certain. Monitor ABCs and vitals, and carry the patient as gently as possible. Rescue breathing for 10 to 15 minutes before movement may prevent ventricular fibrillation.

It may be difficult to find the pulse or respiration rate of a severely hypothermic patient. The heart rate may be 20 to 30 beats per minute, and the breathing rate only 3 to 4 times a minute. Take your time during assessment. Check the heartbeat and breathing for at least 1 minute, carefully watching for the rise and fall of the chest, listening for any breath sounds, and feeling for the pulse at the neck. Ideally, use a cardiac monitor to assess heart rhythm. If in doubt, withhold chest compression and perform rescue breathing.

Causes of Frostbite

- Cold stress
- Low temperatures
- Moisture
- Poor insulation
- Contact with supercooled metal or gasoline
- Interference with circulation of blood:
  —Cramped position
  —Tight clothing (gaiters, wristwatches, etc.)
  —Tight fitting or laced boots
  —Dehydration

FROSTBITE

Frostbite is the freezing of tissue commonly seen on fingers, toes, and ears. Fluid between cells can freeze. The formation of ice crystals draws water out of the cells. Mechanical cell damage also occurs as the crystals rub together. Blood clots form in small vessels and circulation stops, further damaging cells.

A second phase of injury occurs during warming. Damaged cells release substances that promote constriction and clotting in small blood vessels, impairing blood flow to the tissues. Frostbite is not life-threatening, but tissue damage from frostbite can result in loss of function and amputation.

Frostbite is classified as superficial frostbite, also known as frostnip; partial-thickness frostbite; and deep, or full-thickness, frostbite. Many experts classify frostbite only after it has thawed and the extent of the damage is apparent.

Assessment of Frostbite

With frostnip or superficial frostbite, only the outer layer of skin is frozen. It appears white and waxy or possibly gray or mottled. High winds together with cold temperatures create conditions for frostnip on exposed areas of the face, nose, ears, and cheeks.

After the nipped area is warm, the layer of frozen skin becomes red. Over a period of several days, the dead skin peels. As it heals, the appearance of the injury is similar to that of sunburn, a first-degree burn.

Partial-thickness frostbite has progressed from frostnip into the underlying tissues. It may feel hard on the surface, soft and resilient below. Blisters usually appear within 24 hours after warming.

The most serious form of frostbite is deep, or *full-thickness*, frostbite. The injury extends from the skin into the underlying tissues and muscles. The external appearance is the same as frostnip and partial-thickness frostbite, but the frozen area feels hard. After thawing, the area may not blister or may blister only where deep frostbite borders on more superficial damage.

Differentiating partial-thickness from deep frostbite before thawing is difficult. Blisters containing clear fluid, extending to the tips of the digits, and forming within 48 hours

> **Signs and Symptoms of Frostbite**
>
> All forms of frostbite can look similar.
> - The skin is cold, waxy, and pale or mottled.
> - There can be tingling, numbness, or pain.
> - The tissue may be soft if partially frozen, or hard if frozen.
> - Blisters may form if the frostbite has been thawed.

of warming suggest partial-thickness frostbite. Blood-filled blisters that don't reach the tips of the digits, delayed blisters, or the lack of blisters indicates deep frostbite.

Treatment of Frostbite
Frostnip or small areas of partial-thickness frostbite can be warmed by sticking fingers into armpits. Larger areas of partial-thickness frostbite and all full-thickness frostbite should be treated with rapid warming by immersion in warm water between 99° to 102°F (37° to 39°C).

Dangerous folk remedies for frostbite include rubbing the frozen part with snow, flogging the area to restore circulation, and exposing it to an open flame. The treatment of choice for larger areas of partial-thickness and all full-thickness frostbite is rapid warming in warm water.

Many people, including the author, have traveled long distances with frozen feet in order to reach a place where warming could be done once and done well. How long the tissue can be kept frozen without increasing the damage is a matter of controversy. Tissue damage seems to be related to the length of time the tissue stays frozen. Do not keep tissue frozen any longer than necessary.

There are several problems with keeping a frostbitten extremity frozen while evacuation takes place. If the injury occurred from exposure to extreme cold, lack of proper clothing, or in conjunction with hypothermia, the frostbitten area may warm as the problem that caused it is corrected. The activity of traveling may generate enough heat to begin thawing, thus increasing the possibility of further injury from freezing a second time or bruising. Unintentional slow warming is common.

Skin-to-Skin Warming. If the injury is confined to a small area of the body, such as tips of toes or fingers, slow thawing is likely, and skin-to skin warming, hands under armpits or feet on your companion's belly, should be started.

Rapidly Warm in Warm Water. Ideal treatment for frostbite, best done in a hospital, is rapid warming in water between 99° and 102°F (37° and 39°C). Use a thermometer to ensure that the water is the proper temperature. For a rough estimate, 105°F

(40°C) is hot tap water. Cooler water will not thaw frostbite rapidly. Hotter water is very painful and may burn the patient.

Water temperature should remain constant throughout the procedure. This requires a source of hot water and a container large enough to contain the entire frozen part. Do not pour hot water over the frozen tissue. Rather, immerse the frozen area, being careful not to let it touch the sides or bottom of the container. When the water cools, remove the frostbitten part, quickly warm the water, and re-immerse the part.

Thawing frozen fingers generally takes 45 minutes. There is no danger of overthawing, but underthawing can leave tissue permanently damaged. A flush of pink indicates blood returning to the affected site. Warming frostbite is generally very painful. Aspirin or ibuprofen is appropriate for pain relief. If hypothermia is present, it takes priority in treatment.

Post-Thaw Care. Air dry the extremity carefully; don't rub. Swelling will occur, along with blister formation. Inserting gauze between the fingers or toes keeps these areas dry as swelling occurs. Blisters should be kept intact. Once the tissue is thawed, it is extremely delicate, and seemingly minor trauma can damage it. Ibuprofen may be helpful for pain and inflammation.

Prevent freezing a second time after thawing. The freeze-thaw-freeze sequence will produce permanent tissue damage. The seriousness of frostbite injury is increased if freeze-thaw-freeze has occurred or if it is accompanied by fracture or soft tissue injury.

NONFREEZING COLD INJURY

A nonfreezing cold injury results from exposure to continued wet, cold conditions—conditions that many outdoor recreationists avoid. Military operations, like NOLS expeditions, rarely have the luxury of choosing their weather conditions and may spend days in weather conducive to the development of nonfreezing cold injury. Understandably, much of what we know about nonfreezing cold injury—immersion foot, or trench foot—comes from the military. In World War I, when the term "trench foot" was coined, the British Army experienced 29,000 immersion foot casualties in the winter of 1915–16; frostbite and immersion foot casualties for U.S.

Signs and Symptoms of Nonfreezing Cold Injury

- The skin is cold, swollen, shiny, and/or mottled.
- Tingling, numbness, or pain may be present.
- Capillary refill time is slow.
- After warming skin may be warm, red, swollen, and painful.
- In severe cases blisters, ulcers, and gangrene may develop.

forces in Europe in World War II totaled 90,000.

Nonfreezing injury is a local injury that occurs, most commonly to the feet, in cold, wet conditions when blood vessels constrict in response to heat loss, reducing blood flow to the extremity and depriving cells of oxygen and nutrients. The ensuing injury may range from a few weeks of sore feet to permanent muscle and nerve damage. In some cases, victims experience months of pain, disability, and even amputation.

It is common to hear that at least 12 hours of exposure to cold, wet conditions is necessary to produce the injury. Our experience, however, tells us that it can happen more quickly, over a long, wet, cold hiking day, for example, or in a multihour river crossing. Murray Hamlet, DVM, an expert on nonfreezing cold injury, says that the minimum exposure is as little as 3 hours, although he thinks it takes 12 hours to sustain a serious injury. These episodes of short-onset nonfreezing cold injury could be due to individual susceptibility or could be the culminating event of long-term exposure. There are times when our diligence prevents nonfreezing cold injury, although we have chronically cool and constricted feet. Sadly, as little as an afternoon's lapsed attention can undo our best efforts.

Assessment of Nonfreezing Cold Injury

All these classic signs and symptoms are true. You must be alert, however, to subtle forms of nonfreezing cold injury that do not necessarily look mottled, gray, or waxy, nor do you always see poor capillary refill or altered skin color and temperature. All you may see is cool, pale extremities, numbness or tingling, and mild swelling. Pain is unusual in the field, becoming more common after blood flow has returned to the extremity.

Be suspicious about any numbness, tingling, or pain in your feet in cool conditions. Nerves are most susceptible to injury from reduced blood flow. Many of the long-term effects of immersion foot are due to damaged nerves in the feet: pain, numbness, chronic tingling, and itching.

The patient may not notice the constricted condition of the feet until after the trip. We've learned to advise people returning from prolonged wet and cold conditions to avoid long, hot showers or baths. The rapid warming can surprise the unwary with swollen, painful, and red feet.

Treatment of Nonfreezing Cold Injury
- Warm nonfreezing cold injuries slowly at room temperature.
- Elevate the feet to reduce the swelling.

In serious cases, swelling, pain, and blister formation prevent walking. Bed rest, to avoid trauma, is often necessary until the injury heals. Ibuprofen is recommended because of its anti-inflammatory properties. Aspirin and acetaminophen may also help.

Chilblains and Pernio
The nonfreezing cold injuries chilblains and pernio tend to occur on the extremities, especially the hands and feet, and are more common in cold, wet conditions than cold and dry conditions.

The chilblain usually is swollen and tender, itches, and is reddish to purple in color. It has a nodule, bump-like appearance. Pernio, sometimes called the long-term effect of chilblains, can look like chilblains except that there is more of a chance of blisters with a dark crust. Both pernio and chilblains can cause persistent itching, numbness, and pain. The key to treatment, like any cold injury, is prevention.

Prevention of Cold Injury
Our experience is that in prolonged cold, wet conditions, some degree of immersion foot is inevitable. The best footwear-gaiter system is of little help. Prevention is based on the consistent daily interaction of equipment, outdoor skills, and habits of vigilance and assessment.

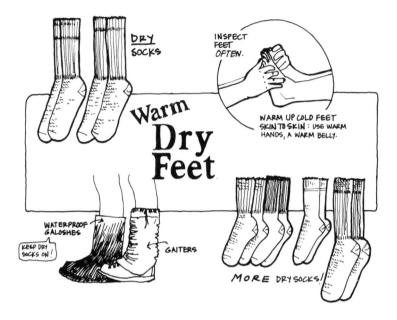

There is no new thing under the sun. In World War I, the British significantly reduced immersion foot casualties (without making major footwear changes) by using techniques that we still follow today: wearing well-fitting boots with heavy wool socks; keeping the body warm; removing wet socks and drying and massaging the feet twice a day; not sleeping in wet footwear; drying wet socks against the skin; keeping feet out of water or mud as much as possible; watching carefully and reacting promptly to any numbness or tingling; and keeping footwear loose to allow for circulation.

What follows are suggestions from NOLS instructors that we have accumulated over the years.

Dry Your Socks. Drying socks is a continual activity on wilderness trips. During the day, we stick wet socks under our shirts to dry them against the skin, and at night, we drape them over our chests and bellies in our sleeping bags. We'll hang them in the sun and dry them over a fire. Keep one pair of dry socks in a dry place, such as in a sleeping bag or a small plastic bag.

Sleep with Warm, Dry Feet. Sleeping with dry feet is very helpful, but there is a false impression that this offers complete protection. People coping with prolonged wet, cold conditions have developed immersion foot by hiking for a single day in wet socks. A single night of sleeping in cool, wet socks has undone weeks of vigilant attention. Go to bed with warm, dry feet and keep them that way all night long.

Use the Environment to Your Advantage. Travel early. Stop before nightfall, leaving time to care for your feet. In spring and summer, use the hardened overnight snowpack to stay on top of the snow. Stop when the snowpack becomes wet and soft, and dry your feet and socks in the afternoon sun. Choose campsites with good sun exposure and campfire possibilities.

Look at Your Feet. Local cold injuries are as much a leadership as a medical problem. When the conditions are ideal for trench foot to occur, the leader may need to check susceptible people frequently; visual checks twice daily are often suggested. Visual checking must be part of the routine. Messages sent to the brain from the feet may be faulty due to nerve damage.

Give Your Feet Top Priority. In some places where people hike and ski, it is impossible to have dry feet all day. The best footwear won't keep you dry in soaking wet tundra or through multiple river crossings. On these days, if your socks are damp and your feet cool, stop, warm your feet, and if possible, change into dry socks.

Warming cool feet on a companion's belly or stopping to change socks in the middle of the day should be routine tasks, not impositions. When you get to camp, get out of your wet boots immediately. Change into a pair of dry socks and begin to actively dry your wet or damp socks. Warm your feet promptly. Don't wait until bedtime.

Use Foot Powder. Foot powder does not seem to be helpful in preventing immersion injury, other than as a discipline in conjunction with changing socks. People with a tendency toward athlete's foot (a fungal infection) have found medicated foot powders helpful.

Display Good Habits. For outdoor leaders, role modeling good foot care on the trail and in camp is essential. To many outdoor enthusiasts, frostbite is the cold injury that is most well known. People are not well informed on the subtleties of nonfreezing cold injuries. Novices often assume that some degree of cooling is unavoidable and acceptable, and inadvertently cross a line from extremity cooling to a cold injury.

Keep Your Core Warm. Poor nutrition, dehydration, wet socks, inadequate clothing, and constriction of blood flow by shoes, socks, gaiters, or tight clothing are all predisposing factors.

Use Proper Equipment. Plastic boots and supergaiters are improvements over leather boots but are not a panacea. Rubber galoshes, though unfashionable, are inexpensive, simple, and helpful in keeping footwear dry. Bring multiple pairs of socks; wear two pairs on your feet and have at least two spare pairs.

FINAL THOUGHTS

The possibility of cold injury is our constant companion on wilderness trips. It's a threat not only in the mountains or in winter conditions, but anytime the environment is cool and wet, be it a fall rainstorm in the east, a cold desert night, or immersion in a cool ocean, river, or lake. The most successful and easiest treatment for hypothermia is prevention by choosing effective insulating material such as wool and synthetics and water- and windproof parkas and pants, using these items properly, eating and staying hydrated, and honing your camping and navigation skills to live comfortably as you travel through the wilderness.

A common thread in many nonfreezing cold injury and frostbite scenarios is people who tolerate cold feet, wait too long before intervening, and are surprised when they discover that they have been injured. If your feet are not definitely warm, you're doing something wrong. Novices may believe that they have to tolerate some level of cold extremities as an unavoidable consequence of camping. Although there is some truth to this, a novice lacks the experience to know how much one can tolerate before an injury occurs, and even an expert can be fooled. Don't be one of those people who rationalize not taking care of their feet by saying, "My feet are cold, but not that cold."

Evacuation Guidelines

Hypothermia:

- Mild hypothermia can be treated in the field. Severe hypothermia needs to be gently and rapidly evacuated for hospital warming.

Frostbite:

- Isolated, small (less than quarter-sized) thawed areas of frostbite can be kept in the field if subsequent freezing can be prevented. In general, larger areas of partial or full-thickness cold injuries should be evacuated. The pain from nonfreezing cold injury usually dictates evacuation.

CHAPTER 10 | HEAT ILLNESS

INTRODUCTION

Our bodies produce heat constantly. When heat production exceeds heat loss, body temperature rises. Factors that reduce heat loss include high ambient air temperature, excessive clothing, and inability to sweat. To survive in a hot environment, human beings must eliminate enough heat to keep the body temperature within acceptable limits—97° to 100°F (35° to 37°C). Vital organs are irreversibly damaged when the body temperature stays at or above 107°F (41.5°C) for any length of time.

Heat illness is unusual on NOLS courses because we are diligent and aggressive about prevention. Outdoor leaders should be knowledgeable about the causes, recognition, and treatment of heat illness. Preventing heat illness, like preventing hypothermia, frostbite, altitude illness, and dehydration, is a 24-hour-a-day leadership task.

PHYSIOLOGY OF HEAT ILLNESS

The body generates 2,000 to 5,000 kilocalories (kcal) of heat per day. Every metabolic function, blink of the eye, and beat of the heart produces heat. Basal metabolism alone would raise the body temperature 1.5°F per hour if heat were not dissipated.

Organs responsible for heat loss are the skin, cardiovascular system, and respiratory system. As discussed in chapter 9 ("Cold

Injuries"), the four main mechanisms by which the body loses heat are radiation, evaporation, convection, and conduction. Of these, radiation and evaporation are the body's primary avenues of heat loss.

Radiation. Under heat stress, the body dilates superficial blood vessels, increases heart rate and cardiac output, and directs more blood to the skin. Normally, one-third to one-half a liter of blood per minute is shunted to the skin and superficial tissues. The body can increase skin blood flow to 4 liters per minute when it is heat stressed.

Radiation accounts for 65 percent of the heat lost when the air temperature is lower than body temperature. In hot environments, radiation is a major source of heat gain. The body can gain up to 300 kcal per hour when exposed to the sun.

Evaporation. Sweating by itself does not cool the body. Evaporation of perspiration cools the body because heat is necessary to change water from liquid to vapor. A heat-acclimatized person can sweat as much as 2 liters per hour for a total loss of 1 million kcal of heat.

Acclimatization. Acclimatizing to heat entails increasing the rate of sweating, decreasing the sweating threshold, improving vasodilation, and decreasing electrolyte loss in the sweat. When acclimatized, we sweat faster and sooner and lose fewer electrolytes in the sweat.

To become acclimatized to a hot environment, the body requires 1 to 2 hours of exercise in the heat daily for approximately 10 days to 2 weeks. To remain acclimatized requires 1 to 2 hours of exercise per week.

Predisposing Factors in Heat Illness. Increased heat production, decreased heat dissipation, and a lack of salt and water are the basic factors that produce heat illness.

Other factors in the development of heat illness are age, general health, use of medications or alcohol, fatigue, and a prior history of heat illness. Patients with underlying problems (illness or injury) may not be able to tolerate heat. Underdeveloped physical mechanisms contribute to the incidence of heat illness in children. Individuals with compromised heart function are less able to adjust when stressed by heat. A study conducted by the U.S.

Army demonstrated a correlation between lack of sleep, or fatigue, and the development of heat illness.

Antihistamines, antipsychotic agents, thyroid hormone medications, amphetamines, and alcohol are among the drugs that have been implicated in the development of heat illness. Some interfere with thermoregulation; others increase metabolic activity or interfere with sweating.

HEAT ILLNESS

A continuum of signs and symptoms provides evidence of heat illnesses that range from heat syncope and cramps to heat exhaustion and heatstroke. Symptoms of heat illness, like those of hypothermia and altitude illness, may be subtle and remain unrecognized until a sudden collapse occurs.

Heat Syncope

Heat syncope is fainting due to heat stress. Shunting of blood to the periphery decreases blood flow to the brain through vasodilation and pooling of blood in the large leg veins. Standing for long periods of time (soldier-on-parade syndrome) is a cause of heat syncope.

Assessment and Treatment for Heat Syncope. Prior to fainting, the person may complain of tunnel vision, vertigo, nausea, sweating, or feeling weak.

Heat syncope is self-limited; leave the patient lying flat, and the fainting will usually promptly resolve. Make sure the patient is hydrated. Conduct an initial assessment and focused exam to check for any injuries that may have occurred as a result of the fall.

Heat Syncope

SIGNS AND SYMPTOMS
- Tunnel vision, vertigo, nausea, sweating, weakness.
- Sudden fainting.

TREATMENT
- Lie flat, elevate legs.
- Hydrate.

Heat Cramps

Heat cramps are painful muscle contractions that follow exercise in hot conditions. We don't know for sure what causes the cramps. They may be caused by a lack of salt (sodium, potassium, calcium), neuromuscular fatigue, or a combination of the two. People who sweat profusely and drink only water to replace lost fluids may be more susceptible to heat cramps.

Assessment and Treatment for Heat Cramps. Calf, abdominal, and thigh muscles can be affected, and muscle spasms in the abdomen can be severe. Treat by moving the patient to a cool spot and replenishing the lost salt. Mix one-quarter to one-half teaspoon of salt in a liter of fluid and have the patient drink it slowly. Tums can be helpful as a source of calcium. Massaging the muscles may make the cramps worse. Try gentle limb straightening instead.

Heat Cramps

TREATMENT
- Rest, lie flat, elevate legs.
- Hydrate.
- Gentle limb straightening.

Heat Exhaustion and Heatstroke

Heat stroke is a life-threatening rise in body temperature secondary to heat stress. Heat exhaustion is a vague term referring to an inability to cope with heat stress. The boundary between heat exhaustion and heatstroke is not completely clear. Some authorities consider heat exhaustion an early stage of heatstroke; others consider it a distinct illness resulting from heat stress and water and electrolyte loss. Sweating, body temperature, and other symptoms may not be clear-cut between the two illnesses. In contrast to common wisdom, heat stroke is not a failure of the sweating mechanism; people with heat stoke can be sweating. The prevailing thought is that a patient with altered brain function—bizarre be-

---

Assessment of Heat Exhaustion and Heatstroke

HEAT EXHAUSTION
- Heart rate elevated.
- Respiratory rate elevated.
- Skin pale, cool, clammy.
- Alert.
- Headache, nausea, weak, tired.
- Temperature normal or slightly elevated.

HEATSTROKE
- Heart rate elevated.
- Respiratory rate elevated.
- Skin pale, warm, clammy.
- Altered mental status.
- Temperature >104°F (39.5°C).

---

havior, confusion, delirium, ataxia, seizure, or unresponsiveness—
should be considered to have heatstroke.

There are two broad classifications of heatstroke: classic and
exertional. Classic heatstroke affects the chronically ill, the elderly,
and infants. It develops slowly and is a health concern during heat
waves. Exertional heatstroke is more likely to affect healthy, fit individuals and to develop rapidly during exercise or hard physical
work.

Assessment for Heat Exhaustion and Heatstroke. The signs
and symptoms of heat exhaustion are believed to be caused by
heat stress and dehydration. The patient complains of weakness,
fatigue, headache, dizziness, thirst, nausea, vomiting, and muscle
cramps. Pulse and respiratory rate may be elevated.

In contrast to heat exhaustion, the onset of heatstroke is usually rapid. The patient develops an altered mental status. The
pulse and respiratory rate are elevated. Prodromal signs and
symptoms are confusion, drowsiness, disorientation, irritability,
anxiety, and ataxia. Heatstroke victims usually have a rectal temperature above 104°F (40°C).

Treatment for Heat Exhaustion. Provide a cool environment,
lay the patient flat, remove excess clothing, and shade the patient
or move him from direct heat. Active cooling is not necessary.

Hydrate. If the patient is mentally alert enough to hold the
glass and drink, allow him to drink. Water, a dilute solution of
sugar drinks with a teaspoon of salt, or a sports drink is fine.

Monitor. Watch the patient. The patient often gets better when
you remove the heat stress and assist them in rest and hydration.

Treatment for Heatstroke. Treatment of heatstroke is rapid
cooling. Both the temperature reached and the length of time it is
sustained can affect the long-term outcome of the disease.

Treatment of Heat Exhaustion and Heatstroke

HEAT EXHAUSTION
- Cool environment.
- Rest, lie flat.
- Hydrate.

HEATSTROKE
- Immediate cooling (cool water and fan).
- Evacuate.

Provide a cool environment, lay the patient flat, remove the patient's clothing, cool with water and fanning. Shade the patient or move him or her from direct heat. Lay the patient flat and remove his or her clothing. Spray the patient with water and fan the body to enhance evaporation. Apply cool cloths to the patient's trunk, armpits, abdomen, and groin, where large blood vessels lie near the skin surface. Immersing the patient in cool water, while protecting his airway, will cool the patient rapidly.

Risk Factors for Exertional Heatstroke

- Overweight
- Overdressed
- Fatigue
- Dehydration
- Alcohol use
- Medications
- Exertion
- High humidity
- High temperature
- Not acclimatized
- Young athlete

Monitor temperature. Hypothermia becomes possible with aggressive cooling, so monitor the patient's temperature for hypothermia as well as rebound hyperthermia. Document how long the temperature was elevated, how high it was, and how long it took to cool the patient. Body temperature may remain unstable even after cooling. Evacuate a heatstroke patient, keeping a close watch on temperature.

Hydrate. Do not give fluids by mouth until the patient is mentally alert and able to hold the glass and drink.

Evacuate. Any patient you suspect of having heatstroke should be evacuated immediately for further evaluation. Internal organ damage may not present itself for several days following the episode of heatstroke.

FINAL THOUGHTS

Prevention of heat-related illness is, of course, the best treatment. Leaders need to be alert for signs of developing heat illness in their groups. Environmental risk factors of high heat and humidity, coupled with dehydration, exertion, the cumulative stress of several days in the heat, and overdressing, should raise caution flags. The vague symptoms of fatigue, headache, weakness, irritability, and malaise should be recognized as indicators of dehydration and heat illness.

Tips for Preventing Heat Illness
- Shade the head and back of the neck to decrease heat gain from the sun.
- Hydrate. Simple indicators of hydration are thirst and the color of your urine. If you are thirsty, drink. The urine should be clear to pale yellow. Dark urine may indicate dehydration.
- The average American diet contains 10 to 12 grams of salt per day, which should be adequate for exercising in hot environments.
- Wear loose-fitting, light-colored clothes. This maximizes heat loss by allowing convection and evaporation to take place.
- Exercise cautiously in conditions of high heat and humidity. Air temperatures exceeding 90°F (32°C) and humidity levels above 70 percent severely impair the body's ability to lose heat through radiation and evaporation.
- Recognize the diseases and drugs that impair heat dissipation.
- Know the warning signs of impending heat illness—dark-colored urine, dizziness, headache, and fatigue.
- Acclimatize. It takes 10 days to 2 weeks to acclimatize to a hot environment.

Evacuation Guidelines
- Heat syncope, cramps, and exhaustion can often be treated in the field.
- Rapidly evacuate any person with suspected heat illness and associated altered mental status.

CHAPTER 11 | ALTITUDE ILLNESS

INTRODUCTION

Each year thousands of people trek in Nepal, South America, and Africa at altitudes over 13,000 feet (3900 meters). In the United States, thousands of people climb Mount Rainier (14,408 feet, 4391 meters) and hundreds attempt Denali (20,320 feet, 6193 meters) each year. Skiers in the Rocky Mountains often ski above 10,000 feet (3000 meters) within 24 hours of leaving low elevations. Studies show that symptoms of altitude illness affect up to 40 percent of these people.

Prevention through acclimatization provides some protection from altitude illness, but there is no immunity. NOLS expeditions have managed life-threatening cerebral edema at 21,000 feet (6400 meters) on Cerro Aconcagua in Argentina and pulmonary edema at 11,000 feet (3300 meters) in Wyoming's Wind River Range. If you travel in mountains, you need to know how to prevent, recognize, and treat altitude illness.

Normally, oxygen diffuses from the alveoli into the blood because the gas pressure is greater in the alveoli than in blood. At altitude, diminished air pressure (barometric pressure) reduces the pressure in the alveoli and decreases the amount of oxygen diffusing into the blood. For example, in a healthy person at sea level, blood is 95 percent saturated with oxygen. At 18,000 feet

(5400 meters), it is only 71 percent saturated; that is, it is carrying 29 percent less oxygen.

As altitude increases, barometric pressure falls. Distance from the equator, seasons, and weather also affect barometric pressure. The greater the distance from the equator, the lower the barometric pressure, given the same elevation. For example, if Mount Everest were located at the same latitude as Denali, the corresponding drop in barometric pressure would probably make an ascent without oxygen impossible.

Air pressure is lower in winter than in summer, and a low pressure trough reduces pressure. Although temperature does not directly affect barometric pressure, the combination of cold, stress, and lack of oxygen increases the risk of cold injuries and altitude problems.

ADAPTATION TO ALTITUDE

The body undergoes numerous changes at higher elevation in order to increase oxygen delivery to cells and improve the efficiency of oxygen use. These adaptations usually begin almost immediately and continue to occur for several weeks. People vary in their ability to acclimatize. Some adjust quickly; others fail to acclimatize, even with gradual exposure over a period of weeks.

When we descend, we begin losing our hard-won adaptations at approximately the same rate at which we gained them; 10 days after returning to sea level, we have lost 80 percent of our adaptations.

Increased Respiratory Rate. During the first week of adaptation, a variety of changes takes place. Respiratory rate and depth increase in response to lower concentrations of oxygen in the blood, causing more carbon dioxide to be lost and more oxygen to be delivered to the alveoli. The increased respiratory rate begins within the first few hours of arriving at altitudes as low as 5,000 feet (1500 meters). The lost carbon dioxide causes the body to become more alkaline.

To compensate for the body's increasing alkalinity, the kidneys excrete bicarbonate—an alkaline substance—in the urine. This compensation occurs within 24 to 48 hours after hyperventilation starts.

Increased Heart Rate. Cells require a constant supply of oxygen, so the heart beats more quickly to meet the demand. Except at extreme altitudes, heart rate returns to near normal after acclimatization.

Fluid Shifts. In the lungs, the pulmonary capillaries constrict, increasing resistance to flow through the lungs and raising pulmonary blood pressure. Dangerously high blood pressure in the pulmonary artery may cause fluid to escape from the capillaries and leak into the lungs (pulmonary edema).

Adaptation to Altitude

EARLY CHANGES
- Increased respiratory rate
- Increased heart rate
- Fluid shifts

LATER CHANGES
- Increased red blood cell production
- Increased 2, 3-DPG production
- Increased number of capillaries

Increased Red Blood Cell Production. As acclimatization continues, the bone marrow contributes by increasing red blood cell production. New red blood cells become available in the blood within 4 to 5 days, increasing the blood's oxygen-carrying capacity. An acclimatized person may have 30 to 50 percent more red blood cells than a person at sea level.

Increased 2, 3-DPG Production. Within the blood cells 2, 3-diphosphoglycerate (DPG) increases. This is an organic phosphate that helps oxygen combine with red blood cells. Production of myoglobin, the intramuscular oxygen-carrying protein in red blood cells, also increases.

Increased Number of Capillaries. The body develops more capillaries in response to altitude. This improves the diffusion of oxygen by shortening the distance between the cell and the capillary.

ALTITUDE ILLNESS

Altitude illness results from a lack of oxygen in the body. Anyone who ascends to high altitude will become hypoxic (the condition of having insufficient oxygen in the blood). Why some people become ill and others don't is not known. It is known, however, that

---

Factors That Affect the Incidence and Severity of Altitude Illness

- Rate of ascent—the faster you climb, the greater the risk.
- Altitude attained (especially sleeping altitude)—the higher you sleep, the greater the risk.
- Length of exposure—the longer you stay high, the greater the risk.
- Inherent physiological susceptibility—some people are more likely to become ill, and we don't know why.
- Ego, peer pressure, and schedules—if you are not acclimatizing, stop ascent until you adjust.

---

most people who become ill do so within the first few days of ascending to altitude.

The three common types of altitude illness are acute mountain sickness (AMS), high-altitude pulmonary edema (HAPE), and high-altitude cerebral edema (HACE). AMS is the most common. It is not life-threatening, but if not treated, it can progress to HACE. HAPE is less common but more serious. HACE is rare but can be sudden and severe.

Treatment of altitude illness is based on four principles: (1) stop ascent when symptoms develop; (2) descend if there is no improvement or condition worsens; (3) descend immediately if there is shortness of breath at rest, loss of coordination, or altered mental status; and (4) don't leave people with altitude sickness alone. The definitive treatment of all forms of altitude illness is descent.

ACUTE MOUNTAIN SICKNESS (AMS)

Acute mountain sickness is a headache in conjunction with recent altitude gain and one or more of the following symptoms: nausea, loss of appetite, lassitude, fatigue, insomnia, disturbed sleep, and unusual shortness of breath.

Signs and Symptoms of AMS

Signs and symptoms tend to start 6 to 36 hours after arrival at an altitude at which we are not acclimatized. Symptoms are worse in the morning, probably due to the normal decrease in the rate and depth of breathing during sleep, which lowers blood oxygen saturation. The cardinal symptom of AMS is a headache. Malaise, an uneasy feeling, drowsiness, and lassitude occur. Loss of appetite and nausea commonly accompany AMS and contribute to the overall sensa-

Signs and Symptoms of AMS

- Headache
- Malaise
- Loss of appetite
- Nausea, vomiting
- Disturbed sleep

tion of feeling lousy. Persons with AMS tend to retain fluid, resulting in edema, especially of the face and hands. During sleep, a person's rate and depth of respiration may gradually increase until it reaches a climax. Breathing then ceases entirely for 5 to 50 seconds. This phenomenon is called Cheyne-Stokes respiration and contributes to disturbed sleep.

Treatment of AMS

Follow the treatment principles for altitude illness. Don't go higher until the symptoms resolve. Stop ascending until signs and symptoms resolve, descend if there is no improvement with rest, and descend immediately if signs of severe AMS appear. Light activity around camp is fine as long as the theme is rest and acclimatization, not more fatigue. Stay well hydrated to help the kidneys excrete bicarbonate. Aspirin, acetaminophen, or ibuprofen may ease the headache. If symptoms worsen, signs of ataxia or pul-

Treatment of AMS

Treatment Principles for Altitude Illness (AMS)

1. Don't go up until the symptoms go down.
   - Stop ascent until s/s resolved.
   - Descend if no improvement over 24-48 hours to last camp without s/s.
   - Descend immediately at first sign of severe AMS.
2. Acclimatize.
   - Light exercise.
   - Maintain adequate hydration.
3. Pain medication for headache is okay. Avoid sedatives.
4. Monitor for shortness of breath, ataxia, altered mental status.

monary edema become apparent, or there is a change in the level of consciousness, descend.

HIGH-ALTITUDE PULMONARY EDEMA (HAPE)

HAPE is abnormal fluid accumulation in the lungs at altitude. HAPE rarely occurs below 8,000 feet (2400 meters). HAPE can be insidious in development yet abrupt in onset and causes the most deaths from altitude illness.

Signs and Symptoms of HAPE

The symptoms of HAPE result from the decreasing ability of the lungs to exchange oxygen and carbon dioxide. The symptoms usually begin 24 to 96 hours after ascent.

HAPE may initially appear with mild symptoms similar to AMS. The patient complains of a dry cough and shortness of breath, and more fatigue than expected. The heart and respiratory rates increase.

As HAPE worsens, the shortness of breath, weakness, and fatigue occur at rest or light exercise. The patient complains of a

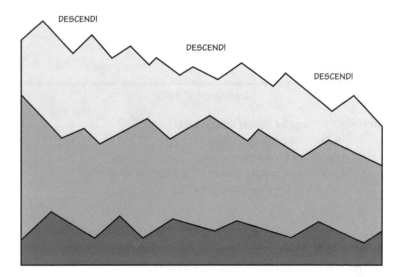

Signs and Symptoms of HAPE

- Signs of acute mountain sickness.
- Shortness of breath on exertion, progressing to shortness of breath at rest.
- Fatigue.
- Dry cough, progressing to wet, productive cough.
- Increased heart rate and respiratory rate.
- Rales, sounds of fluid in the lungs.

---

harsh cough, headache, and loss of appetite. The heart and respiratory rates remain elevated. The nail beds become cyanotic. Rales (rattles) can be heard with a stethoscope. Signs and symptoms may be mistaken for the flu, bronchitis, or pneumonia.

As HAPE becomes severe, rales can be heard without a stethoscope. The patient coughs up frothy, blood-tinged sputum. The patient becomes ataxic, lethargic, or develops an altered mental status.

HAPE, like AMS, becomes worse at night due to Cheyne-Stokes respirations. HAPE is a life-threatening illness.

Treatment of HAPE

Descend to a lower altitude as quickly as possible, minimizing exertion, which can make HAPE worse. Immediate descent is essential. Give oxygen, if available, during the descent. If the symptoms do not improve, descend until they do.

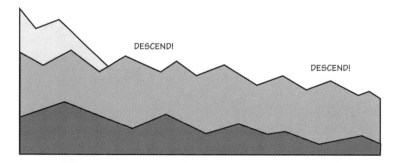

If you are unable to descend but have oxygen available, give the patient 100 percent oxygen at a flow rate of 4 to 6 liters per minute. If the condition does not improve, increase the flow of oxygen. Descend as soon as possible.

HIGH-ALTITUDE CEREBRAL EDEMA (HACE)

HACE is a severe form of AMS with swelling of the brain thought to be caused by hypoxic damage to brain tissue. HACE generally occurs above 12,000 feet (3600 meters).

Signs and Symptoms of HACE

- Signs of acute mountain sickness
- Neurological signs such as vision disturbances, paralysis, seizures, hallucinations
- Ataxia
- Severe lassitude
- Headache
- Altered mental status
- Nausea and vomiting

Treatment of HACE

- Descent
- Oxygen

Signs and Symptoms of HACE

The classic signs of HACE are change in mental status, ataxia, and severe lassitude. The patient may become confused, lose his or her memory, or slip into unresponsiveness.

Ataxia. Ataxia, or difficulty maintaining balance, is a sign—some experts say the most useful sign—of severe AMS or HACE. The test is simple. Have the patient try to walk a line on the ground. If the patient wobbles or falls, he or she has ataxia.

Other obvious signs and symptoms may include vomiting, cyanosis, seizures, hallucinations, transient blindness, partial paralysis, and loss of sensation on one side of the body.

Treatment of HACE

Descend. Do not hope the condition will get better if you wait. Waiting and hoping may be fatal. Descend to a lower elevation as soon as you notice any ataxia or change in mental status. Give oxygen if available.

Acclimatization

- Ascend slowly.
- Climb high, sleep low.
- Hydrate.

Hyperbaric Bags. Portable hyperbaric (greater atmospheric pressure than normal) chambers are used in the treatment of altitude illness. These bags, the best known of which is the Gamow Bag, are made of nonpermeable nylon. Inflated with a foot pump to greater than atmospheric pressure, these bags are believed to increase oxygen diffusion into the blood. They simulate a descent of several thousand feet.

Hyperbaric bags are temporary treatment for emergencies—intended for use during evacuation to lower altitudes or if you are unable to descend immediately.

MEDICATIONS AND ALTITUDE

There are several medications used for the prevention and treatment of altitude illness, including acetazolamide (Diamox) and dexamethasone (Decadron). It is beyond this text to discuss these drugs. Check with your physician advisor for recommendations on their use.

FINAL THOUGHTS

Acclimatization is key. A slow rate of ascent is an sound way to prevent acute altitude illness. General recommendations for an ascent profile include 1,000–1,500 feet (305–610 meters) per day above 10,000 feet (3048 meters) with frequent rest days.

Climb high and sleep low. The sleeping altitude is important. It is best not to increase the sleeping altitude by more then 2,000 feet (600 meters) at a time. Set up camp at lower elevations and take day trips to high points. Ferry loads up to a high camp and then return to the low camp to sleep as you acclimatize.

Stay hydrated. Urine should be clear, not yellow. Over-hydrating does not protect against altitude illness. Avoid sleeping pills, which decrease the respiratory rate, aggravating the lack of oxygen.

Be aware of the influence of ego, peer pressure, and schedules on your rate of ascent. If you are not acclimatizing well, stop, rest, and allow time to adjust. Pushing higher and denying the signs and symptoms of altitude illness is asking for trouble for you and your companions.

Evacuation Guidelines

- Evacuation and/or rapid descent for patients with severe altitude illness (HAPE or HACE).
- Evacuate any patient unable to acclimatize.

CHAPTER 12
POISONS, STINGS, AND BITES

INTRODUCTION

A poison is any substance—solid, liquid, or gas—that impairs health when it comes into contact with the body. Poisoning ranks fifth in causes of accidental death in the United States, and is responsible for approximately 5,000 deaths a year. Approximately 1 million cases of nonfatal poisoning from substances such as industrial chemicals, cleaning agents, medications, and insect sprays occur each year.

Virtually any substance can be poisonous if consumed in sufficient quantity. For example, vitamins can be highly toxic in overdose. A snakebite that kills a child may only produce illness in an adult. Accidental overdoses of aspirin kill more children each year than substances we commonly consider poisons.

A venom is a poison excreted by certain animals. Venomous animals have specialized glands that produce toxic substances for injection into adversaries and prey. All venoms are poisons, but not all poisons are venoms. Most animal venoms are complex mixtures of toxic and carrier (nontoxic) substances. The toxins in various venoms vary in potency, effect, and chemical makeup. They may impair nerve function, destroy cells, or affect the heart or blood.

Much information has been disseminated about the treatment of serpent, spider, and scorpion bites—much of it inaccurate. Outside the United States, there are snakes, spiders, and insects that carry deadly venoms. In the United States, however, snakes and spiders cause relatively few deaths each year. This is not to undersell the potency of these poisons, but rather to emphasize that ill-informed and misguided treatment can be as harmful to the patient as the venom.

POISONS

Poisons enter the body through ingestion, inhalation, absorption, and injection.

Ingested Poisons

Examples of ingested poisons include drugs, toxic plants, and bacterial toxins on contaminated food. The use of poorly labeled fuel bottles as water bottles has led to accidental ingestion of gasoline. Drugs, including nonprescription medications, can be accidentally or intentionally ingested in harmful amounts.

Treatment of Ingested Poisons. Three principles guide the treatment of ingested poisons: call a poison control center, consider inducing vomiting, and evacuate.

If you can, contact poison control and seek advice. They will want to know what substance was ingested, how much was ingested, the time of ingestion, when the victim last ate, and the victim's age, sex, and weight.

Vomiting may help if it is tried early, usually within 30 minutes of ingestion. Do not induce vomiting if the patient has a seizure disorder or if the patient has an altered mental status, as the airway may become obstructed with vomit.

Do not induce vomiting for ingested corrosive chemicals or petroleum products. Vomiting can increase the corrosive damage, as these chemicals burn both on the way down and on the way back up the esophagus. These substances are also extremely harmful if they enter the lungs and can cause a chemical pneumonia.

The wilderness backpacker commonly has to rely on tickling the back of the throat to stimulate the gag reflex.

There is no proven value to diluting an ingested poison with water or other liquids. If it's available, you can also try to bind the toxins to activated charcoal. Activated charcoal isn't the charcoal from a fire. It's a special preparation, usually packaged in 4-ounce plastic bottles or tubes. It's an over-the-counter product that, because of its

---

Treatment of Ingested Poisons

- Call poison control.
- Consider inducing vomiting.
- Evacuate.

---

weight and bulk, and the infrequency of poisoning in the back-country, is rarely carried in wilderness kits. You may find it in a well-stocked base camp or boat medical kit. The patient drinks the slurry, which binds the poison and allows it to be excreted without being absorbed into the body.

In the backcountry, people have died after mistakenly eating poisonous plants and mushrooms. An expert should identify any vegetation you intend to eat. If you suspect ingested plant poisoning, treat by induced vomiting. Save samples for later identification.

Inhaled Poisons

Carbon monoxide is an odorless and colorless gas produced from incomplete combustion and is the most frequently encountered inhaled poison in the United States. Automobiles, portable stoves, lanterns, and heaters are all sources of carbon monoxide. Two climbers on Denali (Mount McKinley) died from carbon monoxide poisoning caused by using a stove in a poorly ventilated tent.

Carbon monoxide combines with hemoglobin in the blood, displacing oxygen and reducing the oxygen-carrying capacity of the blood. This can happen rapidly and without warning. At high altitudes, where less oxygen is available, the potential for poisoning increases. Signs and symptoms of carbon monoxide poisoning range from light-headedness and headache, weakness, nausea, vomiting, loss of manual dexterity, confusion, and lethargy to coma, seizures, and death. A cherry red coloring to the skin is a very late sign of carbon monoxide poisoning and may not occur until after the person has died.

Treatment of Inhaled Poisons. The immediate treatment for any inhaled poisoning is to remove the patient from the source of the poison. Maintain the airway and move the patient to fresh air.

Carbon Monoxide Poisoning

SIGNS AND SYMPTOMS
- Lightheadedness, dizziness, throbbing headache.
- Nausea and vomiting.
- Irritability, impaired judgment.
- Altered mental status.
- Seizures, respiratory failure, coma.

TREATMENT
- Move patient to fresh air.
- Maintain airway.
- If possible, administer oxygen.

Although not readily available in the wilderness, administration of oxygen is standard treatment. A patient who experiences a notable disturbance in alertness or coordination, complains of breathing difficulty, or becomes unresponsive should be evacuated to a physician for evaluation.

Prevent inhaled poisoning by keeping tents or snow shelters well ventilated during cooking or, better yet, by cooking outside.

Absorbed Poisons

Poisons can enter the body through the skin or mucous membranes. Pesticide sprays absorbed through the skin are a common source of poisoning. Toxins secreted into the skin by sea cucumbers and some species of exotic reptiles can cause serious reactions.

Treatment of Absorbed Poisons. If the poison is dry, brush it off, then flush the area with large volumes of water. If the poison is wet, flush the site thoroughly with water, then wash with soap and water. Exceptions are lye and dry lime, which react with water to produce heat and further corrosion. Do not rinse lye or dry lime; rather, brush the powder off the skin.

Injected Poisons

The poisons that enter the body via the injected venoms of stinging insects and reptiles are often complex systemic poisons with multiple toxins. The injected poisons that most concern us in the wilderness are the venoms of snakes, bees, wasps, spiders, and scorpions.

Treatment of Absorbed Poisons

- Dry poisons: brush off, then rinse with water.
- Wet poisons: rinse thoroughly with water.

Bees and wasps cause more deaths in the United States than snakes—approximately 100 deaths a year, usually from the acute allergic reaction known as anaphylactic shock.

Venomous Snakes. Imagine yourself trying to catch a small mammal for dinner, equipped only with a long, limbless body. You might develop the ability to leap quickly to your victim. You might also develop a venom to immobilize the victim. This is how a rattlesnake makes its living: striking quickly and accurately and immobilizing or killing its victims with venom.

Approximately 45,000 snakebites occur in the United States each year, 8,000 of them from venomous snakes. Half a dozen people a year die from these bites, mostly the young, elderly, and infirm. Bites commonly occur on the arms below the elbow and on the legs below the knee. In most cases, the snake is provoked by being handled, antagonized, or inadvertently stepped on.

Prevent snakebite by watching closely where you step. Never reach into concealed areas. Shake out sleeping bags and clothing before use. One NOLS student was bitten on the hand when he attempted to pick up a rattlesnake. Never handle snakes, even if you think they are dead.

Two families of venomous snakes of medical importance in North America are the Elapidae, represented by the coral snake, and Crotalidae (pit vipers), represented by the rattlesnake, copperhead, and cottonmouth, or water moccasin. Elapidae venom primarily affects the nervous system, causing death by paralysis and respiratory failure. Crotalidae venom is a complex mix of substances affecting the nerves, the heart, blood clotting, and other functions.

Coral Snake. The coral snake averages 23 to 32 inches in length and is thin and brightly colored, with adjacent red and yellow bands. It is the creature referred to in the old saying "red and yellow kill a fellow, red and black, venom lack." Coral snakes live in the southern and southwestern states, inhabiting dry, open, brushy ground near water sources. They are docile and bite only when provoked. Their short fangs generally limit their bites to fingers, toes, and loose skin folds.

The signs of systemic poisoning by the neurotoxic venom, which may occur several hours after the bite, include drowsiness,

CORAL SNAKE

THIN, BRIGHTLY
COLORED

23-32" LONG

ADJACENT RED/YELLOW BANDS

SYMPTOMS:

- *LITTLE PAIN OR SWELLING*

- *NEUROTOXIC VENOM POISONING MAY LEAD TO DROWSINESS, WEAKNESS AND OTHER SYMPTOMS and PROGRESS TO POSSIBLE RESPIRATORY FAILURE.*

weakness, nausea, rapid pulse, and rapid respiration progressing to respiratory failure. Treatment is the same as for pit viper bites with one exception—the placing of a wide elastic bandage over the bite site.

Rattlesnakes, Copperheads, and Water Moccasins. These pit vipers have triangular heads, thick bodies, and pits between the eyes and nostrils. Coloring and length vary with the species. Most are blotched and colored in earthy browns, grays, or reds. The number of rattles a rattlesnake might have varies with its age and stage of molt. Rattles are thought to have evolved as a warning device to prevent hoofed mammals from stepping on the snake.

The pit viper's two fangs retract when the mouth is closed and extend during a strike. These snakes periodically shed their fangs. At times, two fangs are present on each side. One is potent, the other not. Venom release is under the snake's control. A pit viper can apparently adjust the volume of venom injected to match its victim's size. The age, size, and health of the snake affect venom toxicity. The same factors affect the victim's response to the venom.

Multiple strikes are possible, and depth of the bite varies, as does the amount of venom injected. Fang marks are not a reliable

RATTLESNAKES

GENERAL CHARACTERISTICS:

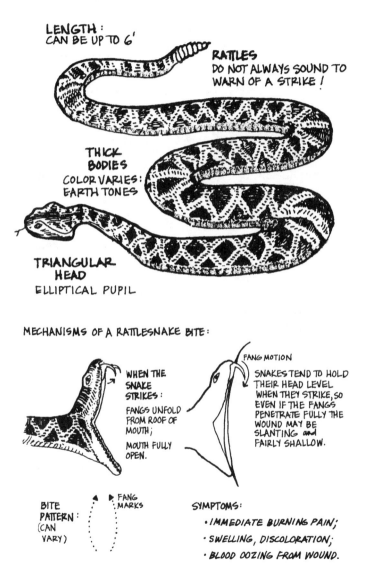

LENGTH:
CAN BE UP TO 6'

RATTLES
DO NOT ALWAYS SOUND TO
WARN OF A STRIKE !

THICK BODIES
COLOR VARIES:
EARTH TONES

TRIANGULAR HEAD
ELLIPTICAL PUPIL

MECHANISMS OF A RATTLESNAKE BITE:

FANG MOTION

WHEN THE SNAKE STRIKES:

FANGS UNFOLD
FROM ROOF OF
MOUTH;

MOUTH FULLY
OPEN.

SNAKES TEND TO HOLD
THEIR HEAD LEVEL
WHEN THEY STRIKE, SO
EVEN IF THE FANGS
PENETRATE FULLY THE
WOUND MAY BE
SLANTING and
FAIRLY SHALLOW.

BITE
PATTERN:
(CAN
VARY)

FANG
MARKS

SYMPTOMS:

• *IMMEDIATE BURNING PAIN;*

• *SWELLING, DISCOLORATION;*

• *BLOOD OOZING FROM WOUND.*

sign of envenomation, as 20 to 30 percent of bites do not envenomate. Pain at the site with rapid swelling and bruising is a better sign that venom has been injected.

Signs and Symptoms of Venomous Poisoning. Signs and symptoms of venomous poisoning include swelling, pain, and tingling at the bite site, tingling and a metallic taste in the mouth, fever, chills, nausea and vomiting, blurred vision, and muscle tremors.

Gently clean the wound with an antiseptic soap and apply a sterile dressing. The goal of treatment is safe and rapid transport to a hospital for evaluation. Keep the affected limb at heart level or below. Keep the patient quiet, hydrated, and comfortable during evacuation. Activity and anxiety accelerate the absorption of the venom. Ideally, immobilize and carry the victim. Walking is acceptable if the patient feels up to it and if no other alternative is available.

A healthy adult may become ill from the envenomation but probably will not die. The patient is often at greater danger from the effects of treatment by misinformed rescuers. Pressure bandages, tourniquets, electric shock, ice, and incision of the area can permanently damage tissue that might otherwise remain unaffected. Pressure bandages are appropriate treatment for some exotic snakebites but not for rattlesnake envenomations, in which local concentration of venom can cause tissue damage.

Non–North American Snakebite. Snakes outside of North America that are significant sources of envenomation are primarily elapids: cobras, mambas, and kraits; Australian brown snakes, tiger snakes, and taipans; and vipers such as death adders and rattlesnakes. The potent neurotoxic venoms of some of these snakes can result in altered mental status, unresponsiveness, blurred vision, paralysis, seizures, and respiratory and heart failure.

Treatment is the same as for pit vipers, with the exception of the use of immobilization and a pres-

---

Signs and Symptoms of Pit Viper Poisoning

- Swelling, pain, and tingling at the bite site.
- Tingling and a metallic taste in the mouth.
- Fever, chills, nausea and vomiting.
- Blurred vision and muscle tremors.

---

sure bandage on the bitten extremity for an elapid bite. To retard venom absorption, the limb is splinted and wrapped with gauze or an Ace bandage. This wrap is firm, but a pulse should still be present in the foot or wrist. In Australia the wound is not washed, to allow for an assay that can identify the venom.

Treatment of Rattlesnake Bites

- Clean wound with antiseptic soap.
- Remove rings and other constrictive items.
- Keep limb at or below level of heart.
- Keep patient quiet, hydrated, and comfortable.
- Evacuate.

Bee Stings. The venom apparatus of most species of bees, located on the posterior abdomen, consists of venom glands, a venom reservoir, and structures for stinging, or injection. The stinger and venom are used in defense and subjugation of prey.

Multiple stings are more dangerous than single stings, and those occurring closely in time are more dangerous than those occurring over a longer duration. Multiple stings, which often re-

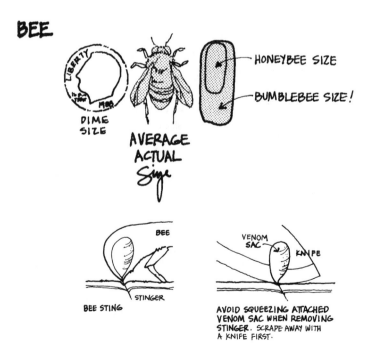

BEE

DIME SIZE

AVERAGE ACTUAL Size

HONEYBEE SIZE

BUMBLEBEE SIZE!

BEE STING

BEE

STINGER

VENOM SAC

KNIFE

AVOID SQUEEZING ATTACHED VENOM SAC WHEN REMOVING STINGER. SCRAPE AWAY WITH A KNIFE FIRST.

Treatment of Bee Stings

- Scrape or flick off stinger.
- Clean wound with antiseptic soap.
- Ice or cool compress may relieve pain.
- If necessary, treat for anaphylaxis.

---

sult from disturbing a nest, can be life-threatening.

Stings from bees and wasps usually cause instant pain, swelling, and redness. If the stinger remains in the skin, scrape or flick it out. A barb prevents the bee from withdrawing the stinger, so the bee's muscular venom reservoir continues to inject until the stinger is scraped away.

Gently clean the wound with an antiseptic soap. Ice or cool compresses may help relieve pain and swelling. The patient should avoid scratching the stings, as this can cause secondary infection. Applying meat tenderizer to relieve the pain is a folklore remedy not supported by any scientific study.

Bee stings cause more anaphylaxis than do the stings of any other insect. Individuals who are allergic to the sting of one species of bee or wasp may also be allergic to that of different species.

Arachnids. Arachnids are mostly terrestrial and wingless and have four pairs of legs. Spiders, scorpions, tarantulas, and ticks are arachnids. There are over 30,000 spider species worldwide. They live in a variety of habitats, and all are carnivorous.

Poisonous spiders inject venom through hollow fangs. The fangs are primarily for subduing and killing prey and secondarily for defense. The venoms are fast-paralyzing agents that contain enzymes to predigest prey, which is then sucked up.

Widow Spiders. The black widow spider has a sinister name, yet kills at most four to six people a year in the United States. A member of the genus *Lactrodectus*, the venomous adult female is 4 centimeters long and is shiny black with a red "hourglass" marking on the bottom of the abdomen. The adult male is not venomous. There are five species of "widow" spiders, all of which have some type of red marking on the underside of the abdomen, but only three of which are black. Black widows are typically found under stones and logs. They are common in desert overhangs, crawl spaces, outhouses, and barns; they are rare in occupied buildings.

BLACK WIDOW SPIDER:

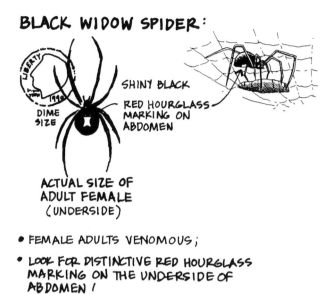

SHINY BLACK

RED HOURGLASS
MARKING ON
ABDOMEN

DIME
SIZE

ACTUAL SIZE OF
ADULT FEMALE
(UNDERSIDE)

- FEMALE ADULTS VENOMOUS;

- LOOK FOR DISTINCTIVE RED HOURGLASS
MARKING ON THE UNDERSIDE OF
ABDOMEN!

The black widow usually bites only when its web is disturbed. The bite is not initially painful—a pinprick sensation with slight redness and swelling, followed by numbness. Ten to 60 minutes may pass before the onset of toxic symptoms. The venom is primarily a nerve toxin that stimulates muscle contraction, causing large muscle cramps. The abdomen may become boardlike and excruciatingly painful. Weakness, nausea, vomiting, and anxiety are common. Systemic signs include hypertension, breathing difficulty, seizures, and, in the very young or old, cardiac arrest.

The pain generally peaks in 1 to 3 hours and can continue over several days. The natural course of the illness is general recovery after several days. Local cleansing and ice may retard pain and venom absorption. Antivenin is available, as are agents to counteract muscle spasm.

Recluse Spiders. The brown recluse spider, genus *Loxosceles*, is rare in the West; it is most abundant in the South and Midwest. It has a violin-shaped mark on its head. The spiders average 1.2 centimeters in length with a 5-centimeter leg span. Unlike the black widow, both sexes are dangerous.

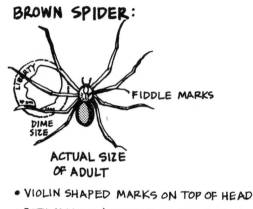

BROWN SPIDER:

FIDDLE MARKS

LIBERTY

DIME SIZE

ACTUAL SIZE OF ADULT

- VIOLIN SHAPED MARKS ON TOP OF HEAD
- BOTH MALE and FEMALE ADULTS VENOMOUS

Recluse spiders live in hot, dry, undisturbed environments, such as vacant buildings and woodpiles. They are nocturnal hunters of beetles, flies, moths, and other spiders, and they are most active from April to October, hibernating in fall and winter. They attack humans only as a defensive gesture.

The venom of the brown spider causes cell and tissue injury. Signs and symptoms vary from a transient irritation to painful and debilitating skin ulcers. Although the bite can be sharply painful, it is often painless. Nausea and vomiting, headache, fever, and chills may be present. In severe envenomations, redness and blisters form within 6 to 12 hours. Within 1 to 2 weeks, an area of dying skin—a necrotic ulcer—forms and may leave a craterlike scar.

Clean the bite site with an antiseptic soap and evacuate the patient to a physician.

Brown spider bites are rare, especially outside the their home range, yet they are a source of myth and frequent misdiagnosis. Likewise, the hobo spider (genus *Tegenaria*) has developed a reputation, perhaps undeserved, as a source of necrotic spider bites.

Tarantulas. Except for some species found in the tropics, tarantulas are not dangerous. The tarantula's fangs are too weak to penetrate very deeply, and the effects of the bite are limited to a small local wound. Tarantula bites are rare.

Scorpions. Scorpions first appeared on the earth 300 million years ago. Grasslands and deserts are primary habitat for more than 600 species of scorpions, some of which carry deadly venoms. In North America, most species are relatively harmless, their stings producing effects similar to those of bee stings.

Only one type of North American scorpion, a small yellowish species of the genus *Centruroides*, is dangerous. It lives in Mexico, Arizona, and New Mexico and has been reported in southern Utah. Fatalities from its venom occur mostly in the young and old.

Scorpions feed at night on insects and spiders, injecting their prey with multiple toxins from a stinger at the tip of the tail. Scorpions like to hide in dark places during the day; beware when reaching into woodpiles or under rocks. Develop a habit of shaking out shoes, clothes, and sleeping bags when in scorpion country.

SCORPIONS

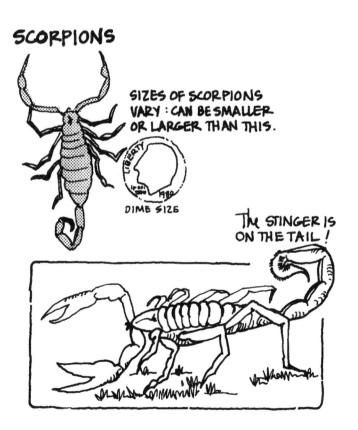

SIZES OF SCORPIONS VARY : CAN BE SMALLER OR LARGER THAN THIS.

DIME SIZE

THE STINGER IS ON THE TAIL !

Treatment of Spider and Scorpion Bites

- Clean wound with antiseptic soap.
- Ice or cool compress to relieve pain.
- If systemic symptoms of envenomation develop:
  —ABCs and supportive care.
  —Evacuate to antivenin.

A scorpion sting produces a pricking sensation. Typical symptoms include burning pain, swelling, redness, numbness, and tingling. The affected extremity may become numb and sensitive to touch.

Treat the sting by applying ice or cool water to relieve the local symptoms. Clean the wound with an antiseptic soap. In the case of severe poisoning, signs and symptoms include impaired speech resulting from a sluggish tongue and tightened jaw, muscle spasms, nausea, vomiting, convulsions, incontinence, and/or respiratory and circulatory distress. Immobilize the extremity and transport the patient to a hospital. An antivenin is available.

Ticks. Ticks are relatives of spiders and scorpions. There are two major families: hard ticks and soft ticks. Most common in the Rockies is the hard tick, genus *Dermacentor*. As with all ticks, it requires blood meals to molt from larva to nymph and from nymph

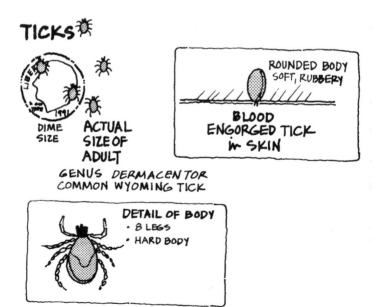

TICKS

DIME SIZE   **ACTUAL SIZE OF ADULT**

ROUNDED BODY SOFT, RUBBERY

BLOOD ENGORGED TICK in SKIN

GENUS *DERMACENTOR* COMMON WYOMING TICK

DETAIL OF BODY
- 8 LEGS
- HARD BODY

to adult. The various diseases the tick carries are transmitted to the host during the blood meal. These diseases include tick fever, relapsing fever, spotted fever, tularemia, babesiosis, and Lyme disease. Tick season in Wyoming is April through July, although ticks are active throughout the warm months.

Preventing exposure is essential in tick-infested areas. Topical tick insecticide is available; look for the chemical ingredient permethrin. A visual inspection of all body parts at least twice daily is recommended, as adult ticks generally stay on the body for a few hours before attaching. Even after a tick has attached itself, prompt removal may prevent the transmission of disease.

To remove a tick, grasp it as close to the skin as possible with tweezers or gloved fingers. Pull the tick out with steady pressure. Clean the bite site thoroughly with an antiseptic soap. Traditional tick removal methods (a hot match head, nail polish, or alcohol) may induce the tick to regurgitate into the wound.

Diagnosis of tick-caused illness in the field is difficult. If a tick bite is accompanied by a rash, fever, flu symptoms, or muscle aches and pains, the patient should be seen by a physician.

Insects. The bites of mosquitoes, blackflies, midges, horseflies, and deerflies tend to be relatively minor. Usually only localized irritation occurs, although anaphylaxis is a possibility. This group is more significant for its capacity to act as vectors of diseases such as malaria and yellow fever. Worldwide, only the mosquito transmits more disease than the tick.

To help reduce mosquito (and other insect) bites, use the following chemical and nonchemical precautions:

- Wearing protective clothing, and avoiding mosquito habitat and times of peak mosquito activity.
- Judicious use of DEET or picardin-based repellents, natural repellents (often made with soybeans or lemon eucalyptus), and insecticides such as permethrin.

Treatment of Tick Bites

- Promptly remove the tick with a gentle, steady pull.
- Clean the bite site with soap and water.
- In cases of rash, fever, flu, or muscle aches following a tick bite, the patient should be seen by a physician.

Controversy persists over the safety and effectiveness of various repellents. The E.P.A. recommends the following general use information for DEET-based products:

- Read the label carefully before use.
- Apply repellent sparingly. Heavy application and saturation are unnecessary for effectiveness. Repeat applications only as necessary and according to label directions.
- Do not apply over cuts, wounds or irritated skin, eyes, or mouth. Discontinue if skin irritation develops.
- Some insect repellents contain a sunscreen. It is recommended that such combination products not be spread as liberally as one might a sunscreen or skin lotion.
- Do not apply to children's hands or allow children to handle the product.
- Avoid DEET use on children under 2, and use only the least concentrated product (10 percent DEET or less).

Poison Ivy, Oak, and Sumac

Poison ivy, oak, and sumac grow in all of the lower 48 states. Poison oak is more common west of the Rockies, poison ivy east of the Rockies, and poison sumac in the southeast. Individuals vary in their sensitivity to urushiol, the oil present on the surface of the plant—some react to very casual contact, others, as they walk through thick patches of these plants, seem immune. Urushiol can be transferred to the skin regardless of whether or not the plant has its traditional shiny three leaves in bloom. Inhaled smoke from burning plants can also cause a significant reaction.

Signs and Symptoms of Urushiol Reaction. This is a contact allergic reaction. The skin becomes red and itchy with a blistered rash and scaly, crusting wounds. Contrary to myth, the blister fluid is harmless. The rash spreads over time, due not to the fluid but to the varying time it takes different parts of our skin to react to the urushiol.

Treatment for Urushiol Reaction. We can't stop this rash. Our efforts at best prevent additional contact and treat symptoms. Try to wash the area immediately after exposure with soap and cool water. You may be able to remove some of the oil before you react.

LIFE CYCLE
of the TICK:

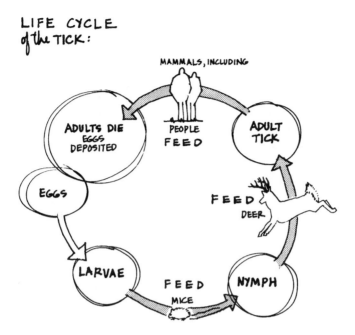

MAMMALS, INCLUDING

ADULTS DIE
EGGS
DEPOSITED

PEOPLE
FEED

ADULT
TICK

EGGS

FEED
DEER

LARVAE

FEED
MICE

NYMPH

Wash all clothes and equipment that may have been exposed. Urushiol persists on clothing, ropes, and plants for years.

Apply a thin layer of 1 percent hydrocortisone cream or calamine lotion, and try oral antihistamines to reduce itching. In severe cases your physician may prescribe a steroid to help reduce the itching and swelling.

Prevention. Learn to recognize poison ivy, oak, and sumac. Nothing works as well as avoiding contact. Barrier creams for hypersensitive individuals may be considered.

Hantavirus

Hantavirus is found throughout North America but is most frequently associated with the southwestern states. It is carried by rodents, primarily deer mice, pinyon mice, brush mice, and chipmunks. The virus produces a serious respiratory disease passed from the rodent reservoir to humans through inhalation of aerosolized microscopic particles of dried rodent saliva, urine, or feces. You can become infected by touching your mouth or nose after handling contaminated materials. A rodent's bite can also spread the virus.

Symptoms are general and flulike: fever, headache, muscle aches, and sometimes nausea and vomiting. Hantavirus infections progress to breathing difficulty, which is caused by fluid buildup in the lungs.

To minimize the risk of hantavirus infection, follow these precautions:

- Check potential campsites for rodent droppings and burrows.
- Do not disturb or crawl around in rodent burrows or dens.
- Avoid sleeping near woodpiles, burrows, or dens that may be frequented by rodents.
- Avoid sleeping on bare ground; use a ground cloth or a tent.
- Store foods in rodent-proof containers and promptly and appropriately dispose of garbage.
- Don't use old cabins until they have been cleaned and disinfected.

FINAL THOUGHTS

Simple Tips for Preventing Poisoning Emergencies
- Read labels for information on toxic substances.
- Cook outside or in well-ventilated tents or snow shelters.
- Identify plants before you eat them.
- Be aware of foot placement.
- Look before you reach under logs or overhangs or onto ledges.
- Shake out clothing, footwear, and sleeping bags.

Evacuation Guidelines
- Consider evacuation for anyone who has ingested a potentially harmful substance.

- Evacuate rapidly any poisoned patient who has an altered mental status or shows signs of respiratory distress.
- Contact the American Association of Poison Control Centers at 1-800-222-1222 for advice.
- Evacuate all patients bitten by a poisonous snake; expedite evacuation if the patient shows signs of envenomation.
- Rapidly evacuate patients bitten by spiders if slurred speech, difficulty swallowing, blurred vision, seizures, respiratory or cardiovascular involvement are present.
- Evacuate any patient with a history of an imbedded tick who develops a fever, rash, and flulike symptoms.

LIGHTNING INJURIES

INTRODUCTION

Injuries can occur from the high voltage (200 to 300 million volts), secondary heat production, or the explosive force of the lightning. A person can be injured by lightning in five ways:

- Direct hit: Actually being struck by lightning.
- Lightning "splash": Lightning hits another object and splashes onto objects or people standing nearby.
- Direct transmission: Being in contact with an object that has been hit directly.
- Ground current: Receiving the ground current as it dissipates from the object that has been hit is believed to be the most common mechanism of injury.
- Blunt trauma from the explosive force of the shock wave.

Most victims are splashed by lightning or hit by ground current. Very few people actually sustain a direct hit. Although a direct hit can deliver 200 to 300 million volts, the duration is short (1 to 100 milliseconds), and severe burns are uncommon.

Lightning burns form distinctive patterns. Superficial linear burns follow areas of heavy sweat concentration. A linear burn may begin beneath the breasts, travel from the sternum to the abdomen, then split down both legs, or it may follow the midaxillary line (an imaginary line drawn through the middle of the armpit to the waist).

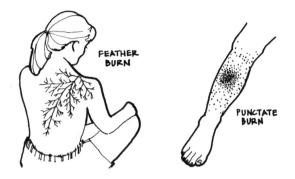

Lightning-caused punctate burns are circular, ranging in size from a few millimeters to a centimeter in diameter. Also, feather-like patterns, which are not true burns, leave imprints on the skin. Most lightning burns are superficial or partial thickness, with some of the punctate burns being full thickness.

Most lightning burns are superficial, but lightning strikes may throw victims a considerable distance, causing head and spinal injuries, dislocations, fractures, and blunt chest and abdominal trauma. The respiratory center in the brain may also be injured, causing respiratory and cardiac arrest.

Lightning can knock its victims unresponsive. Some patients will become temporarily paralyzed and have one or both eardrums ruptured. Other signs and symptoms are confusion, amnesia, temporary deafness or blindness, and mottling of the skin. Pulses may decrease or disappear in the lower extremities due to injury-induced spasms of the blood vessels.

Treat cardiac arrest with CPR. The heart may start beating again before respirations begin. Artificial respiration (rescue breathing) may need to be continued due to paralysis of the respiratory center in the brain.

Risk Management for Lightning
There is no safe place outdoors in a lightning storm. Lightning is an unpredictable and immensely powerful force of nature. At best we can manage the risk by reducing our exposure.

FREQUENT STRIKES
EXTREMELY
HAZARDOUS

OCCASIONAL
STRIKES
HAZARDOUS

RELATIVELY
SAFE

LARGE CAVE
(NOT SHALLOW) SAFE
ONLY IF WALLS /
ENTRANCE AVOIDED.

SIT ON SOMETHING DRY and
NON- CONDUCTING (FOAM PAD,
ROPE, DAY PACK)

SQUAT WITH FEET FACING DOWNHILL.
TRY TO KEEP HANDS
OFF the GROUND!

- Know the local weather patterns:
  —Plan wisely to avoid being exposed in dangerous
    places.
  —Pick your campsites with prevention in mind, among a
    uniform stand of trees or low rolling hills being optimal.
- Know when to seek a better location:
  —Monitor approaching storms. Lightning can strike miles
    ahead or behind a storm.
  —Thunder, a clear sign of danger, can be heard for 10
    miles in calm air, much less in turbulent stormy air.

LIGHTNING Safety

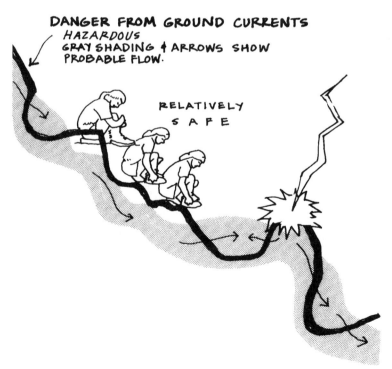

DANGER FROM GROUND CURRENTS
HAZARDOUS
GRAY SHADING & ARROWS SHOW
PROBABLE FLOW.

RELATIVELY
SAFE

—Flash-bang ranging systems are based on sound traveling 1 miles every 5 seconds (1 km/3 sec). It assumes you are correctly matching the flash with its bang, and does not take into account the speed of the approaching storm.
- Avoid dangerous locations:
  —Places higher than surrounding terrain: peaks, ridges, hills
  —Isolated tall objects such as lone trees
  —Open terrain such as meadows
  —Large bodies of water, especially the shoreline
  —Shallow overhangs and caves
  —Places obviously struck before
  —Long conductors: pipes, wires, wire fences, wet ropes
- Seek uniform cover: trees about the same height and rolling hills, insulate yourself from ground current, stay low (lightning position), and disperse a group to limit casualties.
- When it is impractical to move to a safer location, insulate yourself from ground current, stay low (lightning position), and disperse a group to limit casualties.

Evacuation Guidelines
- All lightning injury patients should be evacuated for further evaluation and treatment.

CHAPTER 14 | DROWNING AND COLD WATER IMMERSION

INTRODUCTION

The body's responses to cold water immersion are many. Sudden immersion in cold water causes a gasp for air, constriction of blood vessels in the extremities, and an increase in breathing and heart rate. The initial gasp may result in water inhalation, and the rapid breathing rate makes it more difficult to hold the breath underwater.

Death caused by heart rhythm abnormalities is possible; and as strength and coordination diminish, the chance of drowning increases. What's more, as the brain cools, we think less clearly and may do foolish things, such as removing a personal flotation device (PFD) or swimming aimlessly.

The danger of cold water immersion is widely present in the wilderness environment. Water conducts heat 25 times faster than air. In North America, most water remains below 77°F (25°C) year-round. Lakes in the Rocky Mountains warm only to the mid-50s (13°C) in summer. In Mexico, the Sea of Cortez averages 58°F (14.5°C) in winter. We are unable to remain warm at any of these temperatures unless we wear protective clothing.

DROWNING

Drowning is the second most common cause of accidental death in children, and the third leading cause of death in young adults.

A majority of drowning victims are young males. Alcohol is involved in over half of drowning accidents. Freshwater drowning, especially in pools, is more common than saltwater drowning.

ASPECTS OF A TYPICAL DROWNING

Drowning often begins with an unplanned submersion followed by breath holding, struggle and panic, hypoxia, loss of responsiveness, and respiratory then cardiac arrest. Often victims are first seen floating motionless, sinking silently below the surface or are observed to dive into water and never surface.

Treatment of Drowning

For first aid purposes, the type of water (salt, fresh, clean, dirty) does not matter. Airway maintenance and, if necessary, rescue breathing and chest compressions are essential to the treatment of unresponsive drowning victims. If you have any doubts about how long the victim was submerged, attempt resuscitation. There are rare case reports of people surviving submersion in ice water for more than 15 minutes, with 66 minutes being the longest documented survival.

The goals of treatment are to remove the victim from the water, protect the cervical spine, prevent cardiac arrest, and stabilize the patient's temperature.

Remove the Victim from the Water. Remove the victim from the water as quickly as possible. Rescuer safety is a priority. Remember the lifesaving adage "reach, throw, row, tow, and go." First try reaching for the victim, remaining in contact with the shore or boat. Second, throw a lifeline. Third, row or paddle to the victim. Attempt a swimming rescue only as a last resort.

Handle the Patient Gently. A patient who was submerged in cold water may be hypothermic.

Check the ABCs. Assess and check the ABCs. Aggressive initiation of airway, breathing, and circulation is the standard in drowning rescue. If available, administer oxygen.

Protect the Cervical Spine. Unless injury can be ruled out, assume that the victim has a neck injury and use the jaw thrust technique to open the airway. Neck injuries can be caused from surfing, diving in shallow water, or flipping a kayak or decked canoe in rapids.

Perform a Focused Exam and History. A complete patient exam is warranted to assess for injury.

Treat for Hypothermia. Remove wet clothing and dry and insulate the patient to prevent further heat loss.

Treatment of Drowning

- Remove the victim from the water.
- Handle gently.
- Check the ABCs.
- Protect the cervical spine.
- Perform a focused exam and history.
- Treat for hypothermia.
- Monitor vital signs.

Evacuate the Patient. Outside the wilderness, any victim of involuntary submersion should be evaluated by a physician, as lung injury from inhaled water may not be immediately evident. In the wilderness, we don't evacuate every asymptomatic person who swims through a rapid or takes a dunking during a river crossing and comes up coughing. Evacuate the victim of a submersion incident if that person required resuscitation, was unresponsive in the water, exhibits shortness of breath or other symptoms of respiratory difficulty, or has a history of lung disease.

The mode of transport and speed of the evacuation should be based on the seriousness of the patient's condition. For example, a patient who is unresponsive following submersion should be quickly evacuated.

IMMERSION HYPOTHERMIA

It's a common misperception that we quickly become hypothermic and drown when immersed in cold water. In fact, while cold water is very uncomfortable, and we can quickly cool to the point where meaningful movement is difficult, actual hypothermia takes a while to develop. Dr. Gordon Giesbrecht of the University of Manitoba, Canada, is a leading researcher into immersion hypothermia. Dr. Giesbrecht's simple message is "1 minute, 10 minutes, 1 hour." We need to control our breathing and survive the first minute. We have 10 minutes to move carefully and thoughtfully before we will become incapacitated by the cold. We have an hour before we will become unresponsive due to hypothermia. Knowing this, while we still need to promptly rescue people and treat hypothermia, we know we should not panic and we have time to plan correct actions.

Treatment of Immersion Hypothermia

Although there may be subtle differences between hypothermia on land and in the water, these differences are not relevant to field treatment. Treat immersion hypothermia by removing the victim from the water. Handle the patient gently, as rough handling may trigger lethal heart rhythm abnormalities and a phenomena known as circum-rescue collapse. Treat the patient for hypothermia as discussed in chapter 9 ("Cold Injuries"). Dry and insulate the patient; prevent further heat loss; ensure adequate airway, breathing, and circulation; and place the patient in a sleeping bag, possibly with another person or with hot water bottles as heat sources.

FINAL THOUGHTS

Safety around lakes, rivers, and the ocean begins with respect for the power of moving water and the debilitating effects of cold water. Cold water, failure to wear a personal flotation device (PFD), and the inability to swim are, according to the Coast Guard, the most common factors in white-water deaths.

In two out of three drownings, the victims could not swim, had no intention of entering deep water (and thus were ill prepared), and were affected by alcohol or drugs. Most drownings occur 10 to 30 feet from safety; only 10 percent of drownings occur in a guarded pool.

While awaiting rescue, assume the HELP (heat escape lessening posture) position by bringing your knees to your chest and crossing your arms over them. If you're with a group of people awaiting rescue, everyone in the group should face inward and huddle with arms interlocked. You must be wearing a PFD to assume either of these positions. If possible, get out of the water onto an overturned or partially submerged boat. It is always better to keep as much of yourself or the victim out of the water as possible, even when the wind is blowing.

Clothing selection for paddling or other activities around water requires finding a balance between overdressing—and

Risk Factors Related to Drowning

- Age—toddlers and teenage males are at highest risk.
- Location—private swimming pools, small streams, ponds, and irrigation ditches are common drowning sites.
- Gender—males dominate all age groups.
- Alcohol—a factor in one-third to two-thirds of drownings.
- Injury—cervical spine injury, as from diving or surfing.
- Seizure disorder—risk is greatest if poorly controlled; hyperventilation may cause predisposition to seizures.
- PFD—failure to wear one.

overheating—and protecting the body against sudden immersion in cold water. Extra clothing should be easily accessible in the cockpit of your boat or in your pack and should be put on if developing conditions increase the likelihood of a cold dunking.

Well-developed safety and rescue programs exist for swimming, sea kayaking, white-water boating, and sailing. If you're involved in any of these activities, seek out these programs for further training.

Evacuation Guidelines

- Evacuate any person who required resuscitation, was unresponsive in the water, exhibits shortness of breath, or has a history of lung illness.

CHAPTER 15 | MARINE ENVENOMATIONS

INTRODUCTION

Injuries from marine organisms are rarely the result of an aggressive, unprovoked attack. Most injuries occur as a result of accidental contact or when a threatened animal reacts in self-defense. This chapter discusses two broad categories of injuries from aquatic animals: marine spine envenomations and nematocyst sting envenomations. Treatment for these two types of injuries is very different: injuries from spines are treated with hot water immersion; stings are rinsed in vinegar.

Marine Spine Envenomations

Marine animals with venom known to be harmful to people include the zebra fish, scorpion fish, stonefish, sea urchin, and stingray, which deliver venom through spines, and the cone shell, which injects venom through a proboscis. Envenomation may cause life-threatening injury or mild irritation, depending on the species, the number of punctures, the amount of venom, the health of the victim, and other factors.

Signs and Symptoms of Marine Spine Envenomation. Signs of marine venom injury include local discoloration, cyanosis, and laceration or puncture wound. Symptoms include numbness, tingling, and intense local pain. In serious envenomations, nausea, vomiting, paralysis, respiratory distress, heart rhythm irregularities, and shock can occur.

Treatment of Marine Spine Envenomation. Treat marine envenomations by controlling bleeding, removing imbedded spines, cleaning the wound, and controlling pain with hot water soaks.

Immerse the Injury in Hot Water. Immerse the injury in water as hot as the patient can tolerate (usually 115° to 120°F, 46° to 49°C) for 30 to 90 minutes or until the pain is gone. This therapy is thought to inactivate heat-sensitive proteins in the venom. Immersion in a large pot or a plastic bag filled with hot water is best, but hot compresses can also be used.

Clean the wound with irrigation. Remove obvious imbedded spines carefully. Elevate the extremity to help control swelling. Remedies such as meat tenderizer, papain, or mangrove sap are not scientifically confirmed and may irritate the wound.

Removing imbedded spines is against standard treatment for impaled objects; however, the spines are a source of infection and a continued source of venom. Their presence also retards healing and may cause further injury. Removing them is often difficult; the spines are brittle and break easily, leaving a foreign body that may cause infection. Use tweezers or fingers (wear gloves) to remove the spines. If the spine is hard to remove, leave it in place and evacuate the patient. Medications to control pain are appropriate.

Monitor the patient for signs of generalized envenomation. With severe envenomation, signs and symptoms of shock and respiratory distress will develop. In these cases, our treatment is supportive care and evacuation.

Treatment of Marine Spine Envenomations

- Control bleeding.
- Immerse the injury in water as hot as the patient can tolerate (usually 115° to 120°F, 46° to 49°C) for 30 to 90 minutes or until the pain is gone.
- Remove imbedded spines.
- Irrigate the wound.
- Clean the wound.
- Elevate the extremity to help control swelling.
- Monitor for signs of infection or envenomation.
- Medications for pain.

Scorpion Fish

There are three genera in this family—stonefish, zebrafish, and scorpion fish—and several hundred species. The stonefish, inconspicuous and possessing a highly toxic venom, is considered to be among the most dangerous of all venomous creatures.

Zebra fish are spectacularly colored; stonefish and scorpion fish are less so. All members of the family are found in shallow waters. Zebra fish are free swimmers; stonefish and scorpion fish often hide in cracks, near rocks, or among plants. The stonefish may bury itself under sandy or broken coral bottoms. A dead stonefish is still dangerous! Its venom remains active for 48 hours after death.

The immediate intense pain of stonefish envenomation peaks in 60 to 90 minutes and can persist for days, despite treatment. Stonefish wounds are slow to heal and prone to infection.

Sea Urchins

Sea urchins are nonaggressive, nocturnal, omnivorous feeders that move slowly across the ocean bottom and are often found on rocky bottoms and burrowed in sand and small crevices. The hard spines protecting their vital organs can envenomate victims if the urchin is stepped on, handled, or inadvertently bumped. Their grasping organs, called pedicellariae, can also envenomate.

Symptoms are usually local and mild; however, infections are possible if pieces of imbedded spines remain in the skin or joint capsules. Spines imbedded in joints or large fragments left in soft tissues should be evaluated by a physician. Severe reactions are rare.

Spines lodged in the skin often turn it a brownish purple color. This reaction is harmless and can be seen regardless of whether a spine has broken off and remains imbedded or not.

Starfish

The venomous crown-of-thorns starfish is found in the Indo-Pacific area, the Red Sea, the eastern Pacific, and the Sea of Cortez. Starfish are scavengers that feed on other echinoderms, mollusks, coral, and worms. The upper surface of the crown-of-thorns starfish is studded with sharp, poisonous spines that can penetrate even the best diving gloves.

CONE SHELL:

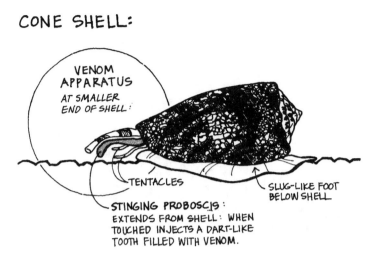

VENOM APPARATUS
AT SMALLER END OF SHELL:

TENTACLES

SLUG-LIKE FOOT BELOW SHELL

STINGING PROBOSCIS:
EXTENDS FROM SHELL: WHEN
TOUCHED INJECTS A DART-LIKE
TOOTH FILLED WITH VENOM.

Cone Shells

The shells of these animals, which live in shallow waters, reefs, and tide pools, are beautiful but hide a nasty sting. Cone shells project a long proboscis from the narrow end of the shell and inject venom from its tip. Toxicity to humans varies, but it rarely causes death. Do not handle cone shells. Drop them immediately if the proboscis is observed. Almost all reported envenomations have come from collectors handling the shells.

The injury resembles a bee sting with pain, burning, and itching. Serious envenomations produce cyanosis and numbness at the injury site, which progresses to numbness around the mouth, then generalized paralysis.

Treatment of cone shell stings is largely supportive care. Clean and thoroughly irrigate the puncture wound. The benefit of hot water soaks is unproved, but they may provide pain relief. Likewise, the value of circumferential pressure bandages is unconfirmed, but they may slow the spread of the venom.

Stingrays

Stingrays are bottom feeders, often found in shallow waters lying on top of or partially buried under sandy bottoms. Most stingray envenomations occur when a careless swimmer or wader steps on a buried ray. The stingray's tail whips up, and its serrated barbs

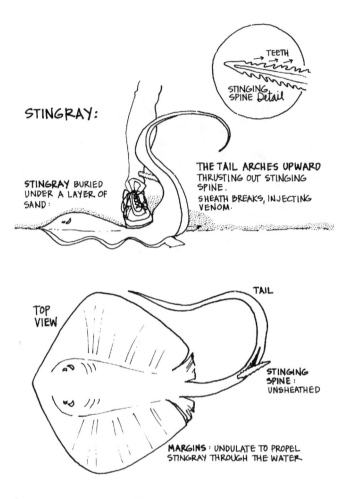

STINGRAY:

STINGRAY BURIED UNDER A LAYER OF SAND:

THE TAIL ARCHES UPWARD THRUSTING OUT STINGING SPINE.
SHEATH BREAKS, INJECTING VENOM.

STINGING SPINE *Detail*

TEETH

TOP VIEW

TAIL

STINGING SPINE : UNSHEATHED

MARGINS : UNDULATE TO PROPEL STINGRAY THROUGH THE WATER

inflict a nasty wound. Such defensive attacks usually cause wounds to the leg or ankle, and pieces of barbs may remain imbedded in the wound. Wounds often take the form of bleeding soft tissue lacerations or punctures. Intense local pain may last up to 48 hours.

NEMATOCYST STING ENVENOMATIONS

Nematocysts are specialized stinging capsules found in members of the phylum Coelenterata, which includes the sea anemones, jel-

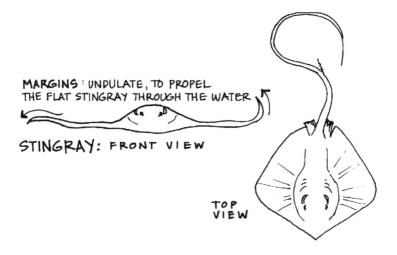

MARGINS : UNDULATE, TO PROPEL
THE FLAT STINGRAY THROUGH THE WATER

STINGRAY: FRONT VIEW

TOP
VIEW

lyfish, Portuguese man-of-wars, and some corals. The nematocyst discharges an incapacitating venom, allowing the animal to kill and digest its prey. Some nematocysts produce a sticky venomous substance; others deliver a barbed, venomous stinger.

Nematocyst discharge is triggered by contact with the skin or by changes in osmotic pressure, as can occur when the nematocyst is rinsed with fresh water. Nematocysts are generally found around the animal's mouth or on the tentacles, and nematocysts from dead jellyfish can still envenomate.

Signs and Symptoms of Nematocyst Sting Envenomations

Signs and symptoms range from mild skin irritations to rapid death, and vary considerably with the venomous species. In general, contact with a nematocyst produces painful local swelling, redness, and a stinging, prickling sensation that progresses to numbness, burning, and throbbing pain. Pain may radiate from the extremities to the groin, abdomen, or armpit. The contact site may turn a reddish brown-purple color, marked by swelling. In more serious cases, blisters may occur.

Severe envenomation may produce headache, abdominal cramps, nausea, vomiting, muscle paralysis, and respiratory or cardiac distress.

Treatment of Nematocyst Sting Envenomations

- Rinse with sea water to remove remaining nematocysts.
- Soak in vinegar for at least 30 minutes.
- After soaking, remove all visible tentacles.

Treatment of Nematocyst Sting Envenomations

Treat nematocyst injury first by protecting yourself and second by inactivating and removing nematocysts from the skin. Rinse the injury with sea water to begin removing remaining nematocysts. Do not scrape, rub, or rinse with fresh water, as this will cause any nematocysts on the skin to release more venom. Soak the injury in vinegar (5 percent acetic acid) for at least 30 minutes. Vinegar should not be used without first testing a small area of the sting for adverse effects—in a few species it may trigger further nematocyst discharge. Alcohol, meat tenderizer, and baking soda are less effective, although a baking soda slurry is effective in treating the sting of the Chesapeake sea nettle.

After soaking, remove all visible tentacles with tweezers. Sticky tentacles may be easier to remove if you first apply a drying agent such as baking soda, talc, or sand. Nematocysts can also be removed with adhesive tape or by shaving gently with a razor and shaving cream. Be careful. Rescuer injury is common both in the water and when removing nematocysts on shore.

Anemones
Stinging cells surround the mouths of these sessile organisms. Contact often occurs from accidentally brushing into the anemone. Anemone nematocysts usually produce only very mild local symptoms.

Jellyfish
These animals vary in size from tiny (2 millimeters) to big (2 meters with 40-meter tentacles). Most produce mild local signs and symptoms; however, some produce very potent venom. The box jellyfish (*Chironex fleckeri*), found in the Pacific Ocean off Australia, can cause death within 1 minute.

Portuguese Man-of-War
This large colony of animals usually lives on the surface of the open ocean, its long, transparent tentacles dangling for prey. It is

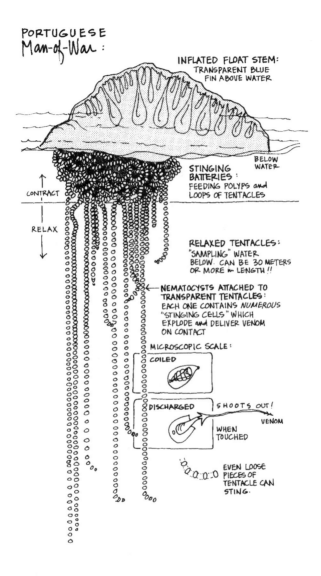

PORTUGUESE
Man-of-War :

INFLATED FLOAT STEM:
TRANSPARENT BLUE
FIN ABOVE WATER

BELOW
WATER

STINGING
BATTERIES :
FEEDING POLYPS and
LOOPS OF TENTACLES

CONTRACT

RELAX

RELAXED TENTACLES :
"SAMPLING" WATER
BELOW. CAN BE 30 METERS
OR MORE in LENGTH !!

NEMATOCYSTS ATTACHED TO
TRANSPARENT TENTACLES :
EACH ONE CONTAINS NUMEROUS
"STINGING CELLS" WHICH
EXPLODE and DELIVER VENOM
ON CONTACT

MICROSCOPIC SCALE :
COILED

DISCHARGED   SHOOTS OUT !
VENOM
WHEN
TOUCHED

EVEN LOOSE
PIECES OF
TENTACLE CAN
STING.

transported by winds and currents, and the animal or pieces of its
tentacles can sometimes be pushed into coastal waters. Contact
with pieces of tentacle usually causes only mild, superficial reactions. Contact with a large number of tentacles from an intact animal, however, can provoke massive envenomation and cause
serious reactions.

Fire Coral

Fire corals are so named because they make you feel as if you've touched hot coals. They are found in coral reefs in tropical waters. Their nematocyst sting causes immediate pain, often described as burning, and small raised red areas on the skin. The localized pain usually lasts 1 to 4 days.

Hard Coral

Hard corals are not highly venomous but often have very sharp edges that can cause abrasions or even lacerations. The wounds heal slowly, especially if pieces of coral are imbedded in the skin. Some species can cause rashes. Vigorous irrigation of the wound is helpful to remove coral pieces. Imbedded pieces of coral often cause slow-healing wound infections.

Sea Cucumbers

These creatures are bottom scavengers found in both shallow and deep water. Sea cucumbers often feed on nematocysts, so they may secrete coelenterate venom as well. They also produce a liquid toxin that causes skin irritations and often severe inflammatory reactions (swelling, raised patches, itching, oozing). To treat, rinse the skin thoroughly with water and soak the injured area in vinegar.

FINAL THOUGHTS

Learn to identify marine animals and to understand their habits. When wading, shuffle your feet to alert stingrays to your presence. Touching marine animals or coral formations is not necessary to enjoy them. When swimming and diving, avoid standing or walking on coral reefs or banging against them. A minimum-impact approach protects not only you but also the fragile underwater environment.

Evacuation Guidelines
- Evacuate any patient with a large soft tissue wound, imbedded spine, unmanageable pain, or systemic signs and symptoms of envenomation.

MEDICAL EMERGENCIES

When we venture into wilderness, we bring with us our clothing and camping gear, our companions, enthusiasms and aspirations, and our medical history. The NOLS incident data shows the variety of illness, from flu-like symptoms to chest pain, allergies to abdominal pain, that can occur in the wilderness. The wilderness first aider isn't expected to know the details of these complex medical conditions. All we need is knowledge of the treatment principles that prepare us to manage this diversity of medical problems and to identify those requiring evacuation to the care of the physician.

This section also provides guidance in addressing mental health concerns that may arise in the wilderness. In most first aid texts and courses, this is an underappreciated topic, yet any seasoned outdoor leader knows that mental health problems arise on our trips and expeditions. The treatment principles will guide your field care of these patients.

CHAPTER 16 | ALLERGIES AND ANAPHYLAXIS

INTRODUCTION

The immune system is an extensive array of cells, structures, antibodies, and other elements constantly defending us against foreign substances: microorganisms, pollen, dust, food, cat dander—practically all the pieces of the natural world. Normally, the immune system smoothly identifies and neutralizes harmful substances with white blood cells, antibodies, and mild inflammation. It's a wonderful, critical, complex, and efficient system. Among the many things it does is remember a first encounter with a foreign substance, producing antibodies designed to recognize and neutralize the invader the next time it appears.

Normally, this interaction is delicately balanced. An overreaction causes us misery when it triggers an inflammatory response we call an allergy. In an allergic person, reintroduction of the foreign material—an allergen—results in an inappropriately large release of histamine. Histamine causes fluid to leak from blood vessels, resulting in edema and swelling, which can obstruct the airway. It also dilates blood vessels, which can lead to shock.

Signs and Symptoms of Mild to Moderate Allergic Reactions

Allergic reactions range from mild to severe, and they can be immediate or delayed. For most people, the allergic response is mild, though often irritating. Hay fever is one example of a mild allergic

Signs and Symptoms of Mild to Moderate Allergic Reaction

- Local swelling near a sting
- Runny nose, sneezing, swollen eyes, hay fever
- Flushed and itchy skin
- Hives or welts on the skin
- Mild or no breathing difficulty

Treatment of a Mild to Moderate Allergic Reaction

- Remove the allergen from the patient or the patient from the offending environment.
- Oral antihistamines.
- Hydration.
- Monitor for increased breathing difficulty.

response. Hay fever sufferers complain of a runny nose, sneezing, swollen eyes, itching skin, and possibly hives. An allergic reaction may also be local, the result of insect stings or contact with a plant. The local reaction is red, swollen, and itching, perhaps with hives, but stays near the point of contact.

Treatment for Mild to Moderate Allergic Reactions

First remove the allergen from the patient or the patient from the offending environment. It's hard to treat a pollen reaction standing under a tree shedding millions of pollen grains or to treat an allergy to dust in a dusty cabin. Antihistamines are the usual treatment. The antihistamines treat the underlying reaction, the release of too much histamine. Monitor the patient closely for a developing severe reaction.

Signs and Symptoms of Severe Allergic Reactions

An anaphylactic response is a massive, generalized reaction of the immune system that is potentially harmful to the body. Common triggers of anaphylaxis are drugs and some foods; people can also react to bee stings and insect bites. Instead of the mild symptoms of hay fever, anaphylaxis produces rash, itching, hives, flushed skin, swollen and red eyes; large areas of swelling typically involving the face, lips, and tongue; difficulty swallowing, asphyxiating swelling of the larynx with respiratory distress and inability to speak in more than one or two word sentences; gastrointestinal symptoms and signs such as crampy abdominal pain and vomiting; and signs and symptoms of shock. The airway obstruction and shock may be fatal. Onset usually occurs within a few minutes of contact with the triggering substance, although the reaction may be delayed and a second reaction can occur after treatment of the first reaction. Any airway swelling, large areas of swelling, typically involving the face, lips, hands, and feet; respiratory compromise; or shock should be treated with epinephrine.

Treatment of Severe Allergic Reactions

If you catch the allergic reaction while the patient can still swallow, administer oral antihistamines. When the reaction becomes severe the anaphylaxis is treated with immediate administration of epinephrine, a prescription medication, to counteract the effects of the histamine. Most cases of fatal anaphylaxis occur because of delayed administration of epinephrine. Persons who know that they are vulnerable to anaphylactic shock usually carry injectable epinephrine in an TwinJect or EpiPen. Trip leaders should be familiar with their use and seek the advice of a physician advisor when responding to this emergency.

Signs and Symptoms of Anaphylaxis

- Flushed and itchy skin
- Hives and welts on the skin
- Swollen face, lips, and tongue
- Respiratory distress
- Shock

Treatment of Anaphylaxis

- Remove the allergen from the patient or the patient from the offending environment.
- For large areas of swelling, respiratory compromise, or shock, inject epinephrine.
- When the patient can swallow, administer oral antihistamines.
- Watch for a second reaction.
- Evacuate.

Use of an Auto-Injector

1. Remove the auto-injector from its storage tube.
2. Grasp the unit with the injection tip (these are different colors depending on the device) pointing downward. Form fist around the unit with the thumb toward the safety/non-needle end. Avoid placing your thumb or finger over the injection end of the auto-injector.
3. With your other hand, pull off the safety release (these are different colors depending on the device).
4. Swing and jab firmly into outer thigh until it clicks. (auto-injector is designed to work through clothing.)
5. Hold firmly against thigh for 10 seconds.

6. Remove unit from thigh and massage injection area for 10 seconds.
7. Carefully place the used auto-injector in a secure location or case for needle protection after use.

Evacuation Guidelines
- Evacuate rapidly any patient with a severe allergic reaction. Secondary reactions can occur within 12 to 24 hours.

17 | RESPIRATORY AND CARDIAC EMERGENCIES

INTRODUCTION

The topics typically discussed in first aid texts as medical emergencies include heart disease, heart attacks, and congestive heart failure; respiratory illnesses such as asthma, emphysema, and pneumonia; as well as diabetes, epilepsy, and drug and alcohol abuse. These are common emergency runs for ambulance crews but less common on wilderness expeditions, although they do occur. Supported by modern medicine, people with heart and lung disease, seizures, and diabetes are able to enjoy the wilderness.

RESPIRATORY AND CARDIAC EMERGENCIES

A history of asthma, heart disease, or even a heart attack does not, by itself, prevent someone from paddling a river, climbing a peak, or hiking the Wind River Range. The wilderness first responder will see these medical conditions and should be knowledgeable in their assessment and treatment.

Hyperventilation Syndrome

Hyperventilation syndrome is an increased respiratory rate caused by an overwhelming emotional stimulus. The patient becomes apprehensive, nervous, or tense. For example, a person may normally have a fear of heights, and the thought of rock

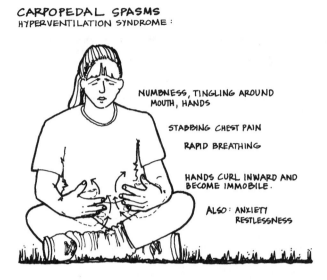

CARPOPEDAL SPASMS
HYPERVENTILATION SYNDROME :

NUMBNESS, TINGLING AROUND MOUTH, HANDS

STABBING CHEST PAIN

RAPID BREATHING

HANDS CURL INWARD AND BECOME IMMOBILE.

ALSO : ANXIETY RESTLESSNESS

climbing triggers a hyperventilation episode, or a climber may fall and suffer a minor injury but begin to hyperventilate out of fear and anxiety. Hyperventilation confounds many injuries and illnesses and can quickly become the major condition affecting the patient.

Signs and Symptoms of Hyperventilation. Signs and symptoms of hyperventilation include a high level of anxiety, a sense of suffocation without apparent physiological basis, rapid and deep respiration, rapid pulse, dizziness and/or faintness, sweating, and dry mouth.

As the syndrome progresses, the patient may complain of numbness or tingling of the hands or around the mouth. Thereafter, painful spasms of the hands and forearms—carpopedal spasms—may occur. The hands curl inward and become immobile. The patient may complain of stabbing chest pain. Rapid respiration increases the loss of carbon dioxide, which causes the blood to become alkaline. The alkaline blood causes the carpopedal spasms.

Treatment for Hyperventilation. To treat hyperventilation syndrome, calm the patient and slow his or her breathing. Coach the patient to breathe slowly. It may take some time before the symptoms resolve. Breathing into a paper bag, once thought to help increase carbon dioxide in the blood, is no longer a recommended treatment.

Pulmonary Embolism

A pulmonary embolism occurs when a clot (usually from a leg vein) breaks loose and lodges in the blood vessels of the lung. Pulmonary embolus is not uncommon outside the wilderness and can be a tough diagnosis. Decreased mobility—lying in a tent waiting out a storm, for example, or long plane flights—may predispose a person to a blood clot. Smoking and a history of recent surgery or illness that kept the patient in bed are also risk factors. There is an increased tendency for blood to clot in arteries and veins at high altitudes. Dehydration, increased red blood cells, cold, constrictive clothing, and immobility during bad weather have been cited as possible causes.

Signs and Symptoms of Pulmonary Embolism. The patient complains of a sudden onset of shortness of breath and pain with inspiration. Respiratory distress may develop, including anxiety and restlessness; shortness of breath; rapid breathing and pulse; signs of shock, including pale, cool, and clammy skin and cyanosis of the skin, lips, and fingernail beds; and labored breathing using accessory muscles of the neck, shoulder, and abdomen to achieve maximum effort.

Treatment for Pulmonary Embolism. First responders can't dissolve the embolism in the field. You can identify the respiratory distress or chest pain, administer oxygen if it is available, and evacuate the patient promptly.

Pneumonia

Pneumonia is a lung infection that can be caused by bacteria, viruses, fungi, and protozoa. The inflammation of the alveolar spaces causes swelling and fluid accumulation. Difficulty breathing can result. People weakened by an illness, chronic disease, fatigue, or exposure are especially at risk. Pneumonia can be a serious infection and is a leading cause of death.

Signs and Symptoms of Pneumonia

- History of upper respiratory infection
- Sweating, fever, chills
- Productive cough
- Pain on inspiration or coughing
- Shortness of breath
- Wet lung sounds
- General illness

Treatment of Pneumonia

- Encourage patients to cough.
- Hydrate.
- Administer oxygen.
- Evacuate.

Signs and Symptoms of Pneumonia. Signs and symptoms of pneumonia are shortness of breath, fever and chills, a productive cough with green-yellow or brown sputum, and pain on inspiration or coughing. The patient may have a recent history of upper respiratory infection and lung sounds, if you can listen with a stethoscope, may be noisy.

Treatment of Pneumonia. Patients with pneumonia should be evacuated. Encourage the patient to cough and breathe deeply to keep the lungs clear. Hydration is important, and oxygen, if available, will be helpful. The patient may be more comfortable sitting up.

Asthma

Asthma is characterized by narrowing of the airways, increased mucous production, and bronchial edema. Asthma's exact cause is unknown. We do know that allergy and environmental (non-allergic) factors such as molds, cold air, chemical fumes, cigarette smoke, exercise, and infections play a role.

Asthma is usually a reversible condition. The airway narrowing can improve spontaneously or in response to medication. A prolonged, severe asthma attack that is not relieved by treatment is an emergency requiring rapid transport. There are other chronic lung diseases, such as emphysema and bronchitis, in which the breathing impairment is persistent because of destruction of lung tissue and chronic inflammation.

Signs and Symptoms of Asthma. Signs and symptoms of mild to moderate asthma are wheezing, chest tightness, and shortness of breath. The heart and breathing rates are increased. When asthma becomes severe, the patient may be hunched over, bracing the upper body and working to breathe. The patient may be able to speak only in one- or two-word clusters. Lung sounds may be diminished or absent. If the patient becomes sleepy or too fatigued to breathe, the situation is dire.

Treatment of Asthma. Usually the patient treats the asthma by self-administering medication, commonly a bronchodilator, with an inhaler. You may need to help the patient relax and use the inhaler properly; shake it first, hold it in the mouth, exhale, and then depress the device and inhale the mist deeply, holding the breath for 5 to 10 seconds before exhaling. To stabilize the initial exacerbation, use of the patient's inhaler 2 puffs every 5 minutes, up to 12 puffs, might be needed. Warm, humidified air can help relax airways and clear mucus. Severe asthma episodes may require medications

---

Signs and Symptoms of Asthma

MILD TO MODERATE ASTHMA
- Chest tightness
- Wheezing and coughing
- Shortness of breath
- Increased heart and breathing rates
- Increased mucous production
- Fatigue

SEVERE ASTHMA
- Use of accessory muscles to breathe
- Decreasing breath sounds progressing to absence of sounds
- Speaking in one- to two-word clusters
- Sleepiness
- Cyanosis

Treatment of Asthma

- Bronchodilators
- Warm, humidified oxygen
- Hydration and rest

(epinephrine and steroids) usually not available in the wilderness, and such patients should be evacuated promptly.

Chest Pain and Heart Disease

Heart disease is a leading cause of death in the United States. Atherosclerosis, a common form of heart disease, slowly builds deposits on arterial walls that narrow the artery and impede blood flow. The narrowed artery can spasm, constrict, or lodge a clot, depriving tissue of blood. If this happens in the brain, the result may be a stroke. If it happens in the heart, it causes chest pain, also known as angina pectoris, or a myocardial infarction, a heart attack. Angina is pain from diminished blood flow. A myocardial infarction is heart muscle damage from blocked blood flow. Sudden death from a heart that beats erratically, or not at all, can be a result of this disease.

Signs and Symptoms of Cardiac Chest Pain

- Persistent chest pain: crushing, tight, pressing, viselike, constricting
- Shortness of breath
- Anxiety and denial
- Pain radiating to arm or jaw
- Nausea and vomiting
- Lightheadedness
- Pale, cool, sweaty skin
- Rapid, slow, weak, or irregular heartbeat
- History of angina, heart attack, or risk factors

Signs and Symptoms of Cardiac Chest Pain. Cardiac chest pain is often described as crushing, tight, pressing, viselike, and constricting. It is below the breastbone and can radiate into the left arm and jaw. Shortness of breath, anxiety, pale sweaty skin, nausea, and dizziness are also common complaints. The pulse may be irregular. If the pain is brought on by physical or emotional stress and is relieved by rest, it may be angina. If it is unprovoked and persists, it may be a myocardial infarction.

Treatment for Cardiac Chest Pain. Figuring out whether nontraumatic chest pain is a heart condition can be difficult under the best of circumstances. Inflammation of the stomach or esophagus, chest muscle strains, rib injury, lung problems, bronchitis, and coughing can all cause chest pain. To complicate the situation, cardiac pain does not always fit the classic pattern and description. Women, the elderly, and diabetics may have fainting, nausea, back pain, weakness, or shortness of breath without classic chest pain. A patient with chest pain symptoms that cannot be attributed to a chest injury, lung problem, stomach upset, or muscle strain should be given one adult aspirin every 24 hours and evacuated. Reduce the demands on the heart by calming the patient and making him or her rest. If available, administer oxygen. If your patient has a history of cardiac chest pain, he or

---

Treatment of Suspected Cardiac Chest Pain

- Reduce anxiety and activity.
- Administer oxygen.
- Administer aspirin.
- Evacuate.

---

she may have nitroglycerin, a medication administered by placing a tablet under the tongue.

Evacuation Guidelines
- Evacuate any patient with chest pain that is not clearly musculoskeletal, pulmonary, or gastrointestinal.
- Expedite evacuation for any patient with chest pain that does not relieve within 20 minutes.
- Expedite evacuation if a severe asthma attack is unresponsive to medications. A patient with severe asthma may need treatment with steroids and epinephrine.

CHAPTER 18 | ABDOMINAL PAIN

INTRODUCTION

The abdomen contains the major blood vessels supplying the lower extremities and the digestive, urinary, and reproductive systems. A lot can go wrong in the belly, and deciding how serious a problem is can be difficult, even for a physician. As first responders, our role is simple: to decide whether the problem is an "acute abdomen," and if so, to support and evacuate the patient. Knowledge of the location and function of the abdominal organs and some of the common abdominal problems can make this determination easier.

ABDOMINAL ANATOMY AND PHYSIOLOGY

The digestive tract processes food to nourish the cells of the body. Secretions within the digestive tract break down food into basic sugars, fatty acids, and amino acids. These products of digestion cross the wall of the intestine and travel to the liver via the veins for detoxification. From the liver, blood circulates nutrients to the individual cells of the body.

Abdominal and Pelvic Cavities. The abdominal cavity, like the chest, is lined by a slippery membrane, called the peritoneum, that covers the organs. The diaphragm separates the chest from the abdomen.

ORGANS OF THE
ABDOMINAL CAVITY

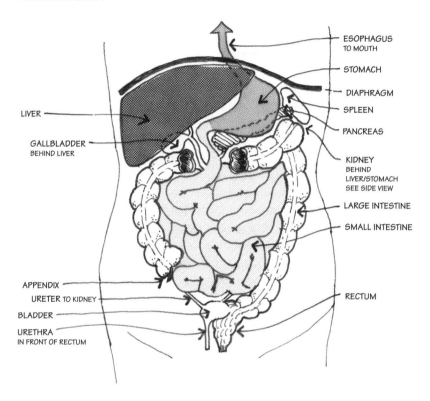

The liver, gallbladder, stomach, spleen, pancreas, appendix, and large and small intestines lie in the abdominal cavity. The kidneys, ureters, adrenals, pancreas, aorta, and inferior vena cava are retroperitoneal. The female reproductive organs, bladder, lower end of the large intestine, and rectum are located in the pelvic cavity.

Digestive Tract. The digestive tract starts at the mouth, where food mixes with saliva—a combination of mucus, water, salts, digestive enzymes, and organic compounds. As food is swallowed, it passes from the mouth into the pharynx. The pharynx divides into the trachea and esophagus. The trachea lies in front of the esophagus. Food could easily go into the trachea, but a thin flap of cartilage, the epiglottis, closes the entrance to the trachea with each swallow.

The esophagus is a 10-inch muscular tube extending from the larynx to the stomach. Contractions of the esophagus—peristalsis—propel food to the stomach.

Stomach. The stomach is a J-shaped organ approximately 10 inches long located in the upper left quadrant of the abdomen. The major function of the stomach is to intermittently store food and move it into the intestine in small amounts. Every 15 to 25 seconds, stomach contractions mix food with gastric juice, turning it into chyme, a thin liquid. Water, salts, alcohol, and certain drugs are absorbed directly by the stomach.

Small and Large Intestines. From the stomach, chyme passes into the small intestine, a tube 21 feet long and 1 inch in diameter. Within the first foot of the small intestine, food mixes with secretions from the pancreas and gallbladder. Ninety percent of the products of digestion (proteins, fats, carbohydrates, vitamins, and minerals) are absorbed in the lower end of the small intestine. Peristalsis moves food through the intestines.

Chyme passes from the small intestine to the large intestine, a tube 5 feet long and 2½ inches in diameter. The appendix is located just below the junction of the small and large intestines. The large intestine absorbs water, forming a solid stool.

The rectum is where feces are stored. The last 2 inches of the intestinal tract forms the anus, which consists of a series of sphincters that move the feces out of the body.

Liver. The liver lies beneath the diaphragm in the upper right quadrant. At 4 pounds in weight, it is the largest solid organ in the abdomen and the one most often injured. There are 500 known functions of the liver, among them detoxifying the products of digestion; converting glycogen, fat, and proteins into glucose; storing vitamins; and producing bile.

Gallbladder. Bile, essential for fat digestion and absorption, is stored in the gallbladder, a pear-shaped organ ¾ inch long. The gallbladder responds to the presence of food (especially fats) in the small intestine by constricting and emptying bile into the intestine.

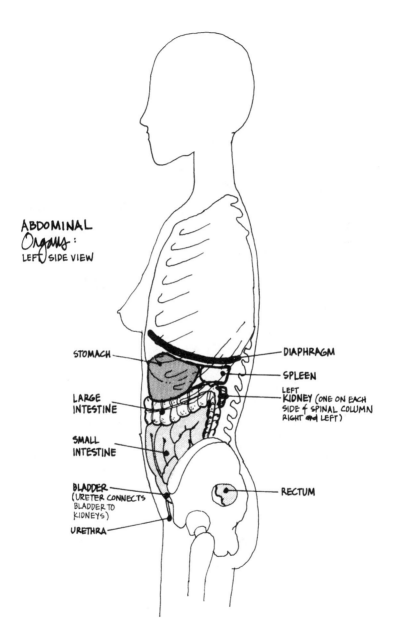

ABDOMINAL
Organs:
LEFT SIDE VIEW

STOMACH

LARGE
INTESTINE

SMALL
INTESTINE

BLADDER
(URETER CONNECTS
BLADDER TO
KIDNEYS)

URETHRA

DIAPHRAGM

SPLEEN

LEFT
KIDNEY (ONE ON EACH
SIDE of SPINAL COLUMN
RIGHT and LEFT)

RECTUM

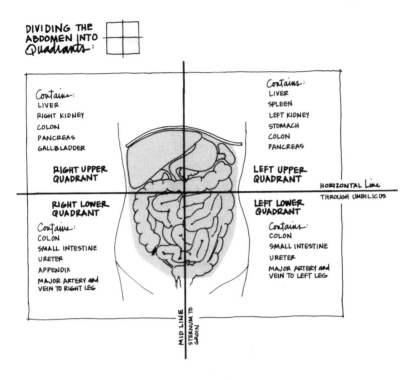

DIVIDING THE ABDOMEN INTO Quadrants:

Contains:
LIVER
RIGHT KIDNEY
COLON
PANCREAS
GALLBLADDER

RIGHT UPPER QUADRANT

Contains:
LIVER
SPLEEN
LEFT KIDNEY
STOMACH
COLON
PANCREAS

LEFT UPPER QUADRANT

HORIZONTAL Line
THROUGH UMBILICUS

RIGHT LOWER QUADRANT

LEFT LOWER QUADRANT

Contains:
COLON
SMALL INTESTINE
URETER
APPENDIX
MAJOR ARTERY and VEIN TO RIGHT LEG

Contains:
COLON
SMALL INTESTINE
URETER
MAJOR ARTERY and VEIN TO LEFT LEG

MID LINE
STERNUM TO GROIN

Pancreas. The pancreas is an oblong organ located in back of the liver. It contains two types of glands. One produces pancreatic juice, which aids in the digestion of fats, carbohydrates, starches, and proteins. The juice flows directly into the small intestine via the pancreatic duct. The other gland secretes chemicals, including insulin, that regulate sugar metabolism.

Spleen. The spleen, located in the upper left quadrant beneath the diaphragm, is the only abdominal organ not involved in digestion. The spleen produces blood cells and destroys worn-out red blood cells.

Urinary System. The urinary system—kidneys, ureters, bladder, and urethra—discharges waste materials filtered from the blood. The two kidneys rid the blood of toxic wastes and control water and salt balance. If the kidneys fail to function, toxic waste will concentrate in the blood, causing death.

Urine flows from the kidneys to the bladder via the ureters. The bladder can hold up to 800 milliliters of urine. At 200 to 400 milliliters, we feel the urge to void. The bladder empties to the outside via the urethra. In women, the urethra is about 1½ inches long; in men, approximately 8 inches.

ABDOMINAL ILLNESS

There are many, many illnesses that can develop within the abdomen. This section is by no means exhaustive, but it does cover problems that, in our experience, we tend to see in the backcountry. The most important part of this chapter is the final section, which reminds us not to worry about diagnosis, but rather to do a sound assessment and decide if the patient meets the evacuation criteria.

Kidney Stones
Kidney stones occur when minerals precipitate from the urine in the kidney. Approximately three-quarters of kidney stones are crystallized calcium. Predisposing factors for kidney stones include urinary tract infections, dehydration, an increase in dietary calcium, too much vitamin D, and cancer.

Signs and Symptoms of Kidney Stones. As a stone passes down the ureter, the patient experiences excruciating pain that comes and goes with increasing intensity. The pain usually begins at the level of the lowest ribs on the back and radiates to the lower abdomen and/or groin. The patient is pale, sweaty, nauseated, and "writhing" in pain. There may be pain with urination and blood in the urine. Chills and fever are not present. The duration of the pain depends on the location of the stone. Pain is severe while a stone is passing from the kidney to the bladder and may stop after the stone has dropped into the bladder. The pain may last as long as 24 hours, but the duration is usually shorter.

Treatment for Kidney Stones. Drinking copious amounts of water may help the patient pass the stone. Pain medication may help. If pain continues for more than 48 hours or if the patient is unable to urinate, evacuate.

Appendicitis

Appendicitis is an inflammation of the appendix causing pressure, swelling, and infection. The highest incidence of appendicitis occurs in males between the ages of 10 and 30.

Signs and Symptoms of Appendicitis. The classic symptoms of appendicitis are pain behind the umbilicus (the navel), anorexia, nausea, and vomiting. They usually develop gradually over 1 to 2 days. The pain then shifts to the lower right quadrant, halfway between the umbilicus and the right hipbone. The patient may have one or two bowel movements but usually does not have diarrhea. When you apply pressure with your hand over the appendix, the patient may complain of pain when you remove your hand. This is called rebound tenderness. A fever and elevated pulse may be present. Due to infection and pain, the patient may lie on his or her side or back with legs tucked onto the abdomen (fetal position). There may also be pain when the patient jumps, walks, or jars his or her right leg or side.

Before the appendix ruptures, the skin over the appendix becomes hypersensitive. If you stroke the skin surface with a pin or grasp the skin between the thumb and forefinger and pull upward, the patient may complain of pain. If the appendix ruptures, the pain temporarily disappears but soon reappears as the abdominal cavity becomes infected (peritonitis). If the infection remains localized (abscess), the patient may only run a low fever and complain of not feeling well. The abscess may not rupture for a week or more.

Treatment for Appendicitis. Appendicitis is a surgical emergency. The patient must be evacuated.

Peritonitis

Peritonitis is an inflammation of the peritoneum. Causes include penetrating abdominal wounds, abdominal bleeding, or ruptured internal organs that spill digestive juices into the abdominal cavity.

Signs and Symptoms of Peritonitis. Signs and symptoms of peritonitis vary, depending on whether the infection is local or general. The patient lies very still, as movement increases the pain. He or she may complain of nausea, vomiting, anorexia, and/or fever. The abdomen is rigid and tender. The infection causes peristaltic activity of the bowel to stop, so the patient has no bowel movements. Shock may be present. The patient appears very sick.

Treatment for Peritonitis. Peritonitis is a severe infection beyond our capability to treat in the wilderness; treat the patient for shock and evacuate.

Hemorrhoids

Hemorrhoids are varicose veins of the anal canal. They may be internal or external. Constipation, straining during elimination, diarrhea, and pregnancy can cause hemorrhoids. External hemorrhoids can be very painful. Internal hemorrhoids tend not to be painful but bleed during bowel movements. The stool may be streaked on the outside with blood. The patient may complain of itching around the anus.

Treatment for Hemorrhoids. Apply moist heat to the anal area. This can be done with a bandanna dipped in warm water. Rest, increased liquid and fruit intake to keep the stools soft, and/or anesthetic ointments (such as dibucaine, Preparation H, or Anusol) help decrease pain and bleeding.

Gastric and Duodenal Ulcers

Decreased resistance of the stomach lining to pepsin and hydrochloric acid, or an increase in the production of these chemicals, may result in ulcers. Stress, smoking, aspirin use, certain bacteria, caffeine or alcohol consumption, and heredity are possible causes.

Signs and Symptoms of Ulcers. The patient complains of a gnawing, aching, or burning in the upper abdomen at the midline 1 to 2 hours after eating or at night, when gastric secretions are at their peak. The pain may radiate from the lowest ribs to the back and frequently disappears if the patient ingests food or antacids.

Is it indigestion, or is it an ulcer? Indigestion symptoms tend to be associated with eating. The patient complains of fullness and heartburn and may belch or vomit small amounts of food. Indigestion worsens when more food is ingested. As time passes and the stomach empties, symptoms disappear. Indigestion tends to be related to a single meal.

Treatment for Ulcers. The primary treatment for ulcers is to take antacids an hour after meals; eat small, frequent meals; and avoid coffee, alcohol, and spicy foods, which increase the secretions of the stomach. Long-term treatment includes rest and counseling to decrease stress. If the ulcer perforates the wall of the stomach, symptoms of peritonitis occur.

ABDOMINAL TRAUMA

Abdominal organs are either solid or hollow. When hollow organs are perforated, they spill their contents into the abdominal cavity. Solid organs tend to bleed when injured. Either bleeding or spillage of digestive juices causes peritonitis.

Blunt Trauma. Inspect the abdomen for bruises; consider how the injury occurred to diagnose what, if any, organs may have been damaged. Pain, signs and symptoms of shock, and a significant mechanism of injury are reasons to initiate an evacuation.

Penetrating Wounds. Assume that any penetrating wound to the abdomen has entered the peritoneal lining. Treat the patient for shock and evacuate.

Impaled Objects. Leave any impaled object in place; removal may increase bleeding. Stabilize the object with dressings. If there is bleeding, apply pressure bandages around the wound.

Evisceration. An evisceration is a protrusion of abdominal organs through a laceration in the abdominal wall. After rinsing the bowel you may be able to gently "tease" small exposed loops back into the abdomen. If not, cover the exposed bowel with dressings that have been soaked in disinfected water. Keep these moist to prevent the exposed loops of bowel from becoming dry. Change the dressings daily. Treat for shock and evacuate the patient.

ABDOMINAL ASSESSMENT

The first responder needs a few simple skills to be able to evaluate the condition of a patient with an abdominal problem.

1. Inspect the abdomen. Position the patient in a warm place, lying down. Remove the patient's clothing so that you can see the entire abdomen. A normal abdomen is

slightly rounded and symmetrical. Look for old scars, areas of bruising, rashes, impaled objects, eviscerations, and distention. Check the lower back for the same. Look for any movement of the abdomen—wavelike contractions may indicate an abdominal obstruction.

2. Listen to the abdomen in all quadrants. Place your ear on the patient's abdomen and listen for bowel sounds (gurgling noises). An absence of noise indicates an injured or ill bowel. You must listen for at least 2 to 3 minutes in all quadrants before you can properly say that no bowel sounds are present.

3. Palpate the abdomen. With your palms down, apply gentle pressure with the pads of the fingers. Make sure your hands are warm and that you palpate in all the quadrants. Cold fingers or jabbing can cause the patient to tighten the abdominal muscles, thereby impeding the assessment. The abdomen should be soft and not tender. Abnormal signs include localized tenderness, diffuse tenderness, and stiff, rigid muscles ("boardlike abdomen").

4. Discuss the patient's condition with him or her. Ask about pain: Where is it located, where does it radiate to, and what is the severity and frequency? What aggravates or alleviates the pain? Are there patterns to the pain (at night, after meals, etc.)? Ask the patient about his or her past medical history. Any past surgery, diagnoses, treatment, or injuries? Any problems with swallowing, digestion, or bowel, bladder, or reproductive organs?

FINAL THOUGHTS

There are many medical problems that cause acute abdominal pain. Determining the actual source of the pain and the urgency of the condition can be difficult, even for a physician. As the leader of a wilderness trip, your task is not to make a diagnosis; it is to decide whether the pain indicates an "acute abdomen," a possible surgical emergency requiring further evaluation. Perform a thorough assessment and decide if your patient triggers an evacuation criteria.

Evacuation Guidelines

Evacuation is recommended for anyone experiencing abdominal pain that is:

- Persistent for more than 12 hours, especially if constant.
- Localized.
- With guarding, tenderness, distension, rigidity.
- With movement, jarring, or foot strike.

Associated s/s that require evacuation may include:

- Blood in the urine, vomit, or feces.
- Persistent anorexia, vomiting, or diarrhea for more than 24 hours.
- Fever greater than 39°C (102°F).
- Signs and symptoms of shock.
- Signs and symptoms of pregnancy.

DIABETES, SEIZURES, AND
UNRESPONSIVE STATES

DIABETES

Diabetes is a disease of sugar metabolism, affecting, by conservative estimates, 10 million Americans. It is a complex disease characterized by a broad array of physiological disturbances. In the
long term, diabetic complications include high blood pressure and
heart and blood vessel disease; it can also affect vision, kidneys,
and healing of wounds. In the short term, the disturbance in sugar
metabolism can manifest itself as too much or too little sugar in
the blood.

Diabetes is thought to be caused by genetic defects, infection,
autoimmune processes, or direct injury to the pancreas. The pancreas produces the hormones, most notably insulin, that help regulate sugar balance. Insulin facilitates the movement of sugar
from the blood into the cells. An excess of insulin promotes the
movement of sugar into the cells, lowers the blood sugar level,
and deprives the brain cells of a crucial nutrient. This disorder is
known as hypoglycemia (low blood sugar).

In contrast, a deficit of insulin results in cells that are starved
for sugar and an excess of sugar in the blood, disturbing fluid and
electrolyte balance. This disorder is known as hyperglycemia
(high blood sugar) or diabetic coma.

A healthy pancreas constantly adjusts the insulin level to the
blood sugar level. The pancreas of a person with diabetes pro-

duces defective insulin or no insulin. To compensate for this, a diabetic takes medication to stimulate endogenous insulin or takes artificial insulin. Treatment plans for diabetics also include diet and exercise.

Hypoglycemia

Hypoglycemia results from the treatment of diabetes, not the diabetes itself. If a diabetic takes too much insulin or fails to eat sufficient sugar to match the insulin level, the blood sugar level will be insufficient to maintain normal brain function.

Hypoglycemia can occur if the diabetic skips a meal but takes the usual insulin dose, takes more than the normal insulin dose, exercises strenuously and fails to eat, or vomits a meal after taking insulin.

Signs and Symptoms of Hypoglycemia. Hypoglycemia has a rapid onset. The most prominent symptoms are alterations in mental status due to a lack of sugar to the brain. The patient may be irritable, nervous, weak, and uncoordinated; may appear intoxicated; or, in more serious cases, may become unresponsive or have seizures. The pulse is rapid; the skin pale, cool, and clammy.

Treatment for Hypoglycemia. Brain cells need sugar and can suffer permanent damage from low blood sugar levels. The treatment of hypoglycemia is to administer sugar. If the patient is awake and able to swallow, a sugar drink or candy bar can help

---

Signs and Symptoms of Hypoglycemia

- Mental status: Weak, disoriented, irritable. Can progress to obvious mental status changes.
- Heart rate (HR): Rapid.
- Respiratory rate (RR): Normal or shallow.
- Skin: Pale, cool, clammy.
- Breath odor: No changes.

Treatment for Hypoglycemia

- If you are unable to distinguish between hypoglycemia and hyperglycemia, give sugar until the patient becomes awake and alert.

increase the blood sugar level. If the patient is unresponsive, establish an airway, then place a small paste of sugar between the patient's cheek and gum. Raising blood sugar by this route takes time. Be patient and diligently watch the airway.

Hyperglycemia

Diabetics who are untreated, who have defective or insufficient insulin, or who become ill may develop a high level of sugar in the blood. Consequences of this may be dehydration and electrolyte disturbances as the kidneys try to eliminate the excess sugar, and acid-base disturbances as cells starved for sugar turn to alternative energy sources.

Signs and Symptoms of Hyperglycemia. Hyperglycemia tends to develop more slowly than hypoglycemia, but it can come on within a few hours if the patient is ill. The first symptoms are often nausea, vomiting, thirst, and increased volume of urine output. The patient's breath may have a fruity odor from the metabolism of fats as an energy source. The patient may also have abdominal cramps or pain and signs of dehydration, including flushed, dry skin and intense thirst. Unresponsiveness is a late and very serious symptom.

Signs and Symptoms of Hyperglycemia

- Mental status: Restless, "drunken"
- Heart rate (HR): Weak, rapid
- Respiratory rate (RR): Increased
- Skin: Warm, pink, dry
- Increased hunger, increased thirst, increased urine output, fatigue
- Breath odor: Acetone, sweet
- Persistent high blood sugar levels

Treatment Principles for Hyperglycemia

- If you are unable to distinguish between hypoglycemia and hyperglycemia, give sugar.
- Hydrate.
- Do not give insulin.
- Evacuate.

Treatment of Hyperglycemia. This patient has a complex physical disturbance and needs the care of a physician. Treatment is supportive: airway maintenance, vital signs, and treatment for shock. Dehydration is a serious complication of hyperglycemia. If the patient is alert, give oral fluids.

Hypoglycemia or Hyperglycemia?

Hypoglycemia usually has a rapid onset; the patient is pale, cool, and clammy and has obvious disturbances in behavior or altered mental status. Hyperglycemia typically has a gradual onset. Often, the patient is in an unexplained coma, with flushed, dry skin, or has a history of recent illness. A fruity breath odor may be present. A patient with hypoglycemia will respond to sugar; a hyperglycemic patient will not, but the extra sugar will cause no harm.

Two questions to ask any diabetic patient are: Have you eaten today, and have you taken your insulin today? If the patient has taken insulin but has not eaten, you should suspect hypoglycemia. The patient will have too much insulin, not enough sugar, and a blood sugar level that is too low to sustain normal brain function. If the patient has eaten but has not taken insulin, hyperglycemia should be suspected. This person has more sugar in the blood than can be transported to the cells.

Most persons with diabetes are very knowledgeable about their reactions and intuitively know if they are getting into trouble. Many diabetics measure their blood sugar levels daily and their urine for ketones. If you're on a wilderness trip with a diabetic, learn his or her medication and eating routines, how he or she measures his or her blood sugar and his or her daily fluctuations in blood sugar level. This can make you familiar with his or her management of diabetes, and helpful if he or she becomes hypo- or hyperglycemic.

When we're sick, we're under stress and we use hormones to fight the infection. Some of these hormones both raise blood sugar and interfere with insulin. The result is that it's more challenging for diabetics to regulate blood sugar when they are sick. A diabetic should have a "sick day" plan, and the trip leader needs to know what that is. The components of a sick day plan include insulin adjustment, food and fluid intake, and decision points for evacuation such as urine ketone, hyperglycemia, and vomiting. Thresholds for evacuation may be several days of illness without relief; vomiting or diarrhea for more than 6 hours; moderate to large amounts of ketones in urine; blood glucose readings consistently greater than normal despite taking extra insulin; early signs of hyperglycemia; loss of a sense of control of blood sugar levels.

It is important for persons with diabetes to eat at regular intervals. If there is a possibility that a diabetic's insulin could be lost or destroyed—for example, by a boat flipping on the river—make sure that someone else in the group is carrying an extra supply. With control and care, diabetics can participate without problems in any activity.

SEIZURES

A seizure is a disruption of the brain's normal activity by a massive paroxysmal electrical discharge from brain cells. The seizure begins at a focus of brain cells, then spreads through the brain and to the rest of the body through peripheral nerves. This electrical disturbance may cause violent muscle contractions throughout the body or result in localized motor movement and possible loss of responsiveness.

The causes of seizures include high fever, head injury, low blood sugar, stroke, poisoning, and epilepsy. Low blood sugar is a cause of seizures in diabetics. Brain cells are sensitive to low oxygen and sugar levels, and if these fall below acceptable levels, a seizure may be triggered. The most common cause of seizures is epilepsy, a disease that manifests as recurring seizures.

The onset of epilepsy is not well understood. Often it begins in childhood or adolescence, but it can also be a consequence of a brain injury. Most persons with epilepsy control their seizures with medication. Interruption of the medication or inadequate dosage is frequently the cause of seizures.

Causes of Seizures

- Overstimulation of the brain
- Eclampsia (a complication of pregnancy)
- High fever and heat stroke
- Brain injury
- High-altitude cerebral edema (HACE)
- Alcohol or drug withdrawal (DTs) or overdose
- Diabetic hypoglycemia

Signs and Symptoms of Seizures

- Aura
- Unexpected and unexplained collapse
- Localized or full body convulsion or temporary disconnection with the present
- Postictal recovery phase

At one time, seizures were attributed to mental illness. The source of these misperceptions may have been the dramatic visual impact of a writhing, moaning person having a seizure. Educating bystanders and group members about epilepsy and seizures can help alleviate such misunderstandings.

Signs and Symptoms of Seizures. The typical generalized seizure begins with a short period, usually less than a minute, of muscle rigidity, followed by several minutes of muscle contractions. The patient may feel the seizure approaching and warn bystanders or cry out at the onset of the episode. The patient suddenly falls to the ground, twitching and jerking.

As muscular activity subsides, the patient remains unresponsive but relaxed. He or she may drool, appear cyanotic, and become incontinent. Pulse and respiratory rate may be rapid. The patient may initially be unresponsive or difficult to arouse, but in time—usually within 10 to 15 minutes—the patient becomes awake and oriented.

Treatment of Seizures. When the seizure has subsided, open the airway, assess for injuries, and take vital signs. Place the patient on his or her side during the recovery phase to help maintain an open airway.

Treatment for a seizure is supportive and protective care. You cannot stop the seizure, but you can protect the patient from injury. The violent muscle contractions of a seizure may cause injury to the patient and to well-meaning bystanders who attempt to restrain the patient. Move objects that the patient may hit. Pad or cradle the head if it is bouncing on the ground. A patient in seizure will not swallow the tongue; however, the airway may become obstructed by saliva or secretions, and the patient may bite his or her tongue.

An accurate description of the seizure tells the physician much about the onset and extent of the problem. In most cases, a seizure runs its course in a few minutes. Repeated seizures, espe-

---

Treatment Principles for Seizures

- Protect from harm, but do not restrain.
- Do not place bite stick or any other object in mouth.
- Place on side to maintain open airway during postictal recovery phase.
- Perform a complete patient assessment to check for other injuries.
- Protect the patient's dignity.
- Administer hi-flow/high-concentration oxygen, if available.

---

cially repeated seizures in which the patient does not regain responsiveness in between, and seizures associated with another medical problem such as diabetes or head injury are serious medical conditions.

An epileptic patient with an isolated seizure requires evaluation by a physician but does not require a rapid evacuation. These occasional seizures are often due to changes in the patient's need for medication or failure to take the medication as prescribed. After recovering from the seizure, the patient should be well fed and hydrated and assessed for any injury that may have occurred during the seizure.

ToStop

To: Toxins
S: Sugar/Seizure
T: Temperature
O: Oxygen
P: Pressure

UNRESPONSIVE STATES

A responsive patient can react to the environment and protect himself or herself from sources of pain and injury. An unresponsive patient or any patient with altered mental status is in danger. He or she is mute and defenseless, unable to rely on even the gag reflex to protect the airway. Many conditions cause unresponsiveness or altered mental status: head injury, stroke, epilepsy, diabetes, alcohol intoxication, drug overdose, and fever.

A patient who is unresponsive or has altered mental status for unexplained reasons poses a difficult diagnostic problem. The medical history may provide clues; use ToStop as a memory aid

---

Treatment Principles for the Unresponsive Patient

- Stabilize the spine.
- Manage the airway, consider positioning the patient on the side.
- Search for clues.
- Consider administering sugar.

---

for common causes of unresponsiveness. Investigate each possibility and look for clues that either rule out or confirm its presence. Since obtaining a history of an unresponsive patient is impossible, carefully question bystanders for any background information they may be able to provide.

Often, all you can do is support the patient and transport him or her to a physician for further evaluation. Care for an unresponsive patient includes airway maintenance and cervical spine precautions unless trauma can be ruled out entirely. If you are unsure why a patient is unresponsive, place some sugar between the patient's cheek and gum. This will help a hypoglycemic patient and won't hurt a patient who is unresponsive for any other reason.

FINAL THOUGHTS

Persons with diabetes and epilepsy routinely participate in wilderness expeditions. The adverse consequences of these diseases—seizures and sugar imbalances—can be prevented through care and education. Paul Petzoldt, NOLS founder, worked with physicians in the early 1970s to support diabetic students attending our remote monthlong wilderness expeditions. At that time, this was a bold initiative. Since then, NOLS students with diabetes have successfully completed our most remote expeditions.

The physical and emotional stress, new physical and social environment, heavy packs, altitude, sun, and battle against dehydration in the wilderness may be new challenges, but they are ones that can be managed.

Discuss the illness beforehand with the diabetic or epileptic person undertaking the expedition. Make sure that you both understand the disease, the timing and side effects of medications, the appropriate emergency treatment, and any other health needs. It is important to inform the rest of the group—especially the person's tent mates—about the condition and how to deal with it in an emergency.

Evacuation Guidelines

Diabetes.

- Evacuation thresholds for diabetes include several days of illness without relief; vomiting or diarrhea for more than 6 hours; moderate to large amounts of ketones in urine; blood glucose readings consistently greater than normal despite taking extra insulin; early signs of hyperglycemia; loss of a sense of control of blood sugar levels.

Seizures.

- Evacuate all people with first time seizures or seizures of unknown origin. Isolated seizures with brief, uncomplicated postseizure periods are not emergencies and can be walked to the road.
- Expedite evacuation for any patient suffering multiple seizures in a short time period.

Unresponsive Patient.

- Unresponsive patients are usually candidates for evacuation. Prolonged unresponsiveness suggests the need to expedite the evacuation.

CHAPTER 20 | GENITOURINARY MEDICAL CONCERNS

INTRODUCTION

Women have participated in NOLS expeditions since the beginning of the school and take their place among the school's most senior field instructors. Both women and men have enjoyed the challenges and rewards of climbing the highest peaks, paddling the wildest rivers and coastlines, and exploring the world's most remote wilderness.

During these trips, people have experienced injury and illness to reproductive and urinary systems. In male anatomy, experience epididymitis and testicular torsion can occur. Female anatomy, which is more complex reproductive anatomy and physiology, may present a variety of medical conditions ranging from changes in menstrual cycles to vaginal infections, pelvic inflammatory disease, and ectopic pregnancy. The wilderness leader should be knowledgeable about the prevention, assessment, and field treatment of these conditions, and know when to evacuate.

MALE-SPECIFIC MEDICAL CONCERNS

Male external genitalia consist of the penis and scrotum. The penis provides a route for urine to be expelled from the bladder and sperm expelled from the testes. The scrotum is a pouchlike structure located to the side of and beneath the penis. The testes

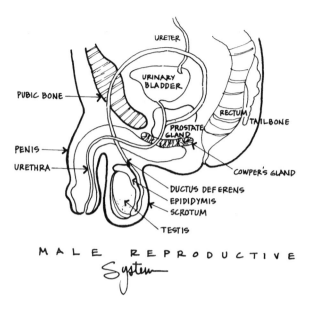

lie within the scrotum and are the site of sperm and testosterone production.

Sperm travels out of the testes via the epididymis, a comma-shaped organ that lies behind the testes. The epididymis is composed of approximately 20 feet of ducts. From the epididymis, sperm travel through the ductus deferens, a tube approximately 18 inches long that loops into the pelvic cavity. Sperm can be stored there for many months.

Epididymitis

Epididymitis is an inflammation of the epididymis and can be caused by gonorrhea, syphilis, tuberculosis, mumps, prostatitis (inflammation of the prostate), or urethritis (inflammation of the urethra).

Signs and Symptoms of Epididymitis. The patient suffers from pain in the scrotum, possibly accompanied by fever. The scrotum may be red and swollen. Epididymitis tends to come on slowly, unlike torsion of the testis, which comes on rapidly.

Treatment of Epididymitis. The treatment is bed rest, support or elevation of the testes, and antibiotics. Diagnosis can be tricky. The pain and swelling often prevent any activity; thus, evacuation

---

Signs and Symptoms of Male-specific Medical Concerns

EPIDIDYMITIS
- Usually more gradual onset.
- Scrotum is swollen, painful, and red.
- Testis may be elevated.

TESTICULAR TORSION
- Usually acute pain.
- Scrotum is swollen, painful, and red.

---

is recommended. Acetaminophen, aspirin, or ibuprofen may decrease the fever and pain.

Torsion of the Testis

Torsion of the testis is a twisting of the testis within the scrotum. The ductus deferens and its accompanying blood vessels become twisted, decreasing the blood supply to the testis. If the blood supply is totally cut off, the testis dies. After 24 hours without blood supply, the prognosis for saving the testis is poor.

Signs and Symptoms of Torsion. The scrotum is red, swollen, and painful, and the testis may appear slightly elevated on the affected side. The patient must be evacuated for treatment.

Treatment of Torsion. If you suspect torsion in the wilderness, there is little to be lost in having the patient attempt to untwist the affected testicle from the medial to lateral direction—since the testicle will die long before anyone gets to the roadhead. Increased pain while untwisting is probably a good indicator that you're going in the wrong direction.

FEMALE-SPECIFIC MEDICAL CONCERNS

Female reproductive organs lie within the pelvic cavity. The vagina, or birth canal, is approximately 3 to 4 inches long. The vagina is continuously moistened by secretions that keep it clean and slightly acidic.

At the top of the vagina is the cervix, a circle of tissue pierced by a small hole that opens into the uterus. The cervix thins and opens during labor to allow the baby to be expelled.

The uterus is about the size of a fist and is located between the bladder and rectum. Pregnancy begins when a fertilized egg

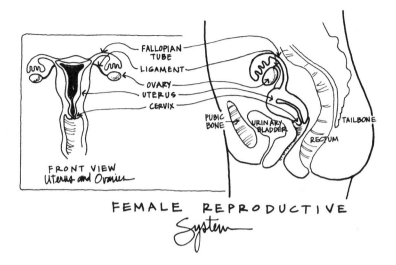

FEMALE REPRODUCTIVE System

implants in the tissue of the uterus. The uterus is an elastic organ that expands with the growing fetus.

On either side of the uterus are the ovaries, which lie approximately 4 or 5 inches below the waist. The ovaries produce eggs and the female sex hormones estrogen and progesterone. Each month an egg (ovum) is released from one of the ovaries and travels down the fallopian tube to the uterus. The fallopian tubes are approximately 4 inches long and wrap around the ovaries but are not directly connected to them. When the egg is released from the ovary, the fimbriae (fingerlike structures at the end of the fallopian tube) make sweeping motions across the ovary, sucking the egg into the fallopian tube.

The Menstrual Cycle
As early as 12 years of age, female bodies can start menstrual cycles, the monthly release of ova. Hormones regulate the cycle, which continues until menopause, or cessation of the menstrual cycle, at approximately 52 years of age.

The endometrial tissue that lines the uterus undergoes hormone-regulated changes each month during menstruation. The average menstrual cycle is 28 days long, with day 1 being the first day of the menstrual period. From days 1 through 5, the endometrial tissue sloughs off from the uterus and is expelled through the vagina. The usual discharge is 4 to 6 tablespoons of blood, tissue, and mucus. During days 6 through l6, the endometrial tissue grows in preparation for implantation of an ovum, becoming thick and full of small blood vessels.

Ovulation usually occurs around day 14; the egg takes approximately 6½ days to reach the uterus. On days 16 through 26, the endometrium secretes substances to nourish the embryo. If conception has not occurred, the hormones progesterone and estrogen decrease, causing the uterine blood supply to decrease and the lining of the uterus to be shed.

Mittelschmerz. Some individuals experience cramping in the lower abdomen on the right or left side or in the back when the ovary releases an egg. The pain is sometimes accompanied by bloody vaginal discharge. This is called mittelschmerz (mittel = middle; schmerz = pain).

Signs and Symptoms. The pain may be severe enough to be confused with appendicitis or ectopic pregnancy, but a careful assessment should allow the first responder to distinguish between the two. Ask the patient where she is in her menstrual cycle. Has she ever had this pain before? Typically, the cramping will be similar to past cycles. Any light bleeding or pain should cease within 36 hours. The abdomen is soft. Individuals taking birth control pills do not ovulate, so they cannot have mittelschmerz.

Dysmenorrhea. Dysmenorrhea is painful menstruation (cramps). Possible causes include prostaglandins, which cause the uterus to cramp, endometriosis (inflammation of the endometrium), pelvic inflammatory disease, or anatomic anomalies such as a displaced uterus.

Treatment. Antiprostaglandins such as ibuprofen reduce the pain as well as the volume of flow and the length of the period. Relaxation exercises such as yoga and massaging the lower back or abdomen help reduce pain. Applying heat to the abdomen or lower back may also help reduce pain.

A change in diet may help. Decreasing the amount of salt, caffeine, and alcohol in the diet while increasing the B vitamins—especially B6 (found in brewer's yeast, peanuts, rice, sunflower seeds, and whole grains)—or drinking raspberry leaf tea (1 tablespoon for each cup) can offer some relief during the acute phase of the cramps. Because exercise causes endorphins (natural opiates) to be released by the brain, many women find that cramps diminish when they participate in strenuous exercise.

Secondary Amenorrhea. Secondary amenorrhea is the absence of menstrual periods after an individual has had at least one period. Causes of secondary amenorrhea include pregnancy, ovarian tumors, intense athletic training, excessive weight loss or gain, altitude, and stress (physical and emotional). Changes in the menstrual cycle are common in the backcountry and may be normal adjustments to unfamiliar stresses.

Vaginal Infection

The normal vagina contains a plethora of microorganisms. Most of the time these organisms are in balance. The normal pH of the vagina is slightly acidic. Vaginal infections can occur when the normal balance of bacteria and the pH are upset. Antibiotics, birth control pills, diabetes, and physical or emotional stress may cause an infection to develop. Cuts and abrasions from intercourse or tampons, not cleaning the perineal area, or not changing underwear can also lead to an infection.

The two most common causes of vaginal infections are candidiasis (yeast) and bacterial vaginitis.

Signs and Symptoms of Vaginitis. Symptoms of a yeast infection generally include curdy white discharge and itching. The vulva may be swollen and excoriated from scratching. Symptoms of bacterial vaginitis include a grayish, milky, thin discharge. The discharge may be malodorous, and the patient may complain of vaginal pain but not itching. For the purposes of field diagnosis, the symptoms are similar, and initial treatment is the same.

> **Signs and Symptoms of a Vaginal Infection**
> - Curdy white discharge or grayish milky discharge
> - Malodorous discharge
> - Redness, soreness, itching of vaginal area

Treatment of Vaginitis. Vaginal infections can be treated with over-the-counter medications such as Gyne-Lotrimin and Monistat 1 (vaginal suppository), or with prescription Diflucan (oral pill). If these treatments don't provide relief within 48 hours, the patient should be evacuated. An untreated infection

Treatment of Vaginal Infection

- Gyne-Lotrimin, Monistat 1, or Diflucan.
- Evacuate if symptoms persist for 48 hours despite treatment.

Prevention of Vaginal Infection

- Stay hydrated.
- Decrease sugar, caffeine, and alcohol intake.
- Wear loose-fitting underwear or running shorts for ventilation.
- Wash perineal area daily.
- Change tampons regularly.
- Decrease stress.

can develop into pelvic inflammatory disease.

Prevention. The best prevention for vaginal infections is education. To help prevent vaginal infections, wipe front to back, clean the perineal area (between the vagina and anus) daily with plain water or a mild soap, and promote ventilation by wearing loose-fitting nylon or cotton underwear or running shorts. Individuals with a history of vaginal infection should decrease their caffeine, alcohol, and sugar intake.

Urinary Tract Infection (UTI)

Urinary tract infections are common in women due to the closer proximity of the urethra to the vagina and rectum and the shorter length of the urethra. The infection can affect the urethra, ureters, or bladder.

Signs and Symptoms of UTI. Urinary tract infections cause increased frequency or urgency of urination and/or a burning sensation during urination. The patient complains of pain above the pubic bone and a heavy urine odor with the morning urination. Blood and/or pus may be present in the urine. Urinary tract infections can progress to kidney infections. If the kidneys are infected, the patient complains of rebound tenderness in the small of the back and may have a fever.

Treatment for UTI. The best treatment (also good for prevention) is to drink lots of water every day and empty the bladder often. A good way to tell if you are drinking enough is by the color of your urine. Unless you are taking vitamins, the urine should be clear, not yellow. Persons taking vitamins tend to have yellow urine.

The perineal area should be cleaned with water or mild soap daily. Taking 500 milligrams of vitamin C daily and/or eating whole grains, nuts, and fruits may help. Curry, cayenne pepper, chili powder, black pepper, caffeine, and alcohol should be avoided because these irritate the bladder. Vitamin B6 and magnesium or calcium supplements help relieve spasms of the urethra.

On extended expeditions, consider carrying antibiotics to treat urinary tract infections. If an infection persists for more than 48 hours despite the use of antibiotics, the patient should be evacuated. Evacuate patients with symptoms of a kidney infection for further evaluation.

Ectopic Pregnancy

Ectopic pregnancies occur outside the uterus, most commonly in the fallopian tubes. Sperm usually fertilizes the egg in the upper two-thirds of the tube. Due to congenital anomalies or scarring caused by infection, the egg starts growing in the tube.

Signs and Symptoms of Ectopic Pregnancy. The classic triad of an ectopic pregnancy is absence of menstruation because of the pregnancy, abdominal pain, and bleeding. The onset of pain is rapid and on one side of the abdomen. The fallopian tube ruptures in 4 to 6 weeks when the embryo becomes too large for the tube. The pain then becomes agonizing, and signs and symptoms of peritonitis develop. The patient may hemorrhage and die from shock, although slow bleeding is more common.

Treatment for Ectopic Pregnancy. Treat for shock and evacuate immediately.

ASSESSMENT TIPS

If you're leading or participating in wilderness trips, you will encounter people with genitourinary medical concerns. An individual experiencing scrotal pain for the first time

---

Signs and Symptoms of Urinary Tract Infection

- Increase in frequency of urination.
- Urgency and a burning sensation during urination.

Treatment of Urinary Tract Infection

- Increase fluid intake.
- Give vitamin B6, calcium, and magnesium supplements to relieve bladder spasms.
- Change diet.
- Avoid sugar and foods that irritate the bladder.
- Antibiotics.

Signs and Symptoms of Ectopic Pregnancy

- Rapid onset of unilateral lower abdominal pain
- Vaginal bleeding
- Signs and symptoms of peritonitis and shock

may be embarrassed and hesitant to inform the leader, especially if the leader is of the opposite gender. Likewise, a person with a urinary tract infection may not know the signs and symptoms or that you have the means to treat it in the field, and she may be reluctant to inform a male trip leader.

If a genitourinary medical problem arises, provide a private place to talk. Be straightforward, respectful, and nonjudgmental. Use proper medical terminology or terms that you both understand—no jokes or slang. A member of the patient's sex should be present before and during any physical exam.

For female patients, gather information about the patient's menstrual and reproductive history. When was her last menstrual period? How long is her cycle? What is normal for her? Does she use contraception? Has she had sexual intercourse in the past? Has she experienced this problem in the past, and if so, how was it treated?

TIPS FOR WOMEN'S HYGIENE IN THE WILDERNESS

Wear loose-fitting shorts that allow for adequate ventilation. With washings, two or three pairs of underwear will be sufficient for a 30-day expedition.

During menstruation, change tampons and pads frequently, and remember to wash your hands prior to inserting a tampon.

If you are prone to vaginal infections, consider decreasing the amount of sugar in your diet. Drink tea instead of cocoa, water instead of fruit drinks, and eat nuts instead of candy bars.

Wipe from the front to the back to limit introduction of bacteria into the vaginal area. Wash the vaginal area with water or mild soap daily.

A "pee rag" has become popular among women backpackers to conserve toilet paper. Usually a bandanna, it's tied onto the outside of the pack while hiking. If it gets rained on, fine. If not, women rinse them out every few days. It makes a big difference in staying clean.

Used tampons and pads are bagged and carried out of the backcountry. Having a designated system makes proper disposal of tampons, pads, and toilet paper easier. A small stuff sack with a couple of extra plastic bags allows personal organization and privacy. Some women prefer wide mouthed water bottles or plastic containers for this. Include a small wad of toilet paper in this kit. An aspirin or two placed in the bag or container will help dissipate odor.

How many extra tampons or pads to bring? Bring a little extra for heavier flow, in case your cycle changes and you experience your period twice in a month-long trip, or if pads or tampons get wet. If a few people in a group brings a bit extra, almost any emergency can be covered by the group without adding a lot of bulk.

An added note: There is no evidence that bears are attracted to people having their periods.

Evacuation Guidelines
- Evacuate any female with signs and symptoms, or the possibility, of pregnancy.
- Expedite evacuation if suspected pregnant patient develops low abdominal/pelvic pain and vaginal bleeding not associated with her regular menstrual cycle.
- Expedite evacuation for suspected testicular torsion, epididymitis, or testicular pain of unknown origin.

CHAPTER 21 | MENTAL HEALTH CONCERNS

INTRODUCTION

When we venture into wilderness, we bring with us our medical and our mental health history. Illness, injury, and mental health concerns that can present back in our urban lives may also present in the wilderness. Outdoor leaders and expedition physicians will tell you that they see mental health issues on Denali, at Everest base camp, on treks, outdoor programs, and personal trips. No one talks much about this in public, but mental health issues ranging from heightened stress to episodes of anxiety, depression, mania, psychosis, or drug reactions can and do occur on wilderness expeditions. More serious episodes will need to be treated by a skilled mental health professional in a more controlled setting. Anxiety, mild depression, some post-traumatic stress responses, and mild drug reactions can often be defused without having to end the camping experience.

We don't expect wilderness first responders to be mental health professionals, but awareness of some of the more common mental health conditions, application of our patient assessment system, and thoughtful, compassionate care can help diffuse these concerns in the field.

STRESS RESPONSES

Stress occurs whenever the mind or body has to adjust to a change in the external or internal world of an individual. Substantial increases in stress typically result in heightened physiological and emotional states. This can exacerbate preexisting physical conditions (e.g., change in blood pressure, greater risk of a cardiac event) and generate symptoms related to anxiety and depression. Stress can also exacerbate chronic mental conditions such as psychotic disorders.

ANXIETY RESPONSES

Anxiety responses can include an acute anxiety disorder (also known as panic attacks), phobias, obsessive-compulsive thoughts/behaviors, and Post-Traumatic Stress Disorder responses. Anxiety often accompanies and can interfere with an accurate assessment of the physical injury. Symptoms may include feelings of fear, apprehension, loss of control, and loss of sanity. Signs, which can mimic a heart attack, include heart palpitations, rapid, irregular heartbeat, rapid breathing, pale skin, and sweating.

First aid for stress and anxiety responses is to calm the patient, try to allay his fears, and complete a PAS to try to rule out physical causes. Patients whose responses abate might be able to stay in the field. An anxiety or stress response that is unpredictable or persistent may be a hazard to the patient and others and may dictate an evacuation.

Signs and Symptoms of Anxiety Responses

- RR Respiratory Rate and HR Heart Rate increased
- SCTM Skin Color Temperature Moisture: PCC Pale Cool Clammy
- Trouble focusing
- Dizziness, trembling
- Stomach distress
- Chest pains
- Tingling sensations
- Excessive fear reactions
- Possible fight/flight/freeze response
- Catastrophic thoughts of dying, losing control or going crazy (with panic episodes)
- Compulsive rituals/thoughts (with obsessive-compulsive disorder)

DEPRESSION

Depression typically manifests itself in withdrawal, isolation, crying, diminished interest in most activities, fatigue or loss of energy, trouble making decisions, feelings of helplessness and hopelessness, and/or a change in eating or sleeping patterns. These are not occasional blue moods. This is a deeper, persistent affective disorder. Depression can also present with agitation, increased motor activity, ruminating thought processes, and compulsive behaviors. If the depression affects other group members, or the ability of the person to participate in the trip, or focus on essential risk management tasks, the patient may need to be evacuated.

Signs and Symptoms of Depression

- Persistent feelings of helplessness, hopelessness, despair (Agitation and anxiety may also be present.)
- Symptoms of withdrawal, isolation, crying, diminished interest in most activities, fatigue or loss of energy, trouble making decisions, irritability, and/or change in eating and sleeping patterns
- LOR Level of Responsiveness Awake+Oriented ×4, HR Heart Rate, RR Respiratory Rate, SCTM Skin Color Temperature Moisture normal for patient

---

MANIA/PSYCHOSIS

Mania and psychoses are generally more serious than anxiety or depression and are more likely to require field consultation with a mental health specialist if available and/or evacuation. Psychotic symptoms can be brought on by heightened stress, change in environment, use of drugs, and/or going off prescribed medications.

Signs and Symptoms of Mania/Psychosis

- Mania: pressured speech, flight of ideas, high energy, decreased need for sleep, and/or altered sense of reality or inability to distinguish internal from external reality
- Psychosis: hallucinations, delusions, and an altered sense of reality

---

Individuals experiencing mania or psychosis are out of touch with reality in some way (e.g., hallucinations, delusions, heightened energy levels), which means that the person suffering from psychotic symptoms cannot distinguish internal reality from external reality. Thus, they are more difficult to manage. Both can be dangerous if they occur in terrain with risk of a fall, or during an activity requiring focus and precise actions, such as paddling a rapid.

SUICIDAL BEHAVIOR

Suicide is the third-leading cause of death among individuals 15 to 24 years of age in the United States. Females tend to have more suicide gestures than males, but males are more likely to complete their attempt to end their life. If someone talks about suicide, pay attention.

If suicidal thoughts are suspected—perhaps the patient is very depressed, feeling hopeless or helpless, or actually talking about harming themselves—talk to the patient. It may be challenging to open this conversation, but talking about suicide does not cause people to commit suicide. Ask the following five questions:

- Are you thinking of harming or killing yourself?
- Have you planned how you would do this?
- Do you have the means with you now to carry out this plan?
- When are you thinking of doing this?
- Do you have a history of past suicide attempts?

The more of these questions that are answered in the affirmative, the higher the risk to that person.

The policy of an outdoor program may dictate what is to be done if an individual demonstrates any suicidal thoughts or behaviors, but in most cases these individuals ought to be evacuated.

TREATMENT PRINCIPLES

Complete your patient assessment (PAS). There may be a physical cause to the problem. Psychological problems can have physical causes such as brain tumors and infections, brain injury, substance abuse, hypoxia, hypoglycemia, hypo- or hyperthermia, to name a few.

Is the patient on any medications? Might they be influencing the problem? Does the patient have any history of this problem? If so, what has made it worse, what has made it better?

Listen carefully. Use a calm voice, slow breathing, eye contact, and patience. Keep questions simple, honest, direct, and respectful. You may need to repeat questions if patient has trouble tracking. Ask the person if he knows what led to his feelings and reactions.

Remain calm and reassure the patient. Focus on the patient's strengths. Discuss what he has done in the past to help correct these feelings/thoughts/reactions, and see if some of these things can be done now. Try to instill hope that he will get better.

Evaluate the risk to yourself, the patient, and others. Inform, don't surprise the patient. Decide if you can manage this patient. Is there danger to yourself, the patient, or others?

Evacuation Guidelines

We don't need to fully understand the problem. We can make a decision based on simple principles used by many field instructors and wilderness trip leaders.

- Does the harm to the expedition outweigh the benefit to the patient?
- Is the mental health condition beyond our ability to manage in the field?
- Is the patient requiring a level of attention or monitoring that is already adversely affecting the cohesion, function, or safely of the group?
- Is the patient a danger to self or others?
- Does the patient believe he is unsafe or unable to continue?

Answering any of these question in the affirmative gives you reason to evacuate the patient and seek a mental health professional.

EXPEDITION MEDICINE

"Judgment in my estimation is the greatest safety factor you can have."

—Paul Petzoldt, NOLS Founder

The first aid we can perform in the field is often limited. The experience and outcome for the patient is strongly influenced by the quality of leadership and expedition behavior, and the decisions we make. Three chapters at the end of the section prepare you for the challenges of leadership, teamwork, communication, decision-making, and the stress of rescue.

This section completes the suite of skills we need to effectively lead wilderness medicine problems and blends the medicine with outdoor leadership. The NOLS incident data shows that flulike illness and gastrointestinal symptoms are by far the most common medical complaints. The chapter on hygiene and water disinfection speaks to this from the perspective of prevention, our most effective treatment. This theme continues as we address hydration, which helps us tolerate heat, cold, altitude, and the exercise that comes with outdoor pursuits.

CHAPTER 22 | HYGIENE AND WATER DISINFECTION

INTRODUCTION

It's common to see signs at wilderness trailheads warning of disease-causing bacteria, viruses, and protozoa in the water. It's become an accepted habit that wilderness water must be disinfected. Yet, it's not clear whether pristine wilderness water harbors diarrhea-causing pathogens. It is clear that on wilderness trips diarrhea and closely-related flu symptoms are the most common illness, but we can't categorically blame the water. Poor hygiene—poor hand-washing habits—is believed to be a prominent cause of these preventable illnesses.

People living in countries with the luxury of clean tap water and effective sanitation systems may not appreciate that in parts of the world water contamination continues to be a major health problem, and diarrheal illness is a leading cause of death. Maintaining strict hygiene practices in pristine wilderness can be difficult and water disinfection may seem unnecessary. Unfortunately, it is not always easy to know when a water source has a low risk of intestinal pathogens and when it has a high risk. Diarrhea is unpleasant. It may be better to be safe than sorry.

WATERBORNE ILLNESS

Worldwide, waterborne microorganisms account for many cases of infectious diarrhea. The microorganisms causing diarrhea include bacteria, protozoa, viruses, and parasitic worms. Diseases that are spread through contaminated water include typhoid, cholera, campylobacteriosis, giardiasis, and hepatitis A.

Although a frequently diagnosed diarrhea-causing microorganism in the United States is the protozoan *Giardia*, other bacteria and viruses are being identified as well. Recently the protozoan *Cryptosporidium* has received attention as a cause of municipal waterborne outbreaks, but it is unclear how much risk it poses in wilderness water sources.

Giardia

Giardia is a microscopic protozoan. It has a two-stage life as cyst and trophozoite. The cyst, excreted in mammalian feces, is hardy and can survive 2 to 3 months in near-freezing water. If swallowed, the warmer internal environment causes the cyst to change into its active stage, the trophozoite. The trophozoite attaches itself to the wall of the small intestine and is the cause of the diarrhea associated with *Giardia* infections.

Humans are a carrier of *Giardia*. It has also been identified in both domestic and wild animals, specifically in beavers, cats, dogs, sheep, cattle, deer, and elk, and in reptiles, amphibians, and fish. It is not clear whether contamination from *Giardia* is increasing or whether it is being diagnosed more frequently as a cause of diarrhea.

Giardia is difficult to diagnose due to the wide variation in symptoms. For a reliable diagnosis, three stool samples should be

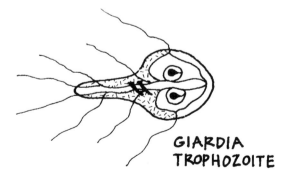

GIARDIA
TROPHOZOITE

examined. Most infections are without symptoms, and the unwitting patient becomes a carrier of *Giardia*, inadvertently spreading the illness.

The incubation period—from ingestion to the onset of infection—is 1 to 3 weeks. Symptoms include recurrent and persistent malodorous stools and flatus, abdominal cramping, bloating, "sulfur burps," and indigestion. Serious infections produce explosive watery diarrhea with cramps, foul flatus, fever, and malaise.

Although drug therapy is available, prevention through hygienic habits and water disinfection makes much more sense. *Giardia* is sensitive to heat, is easily filtered, and can be killed with chemical disinfection.

Cryptosporidium

Also a microscopic protozoan, *Cryptosporidium* is spread by drinking contaminated water, by eating contaminated raw or undercooked food, or by hand-to-mouth transfer of cysts picked up from fecal matter.

Some people may not have symptoms. Most have an illness lasting 1 to 2 weeks that starts 2 to 10 days after infection and includes watery diarrhea, headache, abdominal cramps, nausea, vomiting, and low-grade fever. In persons with suppressed immune systems, such as AIDS or cancer chemotherapy patients, the infection may continue and become life-threatening.

Cryptosporidium cysts are sensitive to heat and can be filtered but are not reliably killed by iodine or chlorine. People with suppressed immune systems should consider boiling water or using a filtration system to protect them from infection.

WATER DISINFECTION

Purifying water eliminates offensive odors, tastes, and colors but does not kill microorganisms. Sterilization kills all life-forms. Disinfection removes or destroys disease-causing microorganisms. What we commonly refer to as water purification is really disinfection. There are three main methods of water disinfection: heat, chemical treatment, and filtration.

Methods OF WATER DISINFECTION:

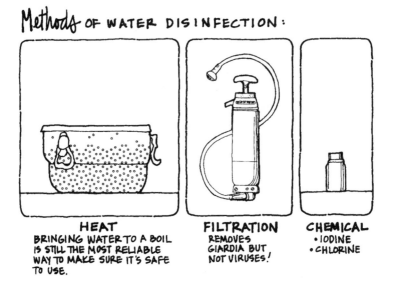

HEAT
BRINGING WATER TO A BOIL
IS STILL THE MOST RELIABLE
WAY TO MAKE SURE IT'S SAFE
TO USE.

FILTRATION
REMOVES
GIARDIA BUT
NOT VIRUSES!

CHEMICAL
• IODINE
• CHLORINE

Heat

Incorrect information persists on how long to boil water before it is disinfected. The common diarrhea-causing microorganisms are sensitive to heat and are killed immediately by boiling water. The protozoa *Giardia* and *Amoeba* (which causes amebiasis) die after 2 to 3 minutes at 140°F (60°C). Viruses, diarrhea-producing bacteria, and *Cryptosporidium* cysts die within minutes at 150°F (65°C). By the time water boils, it is safe to drink.

The boiling point decreases with increasing elevation, but this does not affect disinfection. The boiling point at 19,000 feet (5700 meters) is 178°F (81°C), sufficient for disinfecting water.

The advantage of boiling is its effectiveness. However, it is inconvenient on the trail, takes time, and consumes fuel.

Chemical Treatment

Chemical treatment is the addition of halogens, either iodine or chlorine, or chlorine dioxide to water. If used correctly, halogens and chlorine dioxide can reliably kill viruses, diarrhea-causing bacteria, and most protozoa cysts, with the exception of *Cryptosporidium*. The concentration of halogen and its contact time in water determine the degree of disinfection.

Factors that can affect halogen treatment include pH, chemical binding with material in the water, and water temperature. Halogens are affected by pH, but the pH levels of most natural water sources don't significantly influence the activity of iodine or chlorine.

When iodine or chlorine binds with organic and inorganic particles in water, less halogen is available to destroy the diarrhea-causing microorganisms. Reduce debris before adding halogen; filter murky water with a manufactured filter or use an improvised strainer such as a coffee filter or a clean bandanna. You can also let water sit until the floating particles settle to the bottom or use alum to clear the water. To compensate for halogen bonding with organic matter in cloudy water, increase the amount of halogen (see the recommendations in the table on the next page).

Chemical Water Disinfection Products

IODINE
- Potable Aqua tablets
- Polar Pure crystals
- 2% iodine solution (tincture)
- 10% povidone-iodine

CHLORINE
- Bleach
- Halazone tablets
- Puritabs

CHLORINE DIOXIDE
- Aqua Mira
- Potable Aqua Chlorine Dioxide
- Micropur tablets
- Miox

Halogens are also affected by temperature. Cold water slows the chemical reaction. Compensate for a slower reaction in cold water by increasing contact time. On the safe side, wait 30 minutes in warm water (86°F [30°C]), 60 minutes in cold water (59°F [15°C]).

Iodine. Iodine, the most commonly used halogen, is available as a tablet—tetraglycine hydroperiodide—sold commercially as Potable Aqua iodine tablets. Iodine crystals in PolarPure, 2 percent iodine (tincture), and 10 percent povidone-iodine solutions are also effective.

Iodine is affected less by pH than is chlorine and has less effect on the taste of the water. Wilderness medicine experts believe that at the levels used to occasionally disinfect water, iodine is safe for most people. Iodine is not recommended for persons with thyroid disease, a known iodine allergy, or during pregnancy.

The aftertaste of iodine and chlorine in water can be improved by adding flavoring. The sugar in drink mixes, however, also binds the halogen. Add flavoring after disinfection. An ascorbic acid (vitamin C) tablet, added after disinfection, improves flavor by chemically reducing the iodine and chlorine to iodide and chloride, which have no taste.

Chlorine. Chlorine has been used as a disinfectant for over 200 years. Chlorine bleach (4 to 6 percent) is commonly used to disinfect water. Halazone and Puritabs are chlorine tablets.

Chlorine Dioxide. Chlorine dioxide products such as Aqua Mira, Micropur, Potable Aqua chlorine dioxide, and the MIOX Purifier are newer products that are effective over a broad temperature range and leave less of an aftertaste in the water. They claim to disinfect *Cryptosporidium*, although contact times need to be 4 hours, an inconvenience on the trail.

Ultraviolet Light. There are several products on the market that use ultraviolet light (UV). UV light is a well-established disinfectant. It inactivates viruses, bacteria, and protozoa; does not require chemicals; and does not alter taste. There is no overdose danger, but at the same time there is no residual disinfection power.

Filtration

At this writing there are over 40 different water filtration products on the market. Filtration physically removes solid materials and microorganisms by forcing water through a filter element. Filter elements can be ceramic cartridges, fiberglass, or structured or labyrinth mediums of dense, honeycombed material.

Several types of filters are available with pore sizes small enough to filter *Giardia* and *Cryptosporidium* cysts, as well as bacteria. A 0.2-micron filter (the number refers to the pore size in the filter medium) is a common standard. Most bacteria are removed by 0.2 micron filters, protozoa by 1.0 micron filters. These are believed to be the common waterborne pathogens in the North American backcountry. If you're traveling outside of North America, or in areas with a lot of people and poor sanitation, viruses are more of a risk and a purifier may be the better choice.

Viruses are too small to be reliably eliminated by field water filtration. Some filters, labeled purifiers, kill viruses by passing water through an iodine or chlorine impregnated resin or by trapping them in a filter medium that carries an electrostatic charge.

Filters are more convenient on the trail than boiling water, and filtration may reduce the amount of iodine or chlorine necessary to chemically purify water. Filters can be expensive, costing from $40 to $250. Also, they may clog or develop undetectable leaking cracks.

FOODBORNE ILLNESS

Microbes such as bacteria, viruses, and fungi live everywhere. They're in the soil, in water, on our hands, in our noses and mouths. Many are harmless to us. Some cause illness either through the toxins they produce or as a side effect of colonizing the digestive tract. We can expose ourselves to these organisms by drinking contaminated water or through poor hygiene practices in the kitchen. Bacteria such as *Staphylococcus, Shigella*, and *Salmonella* are common sources of foodborne illness. If we give these creatures a place to live, such as a dirty cookpot, they can quickly multiply or produce enough toxin to make us sick.

With the luxury of modern sanitation, we don't give much thought to hygiene. We're protected by flush toilets, effective waste disposal and sewer systems, reliably disinfected tap water, readily available hot water, and proximity to advanced medical care. Proper human waste disposal, hand and utensil washing, food preparation, and water disinfection need to become habits in the wilderness. A river guide with poor kitchen hygiene was the source of food poisoning for many of the people on his trip. We suspect that most episodes of flulike and diarrheal illness on NOLS courses are caused by poor kitchen and personal sanitation.

Hygiene in the Wilderness Kitchen

These are practices NOLS has found helpful in reducing the incidence of foodborne illness on our expeditions.

Cook Food Thoroughly. Food that is dry or has a high salt or sugar content inhibits bacterial growth. Moist food that is low in salt and sugar is a good medium for growth, especially if it is warm. Protect yourself by cooking food completely; boil your pasta, beans, and rice; cook your meat until it is no longer red (ideally 170°F or 77°C).

Eat Cooked Food Promptly. Heat destroys most bacteria. Cold keeps bacteria from multiplying. Keep cooked food hot or cold, but don't keep it long. The optimal temperature zone for bacterial growth is between 45° and 140°F (7° and 60°C). In only a short period—within an hour in ideal warm and moist conditions—bacteria can multiply to become the source of diarrhea.

Avoid Leftovers. Storing cooked food without refrigeration invites disaster. Plan meals so that all food is consumed when served. Besides promoting bacterial growth, keeping leftovers creates a waste disposal problem and attracts animals such as bears.

Cold weather trips have the advantage of natural refrigeration. If leftovers are quickly cooled in air temperatures that stay below 38°F (3.5°C) and the meal is reheated completely, your risk of foodborne illness is less, but not zero. It's always safer to avoid leftovers. Heat-resistant toxins and microbes may colonize stored cooked food. If you do eat leftover food, make sure that the food is hot throughout the dish, not just on the surface. A crispy exterior does not mean that the interior has been well heated.

Clean Pots, Pans, and Utensils. Dirty pots, pans, and utensils are ideal surfaces for microbial life. Cleaning grease and food in the wilderness can be a challenge, especially if water is scarce. Plan ahead to minimize leftovers. Use sand or snow to scour pots, then rinse with hot water. Hard work to remove food residue can minimize the water needed for a final rinse.

Dish soap helps clean, but it must be rinsed well to avoid diarrhea and must be disposed of properly to leave no trace. Use a strainer to filter out large food particles, which are packed out. Scatter the remaining waste water widely away from camp and water sources.

Boil cooking utensils daily. Immersing clean utensils in your water pot as you boil the morning hot drink water will help continue the sanitizing process. Bacteria, viruses, and protozoa will be killed as the water is disinfected by the heat.

Large groups frequently use group cooking setups with chlorine rinses as an important step in keeping utensils clean. The three-bucket method begins with a hot soapy water scrub, then a warm water rinse, and finally a 1-minute immersion in a chlorine rinse bucket. Prepare this 100 to 150 ppm solution by adding 1 tablespoon of 4 to 6 percent chlorine bleach per gallon of water or one-quarter tablet of Effersan, a commercially available chlorine tablet. Air-dry the cooking gear.

Keep Kitchen Surfaces and Utensils Clean. Keep the food preparation surface and your utensils clean. Between the grocery store and dinner, your food can be contaminated many different ways. Dirty hands can reach inside, touch, and contaminate the food. Avoid this by pouring food from a bag or box. The spoon used to taste the soup may also be the spoon used to stir or serve. The cook may sneeze or cough and spread germs over dinner. The spatula may be placed on the ground or in a grubby food sack, then used to stir your pasta. An organized and clean kitchen reduces the chance of this cross-contamination.

Rinse Fresh Fruit and Vegetables. The surfaces of fruit and vegetables can be contaminated. A rule of thumb is peel it, boil it, cook it, or avoid it.

Protect Food from Insects and Animals. Insects and animals are vectors of disease. Keeping flies and rodents from your food both protects you from disease and keeps the animal from becoming habituated to humans as a source of food.

Don't Share. Sharing your resources, energy, wisdom, and companionship is good expedition behavior. Sharing your microbes with your tent mate is not. Keep your handkerchief, water bottle, cup, bowl, spoon, and lip balm to yourself. Instead of reaching into a plastic bag for a handful of raisins and contaminating the entire bag, pour the raisins into your hand. Serve food with the serving utensil, not your personal spoon. An ill person or one with open cuts on his or her hands should not prepare food. It takes only one person to be the source of a groupwide illness.

Wash Your Hands. Lastly, but most importantly, wash your hands! Keep nails trimmed and clean. Microbes live on the skin. Hands are an excellent and common tool for transporting these creatures from person to person. Regular hand washing does not sterilize your hands, but it does reduce the chance of infection. Ideally, you should use hot water, lots of soap, and a thorough rinse after using the latrine. Practically speaking, in the wilderness, you'll wash with cold water. At a minimum, you should do this before preparing, serving, or eating food. Large expeditions or base camps often set up a hand-washing station near a latrine or outhouse or in a central camp location. Waterless soaps are an option when water is not available or as an extra precaution after hands have been rinsed of grease and dirt.

Using natural toilet paper—leaves, sticks, rocks, or snow—reduces the paper you use and when done properly, this method is as sanitary as regular toilet paper. But you need to be proficient to avoid contaminating your hands with fecal material. And of course, always wash your hands afterward.

FINAL THOUGHTS

Some people think that contaminated water accounts for most infectious diarrhea in the U.S. wilderness. Person-to-person exchange from poor kitchen and personal hygiene practices is also thought to be a leading cause. Outside the wilderness, the most common route for infection is believed to be from person to person via hand-to-mouth contact or from contaminated utensils. Infection rates increase with close contact and poor hygiene. Habits of cleanliness and hygiene are essential to health and safety in the wilderness.

Your choice among boiling, filtering, or chemically disinfecting your water will depend on how contaminated the water might be, personal preference, fuel availability, group size, cost, and reliability. None of the water disinfection methods are foolproof. Each has its limitations, and each must be done correctly. They reduce but do not eliminate the risk of getting sick from drinking water. Their benefit is a reduced chance of becoming ill from bad water.

HYDRATION

INTRODUCTION

NOLS instructors constantly harp on hydration, urging their students to drink. They issue liter water bottles and large insulated mugs. They carry water in the desert and melt snow with a passion in winter environments.

Dehydration as the primary cause of an evacuation at NOLS is rare, but addressing hydration on the trail is a fact of life for wilderness travelers.

Dehydration is a contributing factor to hypothermia, heat exhaustion, heatstroke, and frostbite. Dehydration worsens fatigue, decreases the ability to exercise efficiently, and reduces mental alertness. Often the fatigue, irritability, poor thinking, body aches, and headache at the end of a day are the first signs of dehydration. Even by itself, dehydration can be a life-threatening medical problem.

PHYSIOLOGY OF WATER BALANCE

Humans are bags of water. We hear through a medium of water, the brain is cushioned by fluid, and the joints are lubricated by fluid. Blood is 90 percent water, and every biochemical reaction takes place in a medium of water.

Outside the wilderness, we give little thought to hydration. Air conditioning, heating, and lack of exercise enable us to avoid fluid stress most of the time. In the outdoors, we exercise daily at high levels. Exercise causes water loss through sweating, breathing, and metabolism. In the outdoors, we adjust directly to the environment, whether hot or cold. In the desert, we sweat to lose heat. In the cold, we lose water to moisten the cold air we breathe.

In the outdoors, hydration is not as simple as turning on the tap. It's harder to get water in the outdoors; we lose more of it responding to the environment, and we need more of it to maintain health. In the desert, we carry water, ration water, and spend a lot of time searching for water. Our activity patterns may be altered to reduce loss. We rest during the hours of the hot, midday sun; we work in the cool dawn and evening. In the winter, we must melt the water we drink—a time-consuming process. There is always the difficulty of disinfecting potentially contaminated water sources.

Assessment of Hydration
At L in the SAMPLE History explore fluid intake and output, not just today, but over the past several days. Dehydration can be cumulative. The signs and symptoms mimic altitude illness, hypothermia, fatigue, and heat exhaustion. The key to assessment is suspicion.

General symptoms of a negative water balance are fatigue, heat oppression, thirst, irritability, dizziness, dark concentrated urine, and headache. We experience mental deterioration, decreased group cooperation, vague discomfort, lack of energy and appetite, flushed skin, impatience, sleepiness, nausea. A seriously dehydrated patient—a rare event in the wilderness—appears to have signs of shock: rapid pulse; pale, sweaty skin; weakness; and nausea. Mental deterioration presents itself as loss of balance and changes in mental awareness. Tenting—in which the skin forms a tent shape when pinched—is a sign of serious dehydration. Normal skin is sufficiently hydrated to collapse; the tent stays in place in severe dehydration.

Treatment of Dehydration
A mildly dehydrated patient—and all wilderness travelers—should drink clear water to replace fluids. It is the best fluid for hydration. Cool water is absorbed faster than warm water.

Electrolyte replacement drinks can help, although some people find they are too sweet. Sugar increases the time it takes for fluid to be absorbed from the stomach. Coffee and tea contain caffeine, a diuretic that stimulates the kidneys to excrete fluid. Some experts consider this effect overrated, but regardless, coffee, tea, and alcohol should be avoided when rehydrating. Alcohol also increases urine production and fluid loss.

A severely dehydrated patient may have electrolyte imbalances as well as a fluid deficit. Such a patient cannot be rehydrated in the field and must be evacuated to a hospital for intravenous fluid therapy.

Hyponatremia

Just as it's possible to become dehydrated, we can get into trouble by drinking too much water. The scenario is a hot weather hiker drinking far too much water. You are saturated with water, your blood sodium is low and you have a case of hyponatremia, also known as water intoxication.

Signs and symptoms include impaired exercise performance, nausea and vomiting, headache, and bloating to the hands and feet. Altered mental status and seizures can occur as the brain swells from too much fluid.

The assessment of hyponatremia versus heat exhaustion or dehydration depends on an accurate history. Be suspicious if the patient has a high fluid intake—several liters in the last few hours.

Patients with an altered mental status should be evacuated without any additional fluid intake. Patients with mild to moderate symptoms and a normal mental status can be treated in the field. Have the patient rest in the shade with little to no fluid intake and a gradual intake of salty foods. Oral electrolyte replacement drinks are low in sodium and high in water and may not help as much as you anticipate.

FINAL THOUGHTS

There are several cornerstones to good health in the outdoors: staying warm and dry, eating well, resting, camping comfortably, washing hands, climbing slowly at altitude, and staying hydrated.

How much water should you drink to stay healthy in the wilderness? Hydration needs vary from person to person, climate to climate, activity to activity. Experience is invaluable. Three to 4 liters a day is a good rule of thumb, with another liter added for cold or high-altitude conditions. Thirst is a good indicator. If you are thirsty, drink. Urine color and volume are helpful indicators; darker, smelly, more concentrated urine is an indicator of dehydration.

CHAPTER 24 | DENTAL EMERGENCIES

INTRODUCTION

Enduring a dental problem in the wilderness, several days from a dentist, can be an uncomfortable experience. There are simple field treatments for broken teeth or fillings, toothaches, and gum irritations that can make life more comfortable during the evacuation. Although we do not experience many dental problems on NOLS courses, they account for 10 percent of problems seen among trekkers visiting the Himalayan Rescue Association clinics.

BROKEN TEETH OR FILLINGS

Lost fillings cause discomfort if hot or cold liquids or spicy foods touch the exposed tooth tissue. Exposure of the nerve, pulp, artery, or vein by a lost filling or a broken tooth causes pain. Various temporary filling materials are available for stopgap treatment of broken teeth or fillings. Cavit is a premixed compound available from your dentist. A nonprescription temporary filling available in many dental emergency kits is a combination of zinc oxide powder (not the ointment) and a topical anesthetic. NOLS staff have even had success using sugarless gum and ski wax to cover loose fillings and broken teeth.

Rinse the broken tooth or filling thoroughly before covering with a temporary filling. Roll the temporary material into a small ball and gently press it into the hole in the tooth, sealing the exposed tissue.

A broken or avulsed tooth should be gently rinsed off and slowly and gently placed back in the hole. Irrigate the tooth, but don't scrub it—you may remove tissue that can help the tooth survive. If you can't replace it, save the tooth for replacement. Hank's Balanced Salt Solution, (available as Save-A-Tooth) is the medium of choice. Milk, regardless of fat content, is acceptable (as is powdered milk). Next in line, but still decent choices, are physiological saline, saliva, and water. You can also wrap the tooth in gauze and have the patient carry it between the cheek and gum or in a cool place. For a good prognosis, a tooth must be replaced within 30 minutes and receive the care of a dentist within a week.

If the socket is bleeding, it can be packed to place pressure on the tissue. A slightly moist tea bag makes an acceptable packing material. In fact, the tannic acid in nonherbal tea promotes clotting.

TOOTHACHES

Exposure of the pulp from a dental cavity can cause pain. In the backcountry, treatment is limited to pain medications, antibiotics, and avoiding excessively hot, cold, or spicy foods. A temporary filling material may protect the pulp and any exposed nerve.

ORAL IRRITATIONS AND INFECTIONS

General mouth irritation is usually due to poor hygiene and can be treated with vigorous brushing and rinses with water.

Swelling around teeth or gums is an indicator of an infection. On remote expeditions, treatment with antibiotics and drainage of the infection may be considered. Evacuation to a dentist is the best treatment and the only choice on less remote trips in which there is no access to a physician or antibiotics.

FINAL THOUGHTS

Preparation for a wilderness expedition includes a visit to your dentist to identify and treat any potential problems. In the field, brush and floss regularly. Anyone who has experienced the woes of a toothache, loose filling, or dental infection in the wilderness knows that the need for dental hygiene does not cease when we venture into the woods.

CHAPTER 25 | COMMON NON-URGENT MEDICAL PROBLEMS

INTRODUCTION

These topics are often mislabeled as "common" and "simple" medical problems. They are indeed common. The data NOLS has been keeping for over 28 years on field medical incidents tells us that flulike illness (colds, upper respiratory infections, sore throat, fever, headaches) and gastrointestinal problems (nausea, vomiting, diarrhea, constipation) are 43 percent of reported illness and dwarf all other reported illness categories.

They are not necessarily simple. These symptoms are common to many different medical presentations and can occasionally be the initial symptoms of more serious clinical conditions. Gastrointestinal symptoms (nausea, vomiting, and diarrhea) are usually caused by a "stomach bug," or "stomach flu." Respiratory symptoms (cough, congestion, runny nose, sore throat) are usually viral upper respiratory infections, a "cold" or "flu." All viral illnesses can also cause a headache, malaise, fatigue, low-grade fever, muscle aches, and body aches.

The challenge to the wilderness leader is knowing how to manage these and deciding when someone is sick enough to warrant an evacuation.

FLULIKE ILLNESS

Often these illnesses (colds, upper respiratory infections, sore throat, fever, headaches) are a viral infection of the nasal passages and throat that causes a runny nose, sore throat, cough, sneezing, headache, mild fever, muscle aches, and malaise. "Colds" are self-limiting, but these infections can linger several weeks, despite all of our remedies. They are most often transmitted by contaminated hands and, less com-

Signs and Symptoms of Flulike Illness

- Fever
- Headache
- Muscle aches and malaise
- Nasal congestion and coughing

monly, although possible, as an aerosol. Cover your cough!

Upper Respiratory Infection (URI)

This is a viral or bacterial infection that affects the sinuses, pharynx, larynx, or bronchi. They are uncomfortable for the patient, but usually self-limiting.

Signs and Symptoms of Upper Respiratory Infection

- Increased mucous production
- Cough, sometimes productive
- Sore throat
- Fever
- Malaise

Sore Throat

The most common causes of a sore throat are simple dryness due to altitude and dehydration and viral infections such as the common cold. Strep throat, roughly 10 percent of sore throats, is caused by bacteria (*Streptococcus*) and needs a culture to confirm. We can be suspicious if the throat is beefy red with white pus spots and accompanied by fever, headache, vomiting, and—less likely—accompanied by respiratory signs and symptoms.

Fever

Fever is the body's resetting of our internal thermostat triggered by the immune system's response to an infection. It is usually accompanied by other signs and symptoms of illness.

Headache

The most common cause of headaches in the backcountry is dehydration. Other causes include muscular tension, altitude, vascular disorders, trauma, brain tumor, and carbon monoxide (CO) poisoning.

Treatment Principles for Flulike Illness. The management for flulike illness is based on treating symptoms to help the patient feel better while these illnesses run their course. We also need to recognize when this isn't a common and simple presentation and the patient should be evacuated for evaluation by a physician. Hydration is important, as is hygiene, especially hand washing. These illnesses are communicable, and we want to avoid spreading them through the group.

Rest and patience are cornerstones of treatment. Some of these illnesses may respond to antibiotics, but most are self-limiting—they can take a week or more to resolve. People don't like to be sick, and impatience will drive decisions to try treatments or to leave the wilderness. Pain medications (acetaminophen, aspirin, or nonsteroidal anti-inflammatory drugs) for headache and muscle aches are fine. Decongestants (e.g., pseudoephedrine), and anticough medications can treat upper respiratory symptoms. Bland diets are best for gastrointestinal distress.

Evacuation Guidelines
When are these common problems not simple? Evacuation is recommended for flulike illness if:
- Fever persists for more than 48 hours or is high (>104°F/39°C).
- The patient develops a stiff neck, severe headache, difficulty breathing, or wheezing.
- Signs or symptoms of pneumonia develop. This is usually associated with increasing shortness of breath, decreasing exercise tolerance, worsening malaise, and weakness with a predominance of cough.
- The patient is unable to tolerate any oral fluids more than 48 hours, especially if there are diarrhea volume losses, fever, or vomiting.
- The sore throat is in conjunction with an inability to swallow water and maintain adequate hydration.
- The sore throat is associated with a fever and a beefy red throat with white patches.
- The headache does not respond to treatment, is sudden and severe, or is associated with altered mental status.

GASTROINTESTINAL PROBLEMS

Gastroenteritis is an inflammation of the gastrointestinal system. Diarrhea is persistent loose watery stools. These are common backcountry medical conditions. A recent study on Denali showed that a third of the climbers had diarrhea, and that their hygiene practices could use improvement. We may want to blame it on the water, but fecal-oral contamination is probably a more common cause. Wash your hands!

The signs and symptoms of the "mung," as nausea, vomiting, and diarrhea are often called by NOLS students, are familiar.

Treatment of Gastroenteritis. Hydration is a focus of our treatment. Persistent diarrhea and vomiting can cause dehydration and electrolyte problems. If vomiting has been severe, consider electrolyte replacement solutions. Antiemetic medications (e.g., meclizine, Compazine) can be helpful in managing vomiting. Antidiarrheal medication (e.g., Immodium) can be helpful for persistent diarrhea.

Try a bland diet. If you're in a developing country, check current recommendations for antibiotic use and diarrhea.

Signs and Symptoms of Mild Gastroenteritis

- Gradually increasing, diffuse abdominal discomfort, often worse in the lower quadrants
- Intermittent cramping, usually diffuse and not localized with frequent loose stools
- Hyperactive bowel sounds
- Nausea and vomiting, occasionally low-grade fever
- Usually resolves within 1 to 3 days

Signs and Symptoms of Severe Gastroenteritis

- Persistent or worsening pain over 24 hours, especially if the pain becomes localized and constant
- Inability to tolerate fluids
- Stools with blood and mucus
- Signs and symptoms of shock
- Fever above 102°F (38°C)

Evacuation Guidelines

When are these gastrointestinal problems not simple? Evacuation is recommended if:

- There is bloody or coffee-ground vomit, the vomiting persists despite treatment, or the patient is unable to hydrate.
- The diarrhea becomes bloody or persists despite treatment, or the patient is unable to hydrate.
- Abdominal pain persists or worsens over 24 hours; spiking fever, bloody diarrhea, or dehydration should trigger an evacuation.
- The patient is unable to tolerate oral fluids for more than 48 hours, especially if accompanied by diarrhea or vomiting.

EYE INJURIES

Foreign Body in the Eye

Usually eyelashes, tears, and blinking defend the surface of the eye from foreign particles. If a foreign object, perhaps a speck of dust, dirt, or leaf, lands on the eye or inside the eyelid, it can be painful and irritating.

Examine the eye carefully. Don't rub it. Pull the lower lid down and have the patient look up. This allows you to see the lower part of the eye and inside the lower eyelid. Flip the upper lid over a small stick or cotton applicator and have the patient look down. This allows you to see the upper part of the eye and inside the upper eyelid.

Remove foreign material by irrigating with clean water or—if it's on the eyelid and not the eye itself—with gentle use of a piece of gauze. If the object is stuck, leave it in place. Never try to remove something from the eye with force. Close the eye and bandage it shut with a folded gauze pad or sterile eye patch, and evacuate the patient.

The eye may feel irritated. This may be an abrasion to the surface of the cornea. Irrigate the eye. The patient may be more comfortable if you patch the eye shut. If the irritation is very painful or persists more than 24 hours, take the patient to a physician.

THE EYE

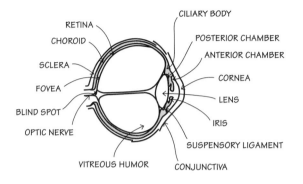

If the foreign object is impaled in the eye, do not remove it. The eye contains precious fluids that may leak out, and extracting the object can cause additional damage. Stabilize the object in place with gauze; cover and protect it against being banged. Because the eyes normally track together—when one moves, the other follows—bandage both eyes to prevent movement. Evacuate the patient.

Subconjunctival Hemorrhage

A subconjunctival hemorrhage is bleeding under the conjunctiva, the outer covering of the eye, and over the sclera, the white part of the eye. A subconjunctival hemorrhage may happen spontaneously after hard coughing, increasing blood pressure, or a direct blow to the eye. Most cases have no specific history and are noticed by someone else. Usually the hemorrhage is on only one side. By itself, it rarely indicates a significant problem and is not a reason for evacuation. If it is the result of a blow to the eye, examination by a physician is advised.

Hyphema is bleeding into the anterior chamber of the eye, often after a blow to the eye. Blood may be seen by looking at the iris or the colored part of the eye. A patient with hyphema should always be evacuated.

Evacuation Guidelines
- Hyphema (blood in the anterior chamber of the eye).
- Any loss of vision, blurred or double vision.
- An object impaled in the eye.
- Acute, severe eye pain.
- A foreign body in the eye that you can't remove.
- Eye irritation that persists more than 24 hours.

LEADERSHIP, TEAMWORK, AND COMMUNICATION

INTRODUCTION

In 1989, the center engine on a DC-10 passenger aircraft with 296 people on board malfunctioned over the Great Plains. Severed hydraulic lines crippled the pilot's ability to control the plane. The three-person crew's response to this crisis was a model of effective communication and teamwork. Working together, and using input from a pilot traveling as a passenger, they improvised a means of controlling the aircraft with the throttles.

Skilled aircrews, rescue teams, and wilderness leaders have found themselves in challenging situations in which communication, teamwork, and leadership are not optimum and things don't work out well. Aircraft have crashed because flight crews failed to perform a routine task or a team member didn't speak up to report a problem. Ineffective communication of snowpack and terrain observation has contributed to avalanche incidents. Maps and headlamps left behind have embarrassed wilderness travelers caught in approaching darkness. Experts have unclipped from their climbing anchors, avoiding a dangerous situation only when their observant partners noticed the error.

Human error is a prominent cause of many accidents and critical incidents in team activities. NASA estimates that 70 percent of airline accidents involve some degree of human error. The Teton Park rescue rangers estimate that human error contributes significantly to most backcountry and mountain incidents. When the airline industry realized that well-trained and technically proficient crews could crash airworthy aircraft because of inadequate crew communication or interaction, it developed a series of programs—known as crew resource management or human factors in aviation—to focus on teamwork, communication, and leadership. The DC-10 crew had this training, and they credit it with helping them manage their emergency.

NOLS LEADERSHIP SKILLS

Leadership at NOLS is timely and effective actions that direct or guide your group to set and achieve goals. In a wilderness medical or rescue scenario, leadership may involve taking charge of a patient or a scene, ensuring a sound assessment and competent treatment, and deciding on the need for and urgency of evacuation. Or it may involve leading a litter carry or technical rescue in remote terrain. The many possible leadership styles—directive, consultative, or consensus building, for example—all use a core group of skills and behaviors. This chapter blends NOLS leadership skills (competence, self-awareness, tolerance for adversity and uncertainty, communication, vision and action), with lessons from crew resource management, and discusses how they apply to leadership, teamwork, and communication in a wilderness medical and rescue.

Competence
Competence is our proficiency in technical (outdoor and first aid) and group management skills. Ideally, our outdoor, first aid, and group management skills are sharp, and we train to keep them fresh.

If he or she is wise enough to capitalize on the abilities of the team, the leader does not need to be a master of every group management or technical skill. For example, in a large rescue operation, a leader may not be the most experienced medical person or the technical rescue system expert. He or she can delegate this task. What the leader needs is sound and timely information from the medical and rescue people to help the leader make good decisions.

Share Knowledge and Experience. A directive leader, a common style in a crisis, does not have to act in isolation. Ideally, the leader utilizes the team's skill and experience to make the best decisions. As with effective air crews, the effective wilderness leader both leads and teaches. He or she takes the initiative and time to make sure that pertinent details on the medical or evacuation plan are shared with team members. Techniques can be explained and practiced before use on the patient. Knowledge and communication strengthen the team. Everyone feels respected and engaged. Higher-quality decisions are more likely to be made.

Self-Awareness

Self-aware leaders learn from their experiences by acknowledging their abilities and successes, facing their limitations, admitting their mistakes, seeking feedback from others, and working to understand themselves. They know themselves well enough to know their bad habits and their tendencies, perhaps they slip into the procrastination syndrome, the hurry-up syndrome, the do-it-all syndrome, or the perfectionist syndrome. The following are some behaviors that help avert these patterns.

Avoid Self-Imposed Workloads. Self-imposed workloads create stress. A lack of situational awareness when mountaineering (e.g., ignoring building afternoon thunderheads) may cause a hasty descent in rain, wind, and lightning. Conversely, watch for a self-imposed and unnecessary hurry-up syndrome—working fast when you don't need to and missing details or failing to complete procedures. There are phases to operations; some need immediate action, others have the time to be careful and thoughtful.

Recognize and Resolve Fatigue. Actively plan and schedule for transition and rest periods. In the excitement of an emergency, you tend to ignore the effect of fatigue on your performance. Plan ahead, and prepare for the night shift. Will you need to rest, feed people, or find fresh folks to help carry the litter? Outdoor leaders and rescue personnel often work in an organizational culture where fitness and competence are valued. They may have unrealistic attitudes about their vulnerability to stress and fatigue. The author learned a valuable lesson when he was assigned to the night shift on a multiday search. Not wanting to rest when others were working hard, he found something to do. The incident commander noticed this, confirmed that he was on his night shift, and told him in no uncertain terms, "It's your job to sleep. I need you at 100 percent tonight."

Recognize and Report Work Overloads. Avoid trying to fix everything yourself and taking on too many tasks. Leaders need to be able to step back and keep their eyes on the big picture. The culture of emergency services and outdoor leadership can drive a strong work ethic and a sense that it is inappropriate for the helper to ask for help. It's a measure of wisdom and maturity to be able to say, "I'm overloaded. Can you help?"

Reflect and Learn from Your Experiences. Identify not only the technical details of an action—snowpack analysis, map reading, the thoroughness of a patient assessment, the gear that worked and the gear that failed—but as well, consider quality of communication and teamwork, the decisions, the distractions of the mosquitoes. What went well, what could have gone better, and when were you more lucky than competent? Reflect on and learn from these experiences.

Tolerance for Adversity and Uncertainty

Wilderness medicine can be a world of lengthy transport times, arduous conditions, inclement weather, and lack of resources—a test of any leader's tolerance for adversity and uncertainty. Wilderness medical leaders must be able to live with uncertainty, endure hard work and challenge, and make do or improvise what they lack.

Prepare for Contingencies. Weather will turn bad. Helicopters will be delayed. Radios will break. Stable patients will take turns for the worse. Spring snow that's firm and supports weight in the morning can become soggy pudding in the afternoon. Stay ahead of the curve by analyzing your plan over and over and asking, what if? What if one of us sprains an ankle? It's sunny and warm now, but can I keep the patient dry if it rains?

Get Ready for the Long Haul. It's easy to be focused during the initial stages of a crisis. In wilderness medicine, however, the rubber often meets the road when you move into the long hours of work in difficult conditions as you carry a litter or wait through a storm for the helicopter. Leaders understand this change. They stay connected to the group, keeping everyone informed and focused on the task. They make sure that team members are eating, drinking, and staying warm and dry. They keep the process moving and energy and enthusiasm high.

Be Comfortable with Uncertainty. Medicine is full of uncertainty. There are times we don't know exactly what injury or illness the patient may have. We often work without the information we need, in uncertain and changing weather, in a fluid and evolving event. Learn to be comfortable in this arena; it's wilderness medicine.

Communication

Effective leaders master communication skills. They have the courage to state what they think, feel, and want and they listen with openness to different viewpoints. Leaders keep their groups informed and give clear, usable, and timely feedback. They provide a safe forum where each group member can discuss ideas and contribute to the decision-making process.

Build a Team Environment. Build an environment that acknowledges and respects the skills, experiences, and contributions of team members. Your team members should clearly understand their roles and tasks: "Sandy, thanks for staying alert for hazards. I'll stay at the head of the patient and monitor the airway and c-spine. Jack, finish the head-to-toe assessment and measure the vital signs. Jill, find a foam pad and sleeping bag for the patient."

Establish a team concept and environment for open communication. If there is an urgent need for action, you may need to focus someone who is rambling or talking about a non-pertinent issue. In general, listen with patience, do not interrupt or "talk over," and do not rush through a discussion. Include as many team members as possible in the communication flow: brief and update them as needed on weather, delays, plans, and schedules. Students in outdoor education groups, clients in guided trips, helpful bystanders, and local rescue personnel may all be part of your team.

Clearly State and Acknowledge Decisions. Clearly state and acknowledge operational decisions to team members. Restate communications, clarify, and question to see if everyone understands: "We're going to rig an anchor here and use it to belay the patient to the ground. Let's go around the group and have everyone say what they will do."

Effective Inquiry: Ask and Listen. Foster an environment where questions are asked regarding actions and decisions. If people do not understand, they should be encouraged to speak up, to ask for clarification of unclear instructions or confusing or uncertain situations. For example:

> I don't understand this technique. . . . I'm not sure what you want me to do. . . . Why are we putting a tourniquet on this snakebite wound? I thought tourniquets weren't indicated for snakebite. . . . You said you can't hear breath sounds. Do you mean it's too noisy to listen or the patient is not breathing?

Give and Accept Appropriate Feedback. Give positive and constructive performance feedback at appropriate times. Make it a positive learning experience for the whole crew—feedback must be specific to the issue at hand, objective, based on observable behavior, and given with respect and politeness. Likewise, accept feedback objectively and non-defensively. Inhibiting communication by having an unreceptive response to feedback has played a role in accidents.

Use Appropriate Advocacy and Assertion. Foster an environment in which your team can speak up and state their information until there is resolution and decision. There are sad tales of a team member or leader making a mistake and another team member having the correct information but not speaking up or asserting his or her perspective. For example: "I'm uncomfortable with your delay in starting an evacuation. John has a persistent high fever. I think we should take him to a doctor."

You may need to provide a forum for communicating views. As a leader, model advocacy by checking in with your team and listening to their responses. "Are you getting enough direction from me about what you need to be doing? If anyone disagrees, please speak up."

Address Conflict. Disagreements may occur. Personalities may clash. Unresolved conflicts can impede communication and cooperation and contribute to accidents. The leader may need to step in, identify the issue, and ask the team to put aside interpersonal differences until the emergency is over, addressing only immediate issues that are impeding progress or affect safety. Later, when the crisis has passed, it's important to debrief these issues and emotions, work to resolve the conflict, and increase the team's ability to deal with its differences. A conflict during a crisis often means that expectations, roles, and responsibilities are unclear. People don't know what is expected of them or others, are missing information, or don't have a sense of the big picture. It's the leader's job to clarify structure and expectations.

Vision and Action

Leaders assure that the group knows the mission. They keep team members informed about the plan and each person's task. They are decisive when the situation requires decisiveness and patient when it is appropriate to wait or gather more information. They are forward looking and flexible, revising the plan as necessary.

Set an Appropriate Tone for the Situation. Set an appropriate tone of urgency. If the situation isn't dire, you may need to slow down your team. "Folks, let's take it easy. We've finished the assessment, and the scene is safe. Next we have to splint Bill's fractured leg and then log-roll him onto a sleeping bag and treat for shock. Let's take it one step at a time." Conversely, you may have to remind them to keep conversation and attention on the situation at hand. "Let's worry about dinner later. Right now, let's RICE and evaluate this ankle sprain." Leaders ensure that nonoperational factors such as social interaction or conversation do not interfere with necessary tasks (e.g., small talk does not interfere with climbing signals).

Scene Awareness. Researchers observing NASA shuttle crews call this vigilance or watchfulness. Many people call it situational awareness. Pause after scene size-up and initial assessment to look over the scene. Seek hazards. Formulate a plan for the next few minutes, but be careful of the trap of creating too much organization. Many scenarios are fluid. Stay alert, and flexible.

Workload Management: State Clear Expectations of Roles and Responsibilities. Make clear roles, responsibilities, and the big picture:

> I'll keep myself visible and in the open in case the rest of the group comes by. John, you're in charge of Fred and Sally. Scout for the best trail through these boulders back to camp. Check back with me before a half hour is up. Allison, you're in charge of patient care. Stay with the patient and monitor vitals. Blow your whistle three times if you need me.

A team works well when people know what they have to do and have a sense of where they fit in the big picture. As well, clear expectations prevent people from doing unnecessary tasks or getting in one another's way. Let others know what you expect of them, and what they can expect from you. "Folks, let's splint this arm first, then move the patient to the litter."

Provide Adequate Time for Completion of Tasks. Half-completed tasks—for example, flaps not adjusted on takeoff—have caused aircraft accidents. Backboard straps left loose when a team stops one task to start another are a real possibility on an emergency scene. Identify your key tasks, tell people what needs to be done, allow enough time, and complete each task—one by one.

Brief Effectively. Briefings are clear, complete, and interesting, and address team coordination and planning for potential problems. The team puts aside social conversation or low-priority tasks, pays attention, and asks clarifying questions. Expectations are set for handling possible deviations from normal operations or unusual conditions. For example: "We sent four people walking to the roadhead to ask for help carrying Pete. They should arrive tonight. If we don't hear from them by tomorrow noon, we'll send a second team."

A briefing should be brief. Short and concise briefings help people remember details. Several two- or three-minute briefings may be more effective than one 20-minute briefing. Keep it simple. Strive for the three-sentence briefing. Brief at phase changes: at the start, when the assessment is done, when you reach an obvious rest stop or obstacle in a litter carry. Brief to keep your team informed. Share information. State decisions and plans. Speak to both who will do it and how they will do it.

A Simple Briefing Format

Leader to team
- Here's what I think we face.
- Here's what I think we should do.
- Here's why.
- Here's what we should keep our eye on.
- Now, talk to me.

After Action Review/Hot Debrief
- What was planned?
- What actually happened?
- Why did it happen?
- What can we do next time?

Stay Vigilant during Both High and Low Workloads. Look around, check details, and check in with people when you're busy and when workload is low. It's easy to focus your attention when you're on duty and in the middle of the event. It's harder in the routine situation or when the initial excitement ebbs and the work of a long but apparently routine situation sets in. Accidents can happen when you overlook the obvious, missing the moment when you could have intervened or prevented a problem. How many of us have walked away from a rest break without looking around and noticing the water bottle and map left on the rock?

Prioritize Secondary Tasks. Prioritize secondary tasks to allow sufficient resources for dealing effectively with the important tasks. Talking about whether you will be able to continue your trip in the face of this illness may be the secondary task, the distraction. Feeding your team, having them gather personal gear, and preparing camp may be the primary tasks. Effective leaders keep their teams' eyes on the ball.

EXPEDITION BEHAVIOR

We have been focusing on leadership, but leaders need teams and teams need good expedition behavior. The two go hand in hand. Expedition behavior is a set of behaviors we value: working together, serving the mission, treating each other with dignity and respect. Expedition behavior is not about leading. It's an intentional choice to be a good teammate, a good follower, a good citizen.

Good expedition behavior is demonstrated by practical tangible tasks done to support the team. It's team members taking care of one another, watching for fatigue and hazards, lending a helping hand without being asked, and asking for help when needed. Good expedition behavior is treating people with respect and politeness. It is acting without being asked, without complaining, and with the good of the group in mind.

Service to the Mission. People engage in search and rescue for many reasons. We want to help people. We enjoy the wilderness. We're proud of using our skills. We want the challenge. Yet sometimes we're assigned boring tasks or we disagree with the plan. Regardless it's our job to see the boring task through to completion. It's our job to work with the team and within the plan. Let us never forget, the mission is the patient.

FINAL THOUGHTS

In my years of wilderness expedition, medicine, and rescue experience I have found that the medicine we can practice in the wilderness is often limited; sick people need doctors and hospitals. The quality of care we provide the patient often hinges, not on our first aid skill, but on the quality of our leadership, teamwork, and communication.

CHAPTER 27 | JUDGMENT AND DECISION-MAKING

INTRODUCTION

Patient care is a series of decisions ranging from the common and simple (whether to treat a blister) to the unusual yet significant (whether to evacuate someone with a bellyache). These decisions affect the patient's health, the safety of your expedition members, and the safety of those who may come to assist in your evacuation or rescue.

Along with the many tales of outdoor leaders showing good judgment when faced with a medical decision are stories of people missing the significance of signs and symptoms and delaying evacuation and tales of rescuers sent needlessly into harm's way. We want to support good judgment by being thoughtful and skilled decision-makers.

Judgment and decision-making are based on a process of forming an assessment, analyzing and comparing the information and options, and then laying down an opinion. Many decisions are simple and routine. We have the information and experience we need and thoughtful people to consult. Yet there are times when we must make decisions in the midst of uncertainty, challenged by missing data, conflicting information, and urgency. We're at the edge of our experience and training, and we're often on our own, making decisions without being able to consult a higher authority.

Humans have developed fascinating and complex ways to reach decisions, and we often do so without giving the process much thought. We may use a rule of thumb, follow a protocol or algorithm, or make a guess. We may act quickly based on experience, or gather information and make a reasoned decision. This chapter takes a brief tour of common ways we make decisions, their pros and cons, and some traps to avoid.

GUESSING

The self-aware decision-maker knows that we guess, sometimes unintentionally, and probably more often than we care to admit. Guessing, using intuition uninformed by data and possibly misinformed by experience, isn't always bad. If consequences are low, it saves time and provides the solace of action. However, when a person's health is at stake, we don't want to guess.

RULES OF THUMB

Heuristics, simple rules of thumb, are common problem-solving aids, mental shortcuts based on collective and personal experience. We use heuristics in everyday decisions, often without thinking. We "measure twice, cut once" to avoid error. We benefit from the cold-weather camping experience of our elders by adhering to the saw to "go to bed warm to sleep warm." We evaluate weather by considering the mariner's rhyme "red in the morning, sailor take warning; red at night, sailor's delight." We avoid the irritation of poison ivy by remembering "leaves of three, let them be."

Using mental shortcuts can be expeditious. We think, then act. Shortcuts are valuable tools as long as they are accurate and relevant to the decision we need to make. We trust heuristics because we assume they are proven over time and supported by statistics or science. But in fact, they may not be accurate in every context. "Red and yellow, kill a fellow. Red and black, venom lack" is used to identify the coral snake found in the United States. Unfortunately, if you cross the border into Mexico and head south, this heuristic doesn't work. There are coral snakes with red and black adjacent bands that are deadly. Be aware when you are using a heuristic, and consider whether it is both accurate and relevant to the situation at hand.

PROTOCOLS, TREATMENT, AND EVACUATION GUIDELINES

Medical professionals use protocols, standing orders, and algorithms to guide treatment and evacuation decisions. These are predetermined decision points that are helpful to guide the novice and remind the expert. They may be the local operating plans, lost person and medical protocols familiar to outdoor leaders. They may be the evacuation guidelines you read in this book.

It can be very helpful to have decisions made before you encounter the situation, especially if they are the work of thoughtful, careful, and experienced professionals. Thank goodness we don't need to choose the compression rate every time we do CPR. We can use the protocol of a minimum of 100 compressions per minute, the heuristic "push hard, push fast," or the memory of practicing to the beat of "Staying Alive."

Yet a word of caution: algorithms useful for classic signs and symptoms can discourage independent and creative thinking when the picture is vague. You may have a patient who does not trigger a protocol—for example, does not meet your program's abdominal pain triggers—but still warrants evacuation. You may be leading a peak climb, knowing you plan to turn around at a certain time, yet decide to descend earlier due to building weather. Protocols are not a substitute for judgment. Cookbooks are best used by thinking cooks who recognize when recipes need to be changed.

EXPERIENCE

We make decisions based on our experience. We recognize specific patterns, find clues within those patterns, and compare this to our experience. Experts intuitively and quickly recognize a situation and evaluate, accept, or reject choices. This is called the expert decision model, expert intuition, natural decision-making, or a pattern recognition model. It's fast: see the pattern, make the decision.

An experienced medical person can look at a patient's appearance, see subtle clues, recognize a pattern, and come up with a hunch as to what is wrong: "This guy is having a heart attack."

An experienced rescuer can look at a map and quickly know whether a litter-carry will be over shortly, or take all night.

The important word is experience. Most of us are outdoor professionals first and medical providers second. We need to be honest about our medical experience, or lack of it. We need to be candid about what we have learned from our experience—learning that often comes from acknowledging errors, which is challenging, as well as successes, which are easier to acknowledge. We need to be careful about reaching conclusions from one or two experiences or from interpretations of our experience that may be inaccurate. We can confuse correlation with cause, or fall into the trap of misperception, thinking the patient had one problem, when in fact he had another.

INFORMATION GATHERING MODEL— THE PATIENT ASSESSMENT SYSTEM (PAS)

The Patient Assessment System is decision-making based on the old-fashioned virtue of careful, deliberate, and systematic thinking. We gather information, weigh alternatives, and then decide.

Gather Information
The initial assessment identifies threats to life and the chief complaint, which will likely be the focal point of the decision. The SAMPLE history and head-to-toe exam complete the gathering of subjective and objective information.

Identify Options, Choices, Alternatives
The assessment, the problem list, catalogs our findings. The plan lists the alternatives and our treatment and evacuation decisions. There are many important decision points in wilderness medicine (such as deciding if abdominal pain warrants an evacuation) and less acute questions (such as determining the usability of an ankle injury), but the ultimate goal is identifying who is sick and who is not—hence the importance of good data-gathering in the PAS.

Are there clear boundaries on this decision, such as limits to your resources or route options? For example, there are no helicopters available or you cannot cross the river on the evacuation route. Do you have treatment or evacuation protocols or orders from your medical director or organization to guide or dictate your decision?

Decide, Implement, and Evaluate

In wilderness medicine we have extended patient contact time, which allows us to repeat our assessment to check unclear findings, to look for changes in our patient's status, and to evaluate the efficacy of our actions. Our decision-making continues throughout our patient care.

An organized analytical approach can be thoughtful, careful, and thorough. It also can be slow. There are certainly times when we don't have the time for this approach, yet consider that in wilderness medicine, we usually don't have the option for rapid transport. We can use time to help us make good decisions.

THE HUMAN HAZARD

There isn't a perfect way to make a decision; every method has its pros and cons. If you're self-aware as a leader, you are honest about your human frailties, tendencies and biases. Here are just a few of the dangers that lie in the fog of decision-making, and some thoughts on how to avoid them.

Cognitive Biases. Cognitive biases are thinking habits, both conscious and subconscious, built up over time and experience. We may think we are being thoughtful, but it's very human to have bias in what information we select, and what we observe. We may anchor our decision on a convenient diagnosis without considering options. We may fill in a blind spot in a pattern with information we desire, but information which is not really there.

Wishful Thinking. Wishful thinking is the familiar trap of making the terrain fit the map. In medicine this can cause us to attach a label to the patient despite discrepancies in the evidence.

Pattern Recognition Error. Cherry-picking only a few features of an illness can cause a pattern recognition error. We close our minds to new information and alternative explanations and solutions.

Common Diagnosis. When we hear "headache" in the wilderness we think "dehydration," the common diagnosis. Common things are common, yet we must be cognizant of the most potentially serious alternative diagnosis. Treat the patient for the statistically probable problems on your list and, in case you are wrong, consider the most serious possibility.

Emotional Hooks. Decision-making is not an objective and rational process free from the intrusion of emotion. Emotional hooks from recent or vivid scenarios affect our cognition and our judgment. Be wary about "going with your gut" when the gut is a strong emotion, positive or negative, about a patient.

"WHAT WERE YOU THINKING?"

Students of decision-making, those who want to be able to answer the question "what were you thinking?" develop the habit of mindful or reflective practice, the ability to think about their thinking. It's an intentional attentiveness to thoughts, sensations, emotions, interpretations, judgments, and heuristics. It's honest self-evaluation, pertinent feedback, attentive observation, an ability to take different perspectives, and presence of mind.

Honest Feedback. Reflective practitioners seek honest feedback. They need to know, as best they can, what really happened. Only by debriefing and reflecting can we truly learn whether the decision made was appropriate, whether it was the actual cause of the outcome and is worth repeating in the future. If we are not open to conflicting information and willing to admit error, we may base future decisions on an inconsequential intervention or a flawed observation.

Tolerate Uncertainty. Reflective practitioners see each situation as unique and avoid prematurely slapping a label on a problem and closing the mind. Clarify unclear information and language. Verify alleged facts. If you are not sure about your history or physical exam, go back and do it again. At the same time, tolerate uncertainty. You may not be able to answer all questions or gather all the data. Make the best decision with the information at hand.

Reflective practitioners are able to see a situation from multiple and opposing perspectives, intentionally considering other explanations and challenging their first impressions. Ask what is common, what is the worst case, and what can be ruled out.

Presence of Mind. Cultivate the presence of mind to be watchful, observant, open, curious, flexible, and present when faced with anxiety, uncertainty, and chaos. Rituals, as simple as pausing and taking a breath, can remind you to be mindful. Repetitive training can give you the confidence to perform tasks with competence, and give you the mental reserve to think.

Self-Aware. Be self-aware. "Did I ignore any data?" "What emotions are operative in me, in this situation?" "What about this situation is different?" "What assumptions am I making?" Everyone stumbles into decision-making traps. Self-awareness and watchfulness give you a better chance to catch yourself before you fall.

Communicate Effectively. Often the first step into the error trap is miscommunication. The medical error literature has many examples of vital signs, medical history, or drug doses incorrectly reported and leading to poor decisions from the cascade of flawed information. Listen actively. Restate key points. Use concise, distinctive speech, without mumbles or fillers, with recognized vocabulary, controlled tone of voice, and minimal jargon.

Use Your Team. Effective teams create a culture where the team members can pool their wisdom by asking questions, clarifying information, and understanding when to advocate for alternate perspectives.

FINAL THOUGHTS

The best wilderness medicine practitioners are lifelong learners. They willingly work on the rough edges of their competency to help them navigate the real world. Knowing that real world decision-making is not as simple as choosing the correct heuristic or protocol, they thrive on practicing both their skills and their judgment.

CHAPTER 28 | STRESS AND THE RESCUER

INTRODUCTION

First aid training has traditionally concentrated on treatment and transport: the nuts and bolts of assessment, splinting, and airway maintenance. The human elements of emergency medical care are equally important. We are beginning to recognize the impact of emergency stress on the rescuer as well as the victim.

Although there is limited data on wilderness rescuers, there is a growing body of literature on the effects of stress on emergency workers. Caring for the ill or injured, having responsibility for the lives and safety of others, is considered a significant stressor. Research is showing that high attrition rates, burnout, and stress-related illness are common in emergency personnel.

EFFECTS OF STRESS

A perceived threat or challenge or a change in the environment can cause stress—a state of physical or psychological arousal. Beneficial stress affects all living creatures and can be a positive factor in change, creativity, growth, and productivity. Healthy exercise that increases your physical capability is a good stress. Continuous hard exercise without rest or adequate nutrition can become a destructive force with negative effects on your health, your family, and your life.

You may be stressed by noises, confined spaces, extremes in weather, and other aspects of the environment. In the social environment, conflicts within a group, and conflicts with the boss or family members are all stressors. You're also stressed by inactivity and boredom.

Stress produces intricate biochemical changes in the body. The brain becomes more active; chemicals secreted by the endocrine system cause muscles to tighten, pupils to dilate, and heart rate, breathing rate, and blood pressure to increase. Protein, glucose, and antibody levels in the blood rise.

These physiological changes prepare you to meet a challenge by making you more alert and ready for physical activity. In the short term, they can be helpful. In the long term, or if the short-term stress is significant, the effects of stress can adversely affect your physical and psychological health by wearing you down and making you susceptible to a variety of physical and psychological problems. The surgeon general estimates that 80 percent of non-traumatic causes of death are actually stress-related disease such as coronary artery disease, high blood pressure, ulcers, and cancer.

STRESS ON THE JOB

The job demands of emergency personnel create an environment in which turnover and stress-related illness are common. Emergency situations may subject workers to noise such as wind, rushing water, screams, and sirens; to the confusion of the emergency scene; to having responsibility for the health and safety of patients and fellow rescuers in prolonged weather extremes; to difficult bystanders who may never be satisfied with the rescuer's performance; to equipment failures and inadequate equipment, which add to the difficulty of the situation; and to long hours of hard physical work. Lengthy rescues, rescues in which the patient dies, multiple-casualty incidents, and incidents in which emergency workers or friends are injured are particularly stressful.

Certainly emergency stress affects an outdoor leader or anyone thrown into the role of rescuer. Experience may help a person cope with these stresses, but it does not make him or her immune.

The leader of a notably difficult expedition experiences significant extra stress when weather, group dynamics, faulty equipment, or complex logistics combine to create a high-pressure situation. In addition to caring for the ill or injured under these difficult conditions, the leader continues to be responsible for the safety and welfare of the group.

ASSESSMENT: RECOGNIZING STRESS REACTIONS

Stress in the short term may produce fatigue, nausea, anxiety, fear, irritability, lightheadedness, headache, memory lapses, sleep disturbances, changes in appetite, loss of attention span, and indecision. These are normal reactions by normal people to abnormal events. A person experiencing an acute stress reaction may wander aimlessly on the scene, sit or stare blankly, or engage in erratic or irrational behavior.

If symptoms last for less than a month, it is an acute stress disorder. If symptoms persist, Post Traumatic Stress might be developing. Long-term effects of stress include difficulty concentrating, intrusive images (recurring dreams or sensations of the traumatic event), sleep disturbance, fatigue, and diseases such as ulcers, diabetes, and coronary artery disease. Emotional signs include depression, feelings of grief and anger, and a sense of isolation. Emergency workers suffering from cumulative stress may respond by avoiding emergency situations, taking excessive sick leave, or being easily aroused or startled. It is beyond the scope of this book to discuss intervention for cumulative stress reactions.

TREATMENT: MANAGING STRESS IN THE FIELD

Preparation for the challenges ahead, before the rescue deploys, includes an honest appraisal of the anticipated difficulties of rescue and of your ability to cope. Rescue work, especially wilderness rescue, can be long and tedious. The outcome is not guaranteed, particularly if the patient is far from modern medical care. Success may need to be measured by reaching a patient, pro-

Acute Stress Reactions

PHYSICAL
- Fatigue
- Muscle tremors
- Nausea
- Glassy eyes
- Chills
- Dizziness
- Profuse sweating

EMOTIONAL
- Anxiety
- Fear
- Grief
- Depression
- Hopelessness
- Irritability
- Anger

COGNITIVE
- Memory loss
- Indecision
- Difficulty problem solving
- Confusion with trivial issues
- Loss of attention span
- Feeling overwhelmed

Delayed Stress Reactions

- Macabre humor
- Excessive use of sick leave
- Reluctance to enter stressful situations
- Intrusive images
- Obsession with the stressful incident
- Withdrawal from others
- Suicidal thoughts
- Feelings of inadequacy

viding comfort, assuring that the patient is not alone and suffering, and completing the rescue without any further injuries.

Among emergency personnel on the scene of a serious rescue, most will experience at least some symptoms of stress. Short-term stress symptoms can be managed by attending to the physical needs for rest, food, and hydration; by briefing the group on the sights, sounds, and emotions they may experience during a long evacuation; and by debriefing the group after the incident.

Acute stress reactions on the scene can be managed by removing an overstressed person from the site. Give simple, clear directions to the stressed person and assign productive tasks that can help shift his or her focus away from the immediate incident. Such tasks might include providing food and drink, building a litter, and setting up tents.

If an emergency caregiver is overly distressed, detached from reality, or disruptive, someone may need to stay with him or her to lend a sympathetic ear. You can help such persons cope by talking with them and offering assurances that their feelings are valid, real, and perfectly appropriate. Provide emotional support with honesty and direct, factual answers to their questions.

FINAL THOUGHTS

The Field Debriefing
Following a rescue, first attend to the physical needs of the rescuers by providing food, water, clean clothing, and shelter. Light aerobic exercise, such as a hike or a game of hacky sack, may help relieve tension built up over the course of the rescue.

Provide emotional support to rescuers, staff, and course participants who experience unusual stress. In wilderness education many of our participants are young and may be experiencing their first real-life stress. Emotional reactions to accidents are perfectly normal and should be expected but people who don't know this may compound their own anxieties, making the stress even worse for themselves. The majority of reactions are short-term, with no lasting consequences.

A simple, voluntary debriefing or a conversation around the fire with a trusted mentor or friend can help people manage the emotions of an event, connect people with their support groups, and identify a person who needs additional help. These conversations can give people a map to work through the emotional and cognitive wilderness after a serious incident. The National Association of EMS Physicians, in a draft position paper on stress in emergency services, recommends "psychological first aid" instead of the more elaborate and controversial critical incident stress debriefings. Psychological first aid entails listening, empathy, assessing needs, ensuring that basic physical needs are met, protecting from additional harm, not forcing people to talk, and accessing family, clergy, or friends for support. Rescuers should understand that their reactions, while uncomfortable, are natural, normal reactions to abnormal events and that healing may take time and assistance. For both patients and rescuers, the emotional first aid we provide is as important to their ultimate recovery as the physical care.

MEDICAL LEGAL CONCEPTS IN WILDERNESS MEDICINE

INTRODUCTION

There are several medical legal concepts that are pertinent to the wilderness first responder. At first glance these legal concepts can be framed as possible trigger points for a lawsuit. They can also be framed as reminders of the style in which we should provide care. They're reminders that we should do what we have been trained to do (and do it well) and that we should treat our patients with respect and politeness.

WILDERNESS PROTOCOLS

Doing your job well and consistent with the standards and practices for which you have trained is excellent protection against lawsuits, as well as assurance that your patient will be treated properly. Medicine uses the phrase "scope of practice" to describe what care a provider can provide, and "standard of care" to describe the yardstick by which that care is measured. The standard of care by which you will be judged is determined in part by your level of training and the protocols under which you practice.

Most of the care provided by wilderness first responders is straightforward and widely accepted first aid. If someone is bleeding, it's expected that we will apply direct pressure and elevation. If we assess a fracture, it is accepted that the prehospital treatment is to immobilize the limb.

Administering medication, relocating dislocations, doing a focused spine assessment, and making evacuation decisions are examples of a few practices that are outside the normal scope of practice of prehospital medicine, yet are very appropriate and the standard of care in wilderness medicine. To clarify the standards of care you should provide, we encourage all our wilderness medicine students who may find themselves in a leadership position to affiliate with a medical director who can develop a set of protocols. Your physician can review your training and experience and provide support for the context in which you will practice medicine. He or she can develop treatment and evacuation protocols that meet your training and your program's needs.

Documentation. In the chapter on patient assessment we discussed written patient notes—the SOAP report. These serve as a form of communication between medical care providers, and they serve as documentation of what you did, when you did it, and how you did it.

Written documentation can be invaluable if your level of care is challenged in a legal process and you try to reconstruct from memory an event in the past. An axiom in medicine is "If you didn't write it down, you didn't do it." This serves as a reminder of the limits of our memory and the importance of documenting our assessment, our treatment, and any changes in the patient's condition while he or she is under our care.

Duty to Act and the Good Samaritan. As a trip leader, whether paid or volunteer, it can be argued that you have a duty to provide assistance in the event of a medical problem. Your patient is not a stranger; you have a prior relationship with him or her if he or she is a participant in an activity you lead. You would also have a duty if you respond as part of a rescue or ambulance team.

You will be a Good Samaritan in the eyes of your society, and in the legal context, if you provide care voluntarily when you don't have a duty to the patient, e.g., if you stop to help an injured hiker by the side of the trail. To encourage us to provide care in this circumstance many states have some form of Good Samaritan legislation that provides legal protection as long as we are not grossly negligent. Good Samaritan laws vary from state to state, but common elements are that we don't have a preexisting duty to the patient and that the care has to be voluntary—often on an unplanned and unforeseen emergency basis.

Consent

It's simple politeness to ask a person for permission to treat. We do this as part of our initial assessment when we introduce ourselves and ask if we can help. It's also a legal principle that people have control of themselves, and we can't practice medicine on them without their permission.

Informed consent is the process, ongoing throughout our care, where a reliable patient agrees to treatment after being informed about the risks and benefits. The dialogue we have while we assess and treat our patient keeps him or her informed, and again is simply being polite and respectful.

The law assumes that an unreliable patient, one with an altered mental status who is not fully alert and oriented to person, place, and time would want help during an emergency situation. This is the concept of *implied consent.*

Implied consent also applies to minors whose parents are not available to give consent. The laws regarding minors are complex and can vary from state to state. If you're working with minors, which in most cases is anyone under the age of 18 years, it's wise to seek legal advice that is pertinent to your program and your state.

Confidentiality

As you assess and treat a patient you will learn aspects of personal and medical history that again, out of politeness and respect, should be considered confidential. The findings from your assessment and care can be communicated verbally, and in writing, to another medical provider who needs to know to continue care for the patient. Outdoor leaders who learn a student's or client's medical history from a routine pretrip screening process have an obligation to only share this information appropriately and must be cautious when discussing medical history with colleagues. Inappropriate disclosure of medical information would breach your "patient to provider" confidentiality. In addition to being disrespectful, in the legal world you may commit slander, defaming a person's character verbally, or libel, defaming in writing.

Be careful about what you say on the radio or to other members of your program or expedition. On the radio state your facts, avoid identifying the patient unless it is necessary, and avoid speculation. For example, you may note the patient's breath odor and odd behavior as facts, but to state he or she is intoxicated without a blood test can be slander, as well as being incorrect.

Abandonment

Abandonment happens when you stop care too soon or transfer the patient to someone who is not able to provide the care the patient needs. This can arise when a trained medical provider begins care and gives the impression he or she will help the patient, then leaves the patient, or turns him or her over to someone with less training. A scenario for this in outdoor education could be a trip leader turning the patient over to a co-leader or a program support person. The trip leader needs to consider the level of care the patient needs and whether the co-leader or program support person can provide that care.

FINAL THOUGHTS

Fear of being sued can restrain people from taking training or responding to an emergency. This is unfortunate when it prevents people from helping one another. We can talk about the legal climate in our society, and the details of law, but there is no argument that if we can help and fail to do so, we violate the expectations of medicine and our society. Legal Advisor Reb Gregg has given us sage advice for years, words that are summarized in the two key points in this chapter: Do what you are trained to do, and treat people with respect and politeness. These simple rules will help you provide the best of care—the key to staying out of court.

FIRST AID KIT

These are the contents of a standard first aid kit designed for a group of twelve on a monthlong trip. (This is the inventory of the NOLS Instructor's Kit.) Obviously, requirements will vary with group size, medical qualifications, trip length, location, and remoteness.

NOLS FIRST AID KIT

General Supplies	No.	Wound Care	No.
Biohazard bag	1	2" x 2" gauze pad	4
Nitrile gloves	1 pair	3" x 4" nonstick gauze pads	2
Latex gloves	4 pairs	Opsite Transparent dressing	2
Micro shield	1	4" x 4" gauze pad	2
Thermometer (digital)	1	Band-Aids	12
Signal mirror	1	Steri-strips	6
Whistle	1	3" gauze roll	1
		Tweezers	1
Foot Repair Pouch	**No.**	Cravats	1
Scissors	1	Oval eye pads	2
Ace bandage	1	Safety pins	2
1" Athletic tape	2	12cc syringe	1
Moleskin	2 (2" x 3")	Bactracin $1\frac{1}{32}$ oz	10
Molefoam	2 (2" x 3")	Cortisone $1\frac{1}{32}$ oz	10
Adhesive knit	2 (2" x 3")	Benzoin 1 oz	2
Second Skin	2 (2" x 3")	Betadine 1 oz	1

Suggestions

Protect the sterile dressings from moisture by sealing them in groups of three or four in clear plastic.

If you have a planned resupply of food and fuel, consider including extra tape and blister material.

The kit should be accessible. Everyone should know its location.

Label all containers. Include instructions for all medications.

Thermometers break easily. A strong package is imperative; a spare thermometer a good idea.

The kit should be packaged in a distinctly colored and labeled bag that is durable, waterproof, and not heavy or bulky.

If your first aid kit is too big, you will have a tendency to leave it behind. Many NOLS instructors carry in their summit packs a small package of the most frequently needed items, including tape, moleskin, Second Skin, and povidone-iodine. Others slide a small roll of tape, cravat, and 4 x 4 into their helmet lining.

NOLS first aid kits do not include premade splints, such as airsplints or SAM splints. Premade splints may be carried in the first aid kit, or suitable splints can be improvised from foamlite pads.

Keep a note pad, pencil, change for phone calls, evacuation report forms, and emergency instructions with the first aid kit.

EMERGENCY PROCEDURES FOR OUTDOOR GROUPS

Evacuations from the wilderness can be complex and pose risks to a patient and rescuers. A little bit of planning can go a long way in supporting an efficient emergency response. Details are important; small omissions in planning can have great consequences. Errors in organization and technique have a tendency to multiply over time. Think and plan. Listed below are a few relevant factors that should be considered in an emergency response plan.

Stabilize the Scene
Patient Assessment: Use this tool to gather information.
Take care of basic needs: Food, shelter, hydration of the rescuers.

Collect Information
Lost Person: SWEET
- Subject information (who, health and fitness, state of mind).
- Weather (present and anticipated).
- Experience (outdoor experience).
- Equipment (what might he have with him? color? shape?).
- Time (when was he seen last?).
- Point last seen (most searches focus on this important location).

- Most likely locations (terrain traps and attractants).
- Original plan (or intention) and Emergency plan (lost person plan).

Injury or Illness
- Prepare and review SOAP Report.
- Determine severity and urgency.

Search Considerations

Search is an emergency. The longer a person is lost the farther they can travel, increasing the difficulty of the search. A lost person can walk approximately two miles per hour. After one hour the search area will be 12 square miles, after two hours 48 square miles, after three hours 108 square miles.

- Start at Point Last Seen.
- Consider geographic containment: rivers, high ridges, steep passes, maintained trails, etc.
- Look for clues: tracks, broken branches, dropped clothing or gear, etc.
- Make the search attractive: fires, whistles, bright clothes, vocal calls, leave notes at trail junctions.
- Search natural attractions: old cabins, mines, hot springs, etc.

Lost Person Behavior: Studies on the behavior of lost persons show the following tendencies:

- If a lost person finds a trail, he tends to stay on the trail and might move fast, convinced he is on the way back, when in fact he might be heading in the wrong direction. Rarely will a lost person reverse his direction on a trail.
- Some lost people will climb/hike to the top of the closest hill for a view.
- The majority of lost people will travel downhill and/or downstream.
- Many lost people will travel at night—even without a flashlight.
- Lost people will rarely move around randomly. They usually move with conviction and hope that they're heading in the right direction.

Evacuation Considerations

Consider the following when determining whether to conduct the evacuation by yourself or with your group, or use local SAR or EMS resources.

- The condition of the patient.
- The distance to the road.
- The difficulty of the terrain.
- The group's strength and stamina.
- The group's technical abilities and experience.
- Your ability to communicate with outside support.
- The support available from your program, EMS, or SAR.
- The suitability of accessible landing or loading zones.

Determine Type of Evacuation

- The patient can travel (walk or ski).
- The patient needs assistance.
- Single person carries.
- Litter carry.
- Horse.
- Helicopter.
- Snowmobile/Boat/Vehicle/ATV.

Requesting Help

Sending a Ground Team

- Send a team: ideally three or four strong persons with bivouac equipment.
- Send a written SOAP note if you have a patient already at hand.
- Send a written plan of your situation and intentions.
- Send in writing an exact location (ideally a marked map).
- Ask in writing for what you think you'll need.

Making a Call

- Know the limitations of your radio, cell phone, satellite phone, or personal locator beacon.
- Prepare your call. Develop a "Headline" report of the problem.
- Be able to describe your location. Use coordinates if possible.
- Make a clear statement of your needs and/or plan.

Helicopters

Mark your location with tightly anchored, brightly colored markings. Yellow, red, blue, and orange are good signal colors, especially if they are Day-Glo. Dull colors are not very useful. Background contrast is important. Use your signal mirror. Landing zones that are 60 feet in diameter are best. Think about a football-field-sized space. Avoid holes under ridges, which can create tricky wind changes for the pilot. Clear loose objects from the landing zone.

- Approach a helicopter only when the pilot motions you to do so.
- Do not walk behind a helicopter. The tail rotor spins fast and is difficult to see.
- Do not approach a helicopter from uphill.
- Be careful on snow. Don't accidentally slide toward the helicopter.
- Stay low when you are near the arc of the rotors.
- Control people on the landing zone.

Pre-Trip Planning, Prevention, and Risk Management

- Have an Emergency Response Plan.
- Have a Lost Person Plan.
- Research local resources (SAR, EMS, etc.).
- Tell someone your travel plan.
- Carry a map, compass, and GPS.
- Carry a communication device with spare batteries.
- Have a first aid kit and a signaling device (mirror, flares, bright colors).
- Always plan for contingencies.

GLOSSARY OF C FIRST AID TERMS

Anaphylaxis. A hypersensitive reaction of the body to a foreign protein or drug.

Anorexia. A lack of appetite.

Appendicular. Refers to the limbs, the legs and arms.

Ataxia. Incoordination of muscles. Usually seen when voluntary movement is attempted; e.g., walking.

Avulsion. A forcible tearing away of a body part. It can be a piece of skin, a finger, toe, or entire limb.

Axial. Referring to the midline through the skeleton, the skull, vertebrae, and pelvis.

Axillary. Referring to the armpit.

Bacteria. Unicellular organisms lacking chlorophyll.

Basal metabolic rate. The metabolic rate of a person at rest. Usually expressed in kilocalories per square meter of body surface per hour.

Basal metabolism. The amount of energy needed to maintain life when the body is at rest.

Brachial. Refers to the arm, usually the brachial artery or nerve.

Brain stem. The portion of the brain located below the cerebrum, which controls automatic functions such as breathing and body temperature.

Campylobacter. A genus of bacteria implicated in diarrheal illness.

Capillary. The smallest of the blood vessels; the site of oxygen, nutrient, and waste product exchange between the blood and the cells.

Cerebellum. The portion of brain behind and below the cerebrum, which controls balance, muscle tone, and coordination of skilled movements.

Cerebrum. The largest and upper region of the brain. Responsible for higher mental functions such as reasoning, memory, and cognition.

Comminuted. A fracture in which several small cracks radiate from the point of impact.

Congenital. A condition present at birth.

Conjunctiva. The mucous membrane that lines the eyelid and the front of the eyeball.

Convection. Heat transferred by currents in liquids or gases.

Cornea. The clear transparent covering of the eye.

Crepitus. A grating sound produced by bone ends rubbing together.

CRT. Capillary refill time. For example, "Capillary refill time is 3 seconds."

Cyanosis. Bluish discoloration of the skin, mucous membranes, and nail beds indicating inadequate oxygen levels in the blood.

Diabetes. A disease resulting from inadequate production or utilization of insulin.

Distal. Farther from the heart.

Electrolyte. A substance that, in solution, conducts electricity: Common electrolytes in our body are sodium, potassium, chloride, calcium, phosphorus, and magnesium.

Embolism. An undissolved mass in a blood vessel; may be solid, liquid, or gas.

Epilepsy. Recurrent attacks of disturbed brain function; classic signs are altered level of consciousness, loss of consciousness, and/or seizures.

Eversion. A turning outward (as with an ankle).

Giardia. A genus of protozoan, a simple unicellular organism that causes an illness that is often characterized by diarrhea.

Globule. Any small rounded body.

Hematoma. A pool of blood confined to an organ or tissue.

Hyperglycemia. High blood sugar.

Hypoglycemia. Low blood sugar.

Intercostal. The area between the ribs.

Irrigate. To flush with a liquid.

Kilocalorie. A unit of heat; the amount of heat needed to change the temperature of 1 gram of water 1 degree centigrade.

LOC. Level of consciousness.

Meninges. The three membranes that enclose and help protect the brain.

MOI. Mechanism of injury for an accident.

Morbidity. The state of being diseased.

Occlusive dressing. A dressing impermeable by moisture.

Palpate. To examine by touching.

Paraplegia. Paralysis affecting the lower portion of the body and both legs.

Paroxysmal. A sudden, periodic attack, spasm, or recurrence of symptoms.

PFD. Personal flotation device (life jacket).

Plasma. The liquid part of blood.

Prodromal. The initial stage of a disease.

Quadriplegia. Paralysis affecting all four limbs.

Rales. Crackly breath sounds due to fluid in the lungs or airways.

RR. Respiratory rate. For example, "RR is 18 and unlabored," or "RR is 22 and shallow and regular."

SCTM. Skin, color, temperature, and moisture. For example, "Skin is pale, cool, and moist," or "Skin is red, hot, and dry."

Seizure. A sudden attack of a disease as in epilepsy.

Signs. An indication of illness or injury that the examiner observes.

Sprain. Trauma to a joint causing injury to the ligaments.

Strain. A stretched or torn muscle.

Symptoms. Pain, discomfort, or other abnormality that the patient feels.

Tendinitis. Inflammation of a tendon.

TRS. Township, range, and section. A grid system used as a legal description of location. The coordinates are available on many topographic maps.

Varicose veins. Distended, swollen, knotted veins.

Vasoconstriction. Narrowing of blood vessels.

Ventricular. Referring to the two lower pumping chambers of the heart, the ventricles.

Vertigo. The sensation of objects moving about the person or the person moving around in space.

Virus. A microscopic and parasitic organism dependent on the nutrients inside cells for its reproductive and metabolic needs.

Wheezes. Whistling or sighing breath sounds resulting from narrowed airways.

BIBLIOGRAPHY

Benenson, Abram S., ed. *Control of Communicable Diseases in Man.* Washington, DC: American Public Health Association, 1990.

Buttaravoli, Philip, and Thomas Stair. *Minor Emergencies: Splinters to Fractures.* St. Louis: Mosby, 2000.

Forgey, William W. *Basic Essentials of Hypothermia.* 2nd ed. Guilford, CT: Globe Pequot Press, 1999.

———, ed. *Wilderness Medical Society Practice Guidelines for Wilderness Emergency Care.* 2nd ed. Guilford, CT: Globe Pequot Press, 2006.

———. *Wilderness Medicine.* 5th ed. Guilford, CT: Globe Pequot Press, 2000.

Fradin, Mark, and John Day. "Comparative efficacy of insect repellents against mosquito bites." *New England Journal of Medicine* 347 (July 4, 2002):13–18.

Giesbrecht, Gordon. "Prehospital treatment of hypothermia." *Wilderness & Environmental Medicine* 12, no. 1 (2001).

Gill, Paul G., Jr. *Pocket Guide to Wilderness Medicine.* New York: Simon & Schuster, 1991.

———. *Waterlover's Guide to Marine Medicine: How to Identify and Treat Aquatic Ailments and Injuries.* New York: Simon & Schuster, 1993.

Gold, Barry, Richard Dart, and Robert Barish. "Bites of venomous snakes." *New England Journal of Medicine* 347, no. 5 (August 1, 2002).

Gookin, John. *NOLS Backcountry Lightning Safety Guidelines.* Lander, WY: National Outdoor Leadership School, 2000.

Hackett, Peter, and Robert Roach. "High-altitude Illness." *New England Journal of Medicine* 345, no. 2 (July 12, 2001).

Houston, Charles. *Going Higher: Oxygen, Man, and Mountains.* 4th ed. Seattle: Mountaineers Books, 1998.

Hultgren, Herb. *High Altitude Medicine.* Stanford, CA: Hultgren Publications, 1997.

Jong, Elaine, and Russell McMullen. *The Travel & Tropical Medicine Manual.* Philadelphia: W. B. Saunders Company, 1995.

Roberts, James R. *Roberts' Practical Guide to Common Medical Emergencies.* Philadelphia: Lippincott-Raven Publishers, 1996.

Schmutz, Ervin, and Lucretia Breazeale Hamilton. *Plants That Poison.* Flagstaff, AZ: Northland Publishing, 1979.

Setnicka, Tim J. *Wilderness Search and Rescue.* Boston: Appalachian Mountain Club, 1980.

Shimanski, Charley. *Helicopters in Search and Rescue Operations: Basic and Intermediate Levels.* Golden, CO: Mountain Rescue Association, 2002.

———. *Search and Rescue for Outdoor Leaders.* Golden, CO: Mountain Rescue Association, 2002.

Smith, David. *Backcountry Bear Basics: The Definitive Guide to Avoiding Unpleasant Encounters.* Seattle: Mountaineers Books, 1997.

Steele, Peter. *Backcountry Medical Guide.* 2nd ed. Seattle: Mountaineers Books, 1999.

Stewart, Charles E. *Environmental Emergencies.* Baltimore: Williams & Wilkins, 1990.

Sutherland, Stuan, and Guy Nolch. *Dangerous Australian Animals.* Flemington, Victoria, Australia: Hyland House, 2000.

Tilton, Buck. *Backcountry First Aid and Extended Care.* 4th ed. Guilford, CT: Globe Pequot Press, 2002.

———. *Basic Essentials of Avalanche Safety.* Guilford, CT: Globe Pequot Press, 1992.

———. *Basic Essentials of Rescue from the Backcountry.* Guilford, CT: Globe Pequot Press, 1990.

———. *Don't Get Bitten: The Dangers of Bites and Stings.* Seattle: Mountaineers Books, 2003.

Tilton, Buck, and Rick Bennett. *Don't Get Sick: The Hidden Dangers of Camping and Hiking.* Seattle: Mountaineers Books, 2002.

Tilton, Buck, and Frank Hubbell. *Medicine for the Backcountry: A Practical Guide to Wilderness First Aid.* 3rd ed. Guilford, CT: Globe Pequot Press, 1999.

Trott, Alexander. *Wounds and Lacerations: Emergency Care and Closure.* St. Louis: Mosby, 1991.

Van Tilburg, Christopher. *Emergency Survival: A Pocket Guide.* Seattle: Mountaineers Books, 2001.

Weiss, Eric. *Wilderness 911: A Step-by-Step Guide for Medical Emergencies and Improvised Care in the Backcountry.* Seattle: Mountaineers Books/Backpacker magazine, 1998.

Wilderness Medicine Institute of NOLS. *Wilderness Medicine Handbook.* 9th ed. Lander, WY: National Outdoor Leadership School, 2005.

Wilkerson, James A., ed. *Medicine for Mountaineering and Other Wilderness Activities.* 5th ed. Seattle: Mountaineers Books, 2001.

———. "Rabies update." *Wilderness & Environmental Medicine* 11, no. 1, (2000).

INDEX

THE AUTHOR

TOD SCHIMELPFENIG

As a wilderness educator since 1973, and a volunteer EMT on ambulance and search and rescue squads for the past thirty-eight years, Tod Schimelpfenig has extensive experience with wilderness risk management. He has utilized this valuable experience by conducting safety reviews as well as serving as the NOLS Risk Management Director for eight years, the NOLS Rocky Mountain Branch Director for six years, and a member for three years on the board of directors of the Wilderness Medical Society (WMS), where he received the WMS Warren Bowman Award for lifetime contribution to the field of wilderness medicine in 2001 and was elected a Fellow of the Academy of Wilderness Medicine. Tod is the founder of the Wilderness Risk Managers Committee, has spoken at numerous conferences on pre-hospital and wilderness medicine, and has taught wilderness medicine around the world. In 2010 he received the Charles (Reb) Gregg Award for lifetime contributions to the field of wilderness risk management. He has written numerous articles on educational programming, risk management, and wilderness medicine topics, and currently reviews articles for the *Journal of Wilderness and Environmental Medicine.* Tod is also currently the Curriculum Director of the NOLS Wilderness Medicine Institute.